THE BATTLE OF SCARY CREEK

MILITARY OPERATIONS IN THE KANAWHA VALLEY APRIL - JULY 1861

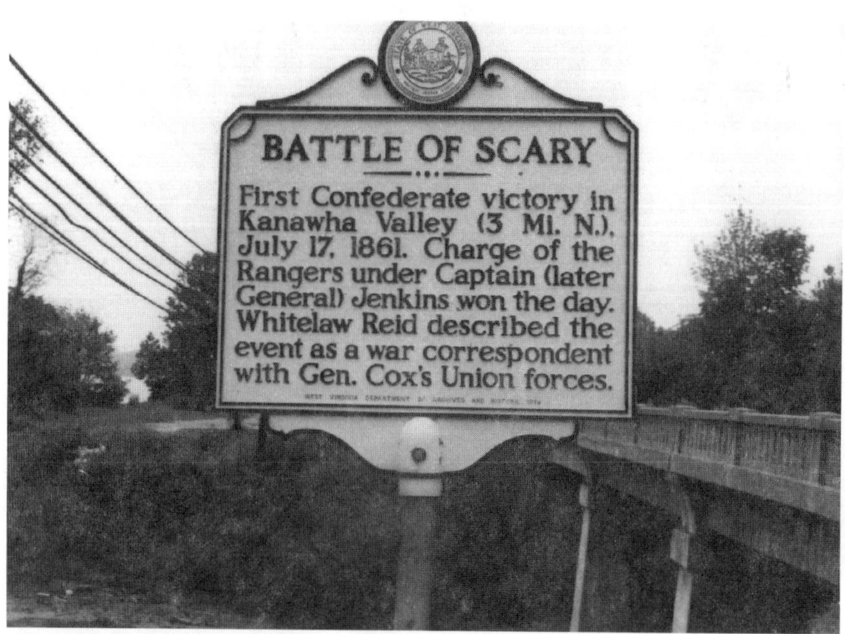

STATE HISTORICAL MARKER AT SCARY CREEK

The sign was originally located 3 miles south, hence the incorrect information.

— Photo by the author

THE BATTLE OF SCARY CREEK

MILITARY OPERATIONS IN THE KANAWHA VALLEY APRIL - JULY 1861

TERRY LOWRY

QUARRIER PRESS
CHARLESTON, WEST VIRGINIA

LIBRARY OF CONGRESS NUMBER 82-081716

ISBN 0-9646197-7-6

Original Edition, First Printing July 1982
Revised Edition, First Printing March 1998

Cover Design and Revised Edition Layout:
Mark S. Phillips/Marketing+Design Group
Original Edition Typography: Arrow Graphics

Printed in the United States of America

Quarrier Press
1416 Quarrier Street
Charleston, West Virginia 25301

CONTENTS

MAPS

INTRODUCTION

On every rock our sentries stood,
Our scouts held post in every wood,
And every path was stained with blood,
From Scary creek to Gauley flood.

—from the poem "Ann Bailey" written by Charles Robb, a U.S. Army cavalryman stationed at Gauley Bridge, printed in the Cleremont, Ohio "Courier" on November 7, 1861

"It was a very insignificant affair, but we exaggerated it into a deed of great valor and importance." This statement, written by former Confederate soldier John S. Wise in 1889 for his book, *The End Of An Era,* referred to one of the many small military actions during the Civil War campaigns in (West) Virginia, and at first glance would seem to be typical of the 1861 Kanawha Valley campaign in particular. With its rugged, mountainous terrain the entire area of (West) Virginia precluded any "successful military operations" of any major size, so the small affairs which did occur, especially those in the Kanawha Valley, have become overshadowed by the larger, more important campaigns of eastern Virginia and elsewhere, and nearly forgotten as a result. Yet historians can't ignore that during the early months of the war the Kanawha Valley was a vital and strategic area to both armies. Situated on the western edge of Appalachia, the (Great) Kanawha River flows from the rustic town of Gauley Bridge, located at the confluence of the New and Gauley rivers, to the equally rural hamlet of Point Pleasant, where it empties into the Ohio River. This area, commonly referred to as the Kanawha Valley proper, involves a total distance of some ninety miles and became one of the most openly contested areas of sentiment at the outbreak of the American Civil War.

This book is basically a study of the military operations within the Kanawha Valley during four months, April through July, of 1861—a time involving the first exposure to warfare by most of the participants involved, a rash of incompetent military officers offset with a few brilliant ones, the first wartime use of artillery in the Kanawha Valley, ragged and poorly trained soldiers waging a war against each other under some of the worst possible geographic and environmental conditions, and the climax of the campaign, the battle at Scary Creek on July 17, 1861, which proved more a comedy of errors than an example of strategic combat. Yet the Kanawha Valley campaign proved a blueprint for most of the remainder of the war: poorly armed and trained Confederate soldiers, outnumbered and led by inexperienced officers, could defeat a larger, well trained Federal army provided they were able to select the best possible position for a defensive action. And when their line of supply became threatened, a retreat was inevitable.

There are those who will argue that the battle of Scary Creek, and the campaign from which it evolved, is not worthy of such a study since the battle was a minor skirmish which had no effect on the eventual outcome of the war. The battle cannot be so easily dismissed. The battle raged on for at least five hours and the casualty lists were light only because the soldiers were "green" and their weapons inefficient. The oddly won Confederate victory would have been headline news in Richmond, had not the enormous battle at Manassas (Bull Run), Virginia taken place only four days later, thereby diminishing the glory of the victors in the Kanawha.

And while it yet can't be explained, the battle held a special place in the hearts of the men who fought it. Men who went on to fight at Gettysburg, Atlanta, Lookout Mountain, Cold Harbor, and so many of the other great blood baths of the war, always seemed to enjoy reflecting back to the battle at Scary Creek. George S. Patton, the commanding Confederate officer at Scary, wrote during the war: "It is now forgotten except by those, who then first met the enemy & who still talk of 'Scary' around their campfires." Patton was most assuredly wrong, for even after the last veteran had passed away, the battle of Scary was, and still is, talked about and written of. Yet there has never been a definitive study, and this work does not claim to be such a piece, but it is the first detailed look into the Kanawha Valley campaign and the personalities who waged it, including many obscure figures who would later rise to prominence during the war. There is much new evidence unearthed and published here for the first time, often altering long accepted views on the campaign.

Admittedly this work is biased. The Confederates receive much more attention than the Federals, and for good reason. Many excellent accounts written by Federal soldiers already exist, the best being Gen. Jacob D. Cox's *Military Reminiscences,* although there are also a number of good regimental histories and independent studies. There is no such readily available source for the Confederates. Also, the Rebels occupied the land encompassing the campaign and, as such, the affair was of a much more personal nature.

Politics and military campaigns elsewhere are avoided except when they directly influenced the Kanawha. Even Gen. George McClellan's activities at such places as Rich Mountain, Laurel Hill, and Corricks Ford in the northern sector of (West) Virginia are barely touched upon, although McClellan formulated the military strategy for the Kanawha. But he did not carry it out—his subordinates did—and this is their story, not his. There are many good accounts already in print of McClellan's adventures; there is no need to rehash them here. This is the time for new information and a new outlook on one of the earliest and most ignored military campaigns of the war.

Some of what you will read is already well known and documented; some has never before been presented; and some can only be based upon conjecture as there are yet many gaps in available information. In this respect, the process of permitting actual participants to speak for themselves is employed, quoting from such sources as actual letters, diaries, and regimental histories. In some instances a group of letters will be presented simultaneously, considered a means of literary padding by some, by others an opportunity to be exposed to many rare and unpublished documents that otherwise would probably never be viewed by the reader. For those bothered by such inclusions, these collections can be entirely avoided without losing any context of the story, although the author does not recommend this procedure.

Of equal importance are the pictures. The quality ranges from excellent to the barely discernible but they all represent an important historical document, many being the only existent pictures. Some have been taken from other publications, hence the poor reproduction quality, while others have come from such fine collections as the Library of Congress, National Archives, and the United States Army Military History Institute. Regardless of quality, they are about all that remain of actual images from the period. Where possible I attempted to use a picture of the figures in their military uniforms but, as many soldiers were never photographed as such, I had to use later post-war views often showing the individual at a much older age and in civilian clothing. As with the manuscript information, many of these have never before been published.

I do have a few regrets. One being that I did not possess the necessary financial resources to hire a grammar specialist to edit my manuscript. Hopefully, the grammar is correct. I also lacked the money to travel to various institutions about the country in order to seek out other unpublished manuscript collections. But my biggest regret is that my father, Charlie Lowry, did not live to see this project completed, although I'm sure he is reading it somewhere in Heaven.

—Terry Lowry

DEDICATED TO

MY FATHER, CHARLIE LOWRY
(9/11/1911 - 5/17/1981)
AND TO
MY MOTHER, RUTH ANN LOWRY

ACKNOWLEDGEMENTS

As usual in such an undertaking there exist those many many people and institutions without whose understanding help such a project would not be possible. Please forgive me for anybody I have accidentally omitted:

The entire staff of the West Virginia State Archives, particularly Emily Neff, library assistant, and Ellen Hassig, manuscripts, West Virginia State Archives and History Division, Charleston, West Virginia.

E. Lee Shepard, assistant curator of manuscripts, and Mrs. Rebecca Perrine, curator of special collections, Virginia Historical Society, Richmond, Virginia.

Edward D.C. Campbell, Jr., director, and Hawson W. Cole, librarian, Museum of the Confederacy, Richmond, Virginia.

Mrs. Toni H. Waller, picture librarian, Virginia State Library, Richmond, Virginia.

Anne A. Hahn, Captain-assistant reference librarian, and Diane B. Jacob, archivist, Preston Library, Virginia Military Institute, Lexington, Virginia.

Peter Gottlieb, assistant curator, West Virginia University Library, Morgantown, West Virginia.

James L. Murphy, reference librarian, and Mrs. Arlene J. Peterson, audio-visual archivist, Ohio Historical Society, Columbus, Ohio.

Virginia Keene, M.R. & R.L. Clerk, Department of Military Affairs, Military Records and Research Library, Frankfort, Kentucky.

Francis Coleman, Kentucky Collection, Department of Library and Archives, State Archives, Frankfort, Kentucky.

Nicky Hughes, curator, Kentucky Military History Museum, Frankfort, Kentucky.

Philip M. Cavanaugh, director, Patton Museum of Cavalry and Armor, Fort Knox, Kentucky.

Lisle G. Brown, curator, Special Collections, Marshall University, Huntington, West Virginia.

Michael Winey and Richard Sommers, United States Army Military History Institute, Carlisle Barracks, Pennsylvania.

Cynthia M. Yeager, librarian, The War Library and Museum (MOLLUS Collection), Philadelphia, Pennsylvania.

Charles A. Shaughnessy, Dale E. Floyd, and Michael P. Musick, Navy and Old Army Branch, General Services Administration, National Archives, Washington, D.C.

Paul T. Heffron, acting chief, Manuscript Division, Library of Congress, Washington, D.C.

Personnel of the Atlanta Historical Society, Atlanta, Georgia.

Herbert Leventhal, Ph.D./Chief, United States Military Academy, West Point, New York.

Carolyn A. Wallace, director, Southern Historical Collection, University of North Carolina, Chapel Hill, North Carolina.

Garland Ellis, Coal River Insurance Company, St. Albans, West Virginia, for photo and information on Valcoulon Place.

Harriet McLoone, assistant curator of American manuscripts, The Huntington, San Marino, California.

Thomas R. Ross, Professor of History, Davis & Elkins College, Elkins, West Virginia.

William Wintz, Upper Vandalia Historical Society, St. Albans, West Virginia.

Mrs. Kenneth D. Swope, archivist, Greenbrier County Historical Society, Lewisburg, West Virginia.

Delmer R. Hite, Jackson County Historical Society, Staats Mills, West Virginia.

Larry L. Legge, of Barboursville, West Virginia, and Roland Hamilton, both of the deactivated re-enactment unit of the 22nd Virginia Infantry, C.S.A.

Mrs. E. Forrest Jones, President, Charleston Chapter of the United Daughters of the Confederacy, Charleston, West Virginia.

Mrs. Leonard Elizabeth Harvey, St. Albans Chapter of the United Daughters of the Confederacy, St. Albans, West Virginia.

Major General George S. Patton (retired), United States Army, Materiel Development and Readiness Command, Alexandria, Virginia, and Ruth Ellen Patton Totten, South Hamilton, Massachusetts, for information on George S. Patton, C.S.A.

Mrs. John T. Morgan of Charleston, West Virginia, for information on the Littlepage family.

Rembrandt Morgan of Morgan's Landing, West Virginia, for information on the John Morgan farm and family.

Lee Mays of Ripley, West Virginia, for information on his father, James H. Mays of the 22nd Virginia Infantry, C.S.A.

Emma Simms Maginnis, Winfield Road, West Virginia, for information on the Simms family, use of the unpublished Simms family history, and use of the William Maginnis photo collection.

Mrs. Murray Shuff and Mrs. M.M. Ralston, both of Beckley, West Virginia, for information on General Alfred Beckley.

S. Louise Bing of Charleston, West Virginia, for use of her Ohio G.A.R. materials.

Dent "Wildman" Myers, Civil War Surplus, Kennesaw, Georgia, for inspiration and patience with me rummaging throughout his store.

Don Marsh of "The Charleston Gazette" and Charles Connor of "The Charleston Daily Mail," both Charleston Newspapers, Inc., Charleston, West Virginia.

Richard Walker, Cabell County Public Library, Huntington, West Virginia.

John D. Stinson, research librarian, New York Public Library, New York, New York.

Fayette County Historical Society, Ansted, West Virginia.

Kanawha County Public Library, Charleston, West Virginia.

Dr. Ida Kramer, History Department, West Virginia State College, for nourishing my historical interest.

Three West Virgninia relic hunters who went above and beyond the call of duty were: Robert Chapman of Huntington, West Virginia; James "Slim" Combs of Charleston, West Virginia; and my good neighbor, William Price, South Charleston, West Virginia, who first introduced me to the hobby of relic hunting

All photos are appropriately credited but much appreciation must be extended to the following: Gary Bays who trampled through many an old Civil War site with me in order to obtain modern views; S. Spencer Moore Photography Department, Charleston, West Virginia; and Gary Brown Photography, Charleston, West Virginia.

And finally there are those who helped in many ways other than research including:

Phyllis Tanner, for both typing and editing the manuscript,
My brother Tim and his family, Nancy, Chuckie, and David, for moral support,
Tina Burcham, for tolerating me during the crucial period,
Dr. John Davidson of Atlanta, Georgia, for retinal surgery on my left eye, and as such I hope this work will serve as some sort of inspiration to others suffering from various eye diseases and injuries.

TERMINOLOGY

Readers must keep in mind that during the Kanawha Valley campaign of 1861 West Virginia was not yet a state, but a part of Virginia. Therefore such designations in this book as (West) Virginia, (West)ern Virginia, etc., apply to the area now known as West Virginia.

For those unfamiliar with Civil War terminology, the following all apply to the Ohio and Kentucky United States troops: Federals, Yankees, Union, while the Confederate States troops are identified as either: Confederates, rebels, secessionists.

In the course of my research I often came across several name variations and misspellings. Any reader further researching this material should keep these in mind. Below you will find the present day, or correct spelling, presented first, followed by the common variations:

Bills Creek (Bill's Creek, Bill Creek, Beales Creek)

Thomas Broun (Brown)

Charleston (Kanawha Court House)

Conrad Hill (Antill Hill, Coonrod Hill)

Capt. James Corns (Coons, Koonz, Koontz, Corn)

Cottageville (Cottage Mills)

Letart (Letarts, Letartsville)

Julia Maffitt (Maffett, Moffitt)

Malden (Kanawha Salines)

George S. Patton (Patten)

Poca (Pocataligo, Pokey, Mouth of Pocataligo, Pocotalico, Camp Poco)

St. Albans (Coalsmouth, Colesmouth, Cole Mouth, Mouth of Coal)

Scary Creek (Scarey, Scurry, Scareytown, Mouth of Scary, Scary's Run, Scary P.O.)

Sissonville (Sessionville, Seissonville)

Christopher Q. Tompkins (Thompkins)

Winfield (Wingfield)

It should also be noted that most of the Virginia troops mentioned in this book were not yet organized into any numerical regiment of the Confederate States Army during the time period discussed herein. Although the designations of a few are mentioned throughout the work, most of them eventually were mustered into the following regiments:

22nd Virginia Infantry
36th Virginia Infantry
46th Virginia Infantry
8th Virginia Cavalry
10th Virginia Cavalry

MOUTH OF SCARY CREEK
JULY 17, 1861 — Shortly after 2 P.M.

Twenty-five year old Lt. James Clark Welch of Hale's Battery, Kanawha Artillery, leaning against his iron six-pounder field piece, taking an occasional glance across the deep ravine cut by the calm waters of Scary Creek, nervously awaited the arrival of the enemy. The weather was hot, and getting hotter by the second. In fact, this was to become one of the hottest summer days the Kanawha Valley had known. The intensity of the heat, coupled with Welch's nervous anticipation, brought sweat beads forth across his face, and with each passing minute his throat became more parched, until, finally, the waters of Scary Creek became most inviting, but to approach that body of water meant exposing himself to enemy guns, which would almost certainly result in death, or at least a horrid and painful wound. Thirst would have to wait. About him his comrades prepared their weapons, waiting for the first blue uniform to appear in the distance across Scary. The war was yet young, the spirit of high adventure was everywhere, the massive casualty lists that would come within the next few years were not even imagined. Most of the soldiers didn't understand the full implications of their presence at Scary—All that mattered was that a Northern aggressor was invading their state and as such it was utterly necessary for them to defend their families and property.

As expected, Federal soldiers, most from the sprawling farms of Ohio, soon emerged from the distant forestry into view. Donning one of those blue uniforms was an innocent nineteen year old boy, Private Elijah Beeman, Company A, 12th Ohio Volunteer Infantry, from Morrow County, Ohio, crouching into a protective position but ready to advance when ordered. As with the men who awaited his arrival, this would be his baptism under fire, and he didn't particularly relish the thought. After all, these Virginians were of his neighbor state but, like his comrades, he was convinced that this military movement was necessary in order to free the Southern people from these vicious rebels. Equally as apprehensive as Welch, his opponent across Scary, Beeman readied his weapon and moved into proper position with Company A.

Some men would soon die, some would be wounded, and some would run away never to be heard of again but most would survive to fight another day. Before the battle of Scary Creek concluded Lt. James C. Welch would lie dead, nearly decapitated by a ricocheting cannonball which made a direct hit on his battery. Others later claimed he caused his own death by spiking his piece so it would not fall into enemy hands. Irregardless of the cause of death, Welch would be gone forever, never having tasted the waters of Scary. Private Elijah Beeman would be luckier. He would partake in an unsuccessful movement against the rebels, survive the battle unscathed, only to be killed by a bullet in his breast at the battle of South Mountain. Maryland, on September 22, 1862. For the moment, though, neither of these two young men, representative of so many others like themselves, knew of their impending fates. Their primary concern was the situation immediately in front of them—the battle of Scary Creek.

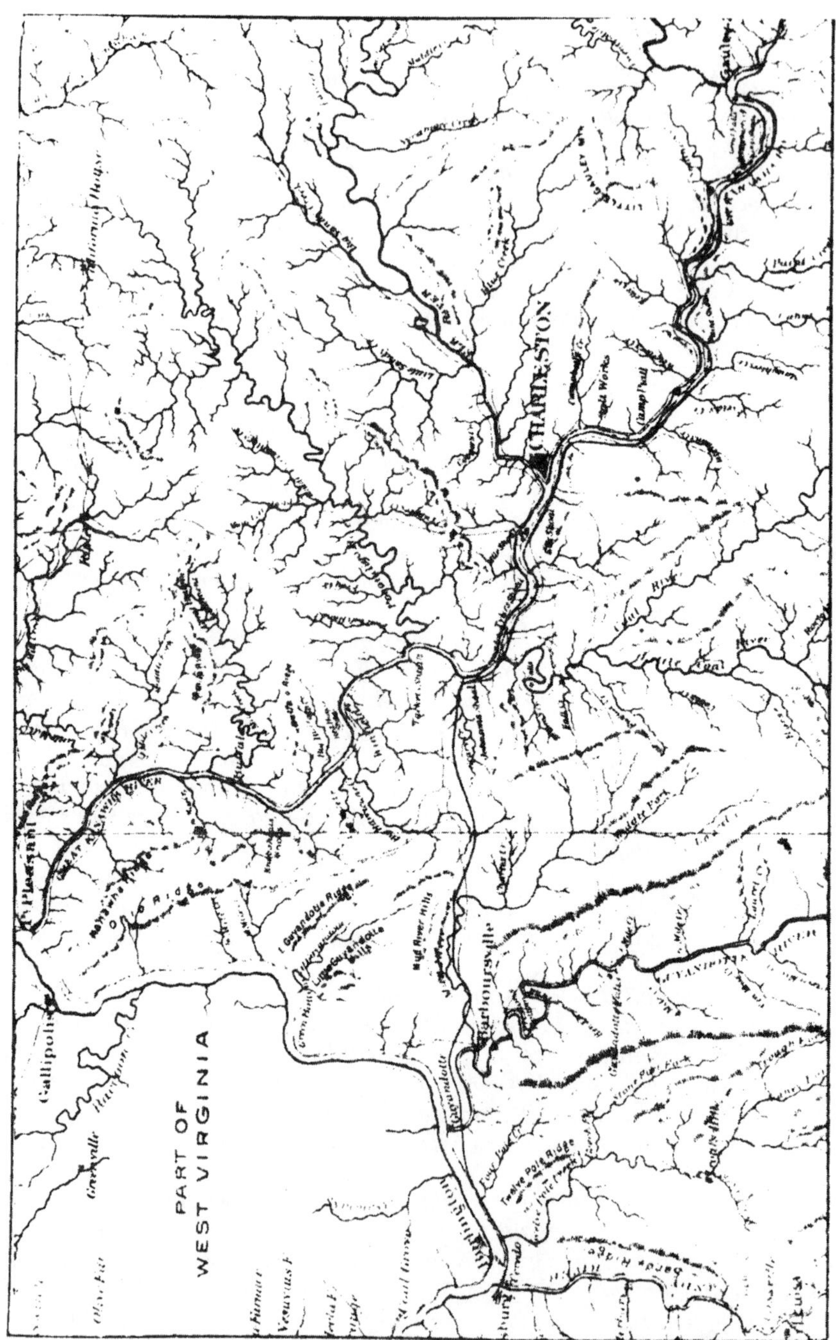

AREA OF OPERATIONS FOR THE KANAWHA CAMPAIGN — APRIL — JULY 1861 *Note that Camp Piatt east of Charleston was a Federal Camp established later in the war.*

CHAPTER ONE

Reflections of Lt. James C. Welch, Kanawha Artillery

Lt. James Clark Welch, like his fellow soldiers, may not have fully understood all the factors which had brought on this sudden civil war where families and neighbors took up arms against each other, but he did realize to some extent his part in this small contained action in the Kanawha Valley of western Virginia, and as the battle of Scary began to unfold he had time to reflect upon these.

Possibly the most important single item was that the military, both North and South, needed salt, primarily for meat preservation, and Welch came from a family involved in the salt industry of the Kanawha Valley. His father's brother had been a salt-maker at Kanawha Salines (Malden) and was engaged as a manager of the shipment and sale of salt. Although coal-oil production had slowly been replacing salt as the chief industry of the Kanawha area at the outbreak of the war, salt manufacturing was still very much present. In fact, "salt furnaces hemmed in the road all the way from Malden to the farmland of Col. Joseph Ruffner" (the vicinity of present day Ruffner Park and Holly Grove).[1]

In addition, the Kanawha Valley was bursting with forest land and agricultural wealth, representing one of the few "rich farming sections in western Virginia, with crops of grain, hay, and fodder, able to constitute both men and horses."[2] This held particularly true in Putnam County, where Scary Creek is located, and in Mason County, both situated on the lower end of the Kanawha River. Here, indeed, were the resources essential to keeping an army on the move.

Even as a novice military man, Jim Welch understood that the Kanawha's geographic location was a plus in itself. From the earliest of times the valley had served as a direct transportation and communications line between Richmond and the Ohio River valley. If Richmond was to be taken by the enemy then this was one of the quickest routes to get there. And the Southern army, by holding this area, could use it to defend their northern frontier, to launch offensive operations, and to inspire neighboring neutrals to flock to the Southern banner.[3] Possession by the Northern troops would mean similar advantages in their favor.

Not to be overlooked was that the Kanawha, as well as the whole of western Virginia, provided a highly potential area of recruitment, the mountain man being in particularly high demand by the Confederate army, as indicated in the April 26, 1861 issue of the *Kanawha Valley Star:*

> *The mountains of Transallegheny are filled with able bodied men—men accustomed from their youth to bear arms, every one of whom has one or more rifles in his cabin, and all of whom are first rate marksmen. These men number legions, and a little drilling would make them the best of soldiers.*
>
> *Should the abolishionists of Ohio send an invading army into Western Virginia, not a soldier of them will ever return alive. The mountain boys will shoot them down as dogs.*

Slavery was not really an issue along the Kanawha. It existed but to a minimal degree. The entire area covered by Kanawha County had only 2,124 slaves according to an 1860 census, a relatively small number compared to other areas of the South. "The rocky hillsides and variable climate of the rugged western plateau were wholly unsuited to the plantation system and its people remained largely hostile to slavery."[4] Yet this attitude failed to prevent constant fears of a slave uprising, as indicated by the April 27, 1861 entry in the diary of Rev. S.R. Houston of Monroe County, which read, "an insurrection among the Negroes on the Kanawha is apprehended" (anticipated).[5] Although some trouble of this sort did develop at Lewisburg, far from the Kanawha Valley, the valley itself never witnessed any such problems.

Sentiment to a particular cause in relation to geographic area also played an important part. During the early stages of the war the Union sentiment was obviously strongest at the points nearest Ohio, and weakened the further eastward one traveled. At Point Pleasant, where the Kanawha empties into the Ohio River, the Union flag soon was flown as volunteers drilled. At Guyandotte, not too many miles to the south of Point Pleasant, the Confederacy reigned for a short while, while at Charleston, the furthest point navigable on the Kanawha River (during low water), feelings were so split on the issue of secession that few dared to raise any flag, but Virginia militia forces, which became part of the Confederate army, took the initiative in the area and gained temporary control. Finally, at Gauley Bridge, where the New and Gauley rivers form the headwaters of the Kanawha, the secessionist army was heartily welcomed. Be it North or South, whoever possessed the Kanawha had a hotbed of indecision to cope with.[6]

And Charleston, the area of strongest uncertainties, principal economic center and largest town on the Kanawha, boasting a population of about 1,500, was Jim Welch's hometown. In that respect, it had to be defended by him. Only a few months after the battle at Scary one Union soldier described Charleston as "quite a pretty place with about 2,000 inhabitants and is located on the beautiful bottom on the northeast bank of the river and is entirely surrounded by lofty hills. There are many pretty residences, but they and the public buildings are built after the old style and have not much pretension to magnificence."[7] Yet one of his fellow soldiers was much less generous with his views: "The general appearance of Charleston is anything but prepossessing. A lot of dingy, old-fashioned, dilapidated buildings, irregular in their relative positions, border some half dozen dirty streets—that is about all there is of it."[8] Even one of Welch's Confederate colleagues remarked that Charleston was nothing more than "a small, dirty looking, country town."[9] But no matter what the physical appearance of Charleston, Welch and his family lived there and he had no intention of that situation changing.

LT. JAMES CLARK WELCH
Hale's Battery, Kanawha Artillery. Killed at Scary Creek.
— Courtesy: Charleston Newspapers

Captain George S. Patton and the Kanawha Riflemen

Since the Kanawha Valley was composed entirely of Virginia soil it was only natural that the state authorities, and later the Confederate government, were the first to attempt recruiting there. But the actual nucleus of the Southern army in the valley, as Lt. James Welch could well remember, had its origination through the foresight of his present military commander, Lt. Col. George Smith Patton (grandfather of General George S. Patton, old "Blood and Guts" of World War II fame). Patton was an 1852 graduate of Virginia Military Institute, had spent time studying law in his father's Richmond office, and during that time, had often peered out the window of that office and watched in inspirational silence the drilling of the Richmond Light Infantry Blues, Virginia's oldest and most distinguished military organization. In fact, this combination of law and the military would help to shape the remainder of his life. In 1856 he and his wife moved to Charleston in order for him to practice law, forming a partnership with Thomas Lee Broun. In his new profession Patton served as Commissioner in Chancery to Kanawha Circuit Court and Kanawha County Court. And, ironically, Patton and Broun both served on the board of directors of the Coal River Navigation Company while William Starke Rosecrans was company president, Rosecrans being the man who later became a Union general and helped to drive the army of Patton and Broun away from the Kanawha Valley.

Upon his arrival in Charleston, Patton purchased a large one-story home known as "Elm Grove," situated on what later became Lee Street, and has been moved twice since and now rests at Daniel Boone Park and is commonly referred to as the Craik-Patton house. Nicknamed "Frenchy" due to his pointed beard (although all photos show him with a full beard), Patton was arrogant, a smart dresser, displayed classic chivalry toward the ladies, and upon formation of his military company, was considered one of the most promising and capable of the early militia commanders. Here indeed was a man destined to rise in military rank.[10]

George undoubtedly anticipated the forthcoming conflict and formed a militia company in the Kanawha in 1856, dubbing it the Kanawha Minutemen. Their formation took place at Brooks Hall (also known as the "Assembly Room") and about a week later they elected officers. The name soon changed to the Kanawha Rifles, and finally in November of 1859, the name was permanently changed to the Kanawha Riflemen. The *Kanawha Valley Star* reported, "This Company is already large and rapidly increasing. It is holding drills regularly."[11] In fact, according to a veteran of the outfit, the earliest organization of the company was a "drilling club,"[12] something Patton was a master at, but their bylaws hinted at their seriousness:

> *No provision is made for the failure of a member of this company to attend in time of war or tumult, for it is naturally supposed that every member will be present. However, should any member fail to answer roll call under such circumstances, and not show good reason therefor, he shall be dealt with as a deserter from the army.*[13]

The Riflemen, obviously patterned after the Richmond Light Infantry Blues, was composed primarily of the socially prominent and wealthy men

GEORGE S. PATTON
22nd Virginia Infantry. Unretouched photo. The uniform has been painted onto the original picture.
— Courtesy: Library of Congress

of the valley, reportedly including some twenty lawyers, and were privately financed. Patton, a harsh disciplinarian, drilled them extensively in the old Mercer Academy Military School lot, and in Joel Ruffner's meadow (present Ruffner Park where a commemorative marker to the Riflemen now rests), and in Brooks Hall (near the present Kanawha County Public Library on Capitol Street). Being as impressive as they were in drill, they often appeared at parades, balls, and social functions, earning a reputation that they could dance as well as, and maybe better, than they could fight, as they had yet to prove themselves in battle. When the Riflemen turned out for manuevers at public outings Patton had the guard mounted and as one of them fondly remembered, "I recall a July 4th celebration and picnic at Ruffner grove, in Slab Town as we used to call the eastern end of the city, and the riflemen turned out en masse. I was one of the mounted guards, marching back and forth for hours in the hot sun, in my new uniform with my rifle on my shoulder—proudly guarding the fried chicken and lemonade."[14]

Life was not always so leisurely for the Riflemen. In 1859 there was talk of sending them to Harpers Ferry to quell the John Brown affair, but this never materialized. However, in the autumn of 1860 another incident nearly erupted into violence for the boys. While the unit was invited to attend the Agricultural Fair at Point Pleasant, two uniformed members took occasion to visit friends at nearby Gallipolis, and soon found themselves jeered and harassed by the citizens of Gallipolis, as the town was a bit strong in Union sentiment at this time. They were quickly rescued by a small detachment of Riflemen but, according to Noyes Rand, one of the unwelcome visitors, if it had not been for the discipline under which the Riflemen had been so well trained by Patton, tempers would have flared and "hostilities would have begun then & there in Gallipolis instead of next Spring at Fort Sumter."[15]

The Riflemen were composed of a fluctuating membership of some 75 to 100 men, and had an excellent brass band led by an English cornetist, but they were best remembered by veterans and residents of the area alike for their flashy uniforms which Patton designed for them. Slightly varying descriptions were recalled, but it basically consisted of brass buttons stamped with the Virginia coat of arms on a uniform of "dark (olive) green broadcloth, matching overcoats, broad gold (some veterans claimed black) stripes down the pantaloons, a fancy headgear which consisted of black hats with ostrich feathers dangling from a wide brim with a gold KR on the front of the cap, the entire headdress covered with oilcloth in bad weather, and white (cotton) Berlin gloves." The "coats were long, with epaulets of gold braid...and a short shoulder cape that graced the coat." It was also remembered that Patton made the men black their shoes regularly. Upon comparison there is but little doubt that Patton's creation was directly influenced by the uniform of the Richmond Light Infantry Blues. When the Kanawha Riflemen were later mustered into the Confederate service as Company H, 22nd Virginia Infantry, the authorities ordered them to dispose of the gaudy uniforms, resulting in an apparent change to "light blue jackets and dark gray trousers with yellow trimmings."[16]

Weaponry of the Riflemen consisted of a various assortment of rifles, including "a short Neiss Rifle, with bayonet, cartridge box and scabbard," Belgian rifles, and a Harper's Ferry Rifle which had a bore of about 45, iron ramrod, and fired with percussion caps, with a grease box located in

ELM GROVE
The Craik-Patton House today. — Photo by the author

the stock.[17] One Rifleman reflected, "Although there is no record of it, I think Patton must have offered the services of the company as a whole to the Governor very shortly after we organized. For had we not been part of the Virginia state militia, and under the command of old Colonel Hogue of Winfield, commandant of this district, we could not have secured rifles from the state. We were inordinately proud of our appearance. After we had learned to drill we never lost an opportunity to turn out, especially after the rifles had come from Richmond. I recall they were locked in Brooks Hall under guard and none of us were allowed to look at those precious rifles at first. I managed to get a peep at them, however, by calling through the door that Colonel Hogue had come and wanted to inspect the guns. When the door was opened, I walked in."[18]

Proud of their Kanawha Riflemen, the fine southern ladies of Charleston bought them a flag which had the regular thirteen stripes and the Virginia coat of arms, but when war came they converted the stripes to the Confederate colors and left the coat of arms.

And so it was that this transplanted Richmond lawyer, only twenty-four years old but full of daring and dash, prepared the Kanawha for its defense well before the outbreak of hostilities. When war finally arrived, George S. Patton and the Kanawha Riflemen, which indirectly included Lt. James C. Welch, were the first to respond. Patton was the type of man, who, if given full command, could possibly lead the Kanawha secessionist army to victory. Unfortunately, he was not given such command.

On April 30, 1861, the *Kanawha Valley Star,* a newspaper run by Kanawha Rifleman John Rundle, published Company Orders #1 for the Kanawha Riflemen, which was primarily a call to hold themselves in readiness for marching orders, a detailed list of items each man was required to possess, and closed with Patton's assumption that: "...in issuing these prepatory orders (there is) but little doubt that the services of this command will be required to aid in driving the invader from the soil of Virginia...and that every Rifleman will respond cheerfully and with alacrity to the call of his State... " (For a complete listing of the Kanawha Riflemen - Company Orders #1 see Appendix).

Patton and his Kanawha Riflemen were not alone by any means. A number of other militia units were organized in the Kanawha Valley prior to the official call for state troops. One of the most prominent was the Kanawha (or Charleston) Sharpshooters, made up of many Kanawha River boatmen and organized in 1859 by Capt. John Sterling Swann, who was assisted by Joel Ruffner, Jr. Completing the leadership of the company was 1st Lt. John R. Taylor, 2nd Lt. Charles Ufferman, 3rd Lt. Dr. A.E. Summers, and James Venable serving as sergeant. This unit, dressed in their gray uniforms, could often be found practicing manuevers in a field belonging to the Welch family.[19] They often worked in conjunction with the Kanawha Riflemen and the Fire department, as illustrated in an 1860 issue of the *Kanawha Valley Star:* "...a handsome appearance was made by Capt. John Swann's Sharp Shooters and Capt. George Patton's Rifle Company. Both of these organizations...attended...the funeral services of Gen. Charles Scott, a kinsman of Gen. Winfield Scott. The services had been conducted by Rev. James Brown of the Presbyterian Church on May 22. The two companies were handsomely uniformed and equipped, presenting an imposing appearance. Capt. Swann's Company has exhibited its heroism frequently in the capacity of a fire brigade, battling at all hours of the night in heat and cold."

Two militia groups existed in Putnam County. One was the Border Guards of Capt. Albert J. Beckett, recruited from the vicinity of Hurricane Bridge. The other was the Buffalo Guards (or Buffalo Blues) led by Capt. William E. Fife, a lawyer and former instructor at the Mercer Academy. Organized in 1859, it included a number of students from the Buffalo Academy at Buffalo, many of them soon to take part in the battle of Scary.

Finally, there was the Coal River Rifle Company, which hardly bears mentioning except for the fact that it did exist. Apparently very little is known about the company except that they organized in December of 1859, probably consisted of men from both Kanawha and Putnam counties, and elected the following officers: Capt. Thomas A. Lewis; Lt. B.S. Thompson; Lt. C.D. Moss; and Sgt. J.F. Hansford. This group, located in the area of Coalsmouth (St. Albans), appears to have either dissolved and faded into obscurity, merged with other outfits, or remained intact but did little to distinguish themselves in order to leave a record of their deeds. B.S. Thompson later showed up at Scary Creek commanding the Kanawha Militia who were perhaps an evolution of the Coal River Rifle Company.[20]

MONUMENT TO THE KANAWHA RIFLEMEN
Ruffner Park, Charleston. — Photo by the author

OVERCOAT OF KANAWHA RIFLEMAN LEVI WELCH
Apparently part of the uniform design by Patton. On display at the West Virginia State Museum. — Courtesy: West Virginia State Archives

KANAWHA RIFLEMAN JOHN RUNDLE
Publisher of the **Kanawha Valley Star**. — From **Confederate Veteran** Magazine

GENERAL [then Captain] ALBERT GALLATIN JENKINS
He helped to turn the tide at Scary.. — Courtesy: National Archives

Captain Albert Gallatin Jenkins and the Border Rangers

Although the Kanawha River does not flow through Cabell County, but does pass through and enter the Ohio River in Mason County, the two neighboring areas contributed one of the most outstanding militia groups to the Kanawha campaign, that being the Border Rangers of Capt. Albert Gallatin Jenkins. As early as December of 1860 a company of militia had been organized at Guyandotte with Cabell County lawyer Ira J. McGinnis serving as captain, but they did nothing more than guard a secessionist flag that had been raised on April 20, 1861 near the banks of the Ohio River in front of Planters Hotel. At about that time Albert Gallatin Jenkins arrived from his nearby farm at Greenbottom and held a general muster, delivering a "stirring speech" to the volunteers. Jenkins, who had just recently turned thirty years of age, was a native of Cabell County who had risen to high ranks in the political world. He was of "medium size, with a flat but good head, light brown hair, blue eyes, immense flowing beard of a sandy hue, and rather a pleasant face."[21] He had attended V.M.I and graduated from Jefferson College in Pennsylvania, then went on to Harvard hoping to eventually practice law. Although properly trained, he never professionally entered the judicial occupation, preferring involvement in politics where he served with the U.S. Congress. Yet when the clouds of war and Northern invasion threatened his home he returned from Washington to aid in Virginia's defense. Undoubtedly, the geographic location of his farm helped to fuel his enthusiasm. "Greenbottom," as his estate was known, was a large plantation with many slaves, located just north of Guyandotte on the Virginia bank of the Ohio River (the original house stands there yet today). If the Northern army invaded via Ohio, which they would, Jenkins' farm would be one of the first places taken.

Once mustered in, the company, which was known as the Border Rangers, marched to nearby Greenbottom Baptist Church where more recruits from Mason and other surrounding counties joined, adding up to an approximate total of 101 men. The volunteers were "armed with obsolete guns, and mounted where horses were available."[22] A rather meager beginning for the men who were to become Company E of the 8th Virginia Cavalry, one of the toughest fighting outfits in the Confederate army. But for now they were just a bunch of farm boys who had formed a cavalry unit to protect their homes. Border Ranger James D. Sedinger later described this period in their development:

> *"...we drilled cavalry drill and thought we could whip the world...our Commissary Department was looked after by the ladies of Cabell and Mason counties who kept us supplied with boiled ham and roasted chicken, baked light bread and biscuit cake and pies. Everything that we could think of to tickle the palate and we enjoyed ourselves better than we ever did afterwards. Our clothing the same way—whenever a wagon would come into camp the boys would make a break for it and he would be certain to find something for him from his sweetheart, sister or mother...."*[23]

After about three weeks of such luxury the Border Rangers were sent to the Kanawha Valley, having marched to Buffalo and camped on the Hall farm en route, arriving at Coalsmouth where they "went into camp in the

Episcopalian parsonage."[24] At this point they remained on picket duty as events continued to develop around them.

Many other counties contributed early, such as Fayette containing the headwaters of the Kanawha, raising such companies as the Dixie Rifles of Capt. Beuhring H. Jones, as well as many others to be later named. Equally representative were the counties not containing the Kanawha River within their boundaries but close enough to be of service to the Kanawha campaign. Typical of these was Nicholas County, where on May 1, 1861 a secessionist flag was raised at the Summersville courthouse. At that time Capt. Winston Shelton raised a 100 man force known as the Nicholas Blues, and on May 15 a Capt. Newman raised another company. Both companies would join the Wise Legion at a later date, but as with so many others of similar background, they would not make their appearance in the Kanawha campaign until a later date, from which time they became an effective part of the Confederate army in the Kanawha.

BORDER RANGERS REUNION

This photo, taken on Feb. 22, 1893 by S.V. Mathews, shows a reunion of Capt. Albert Gallatin Jenkins' Border Rangers, Co. E, 8th Virginia Cavalry. Most, if not all, of these men fought at Scary. 1st row, left to right (standing): 1. Jesse Dodson; 2. James D. Sedigner; 3. Leo Hendrick; 4. James Baumgardner; 5. Sampson S. Simmons; 6. B. Boothe; 7. A.A. (Gus) Handley. 2nd row (sitting): 8. Charles Shoemaker; 9. B.A. (Gus) Wolcott; 10. Thaddeus W. Flowers; 11. W.E. Wilkinson; 12. Lucien C. Ricketts; 13. J.S. Stewart; 14. Geo. W. Hackworth..

— Courtesy: James E. Morrow Library, Marshall University, Huntington, WV

IRA J. MAGINNIS
Original Captain of Jenkins' Border Rangers.

GREENBOTTOM
It is facing the Ohio River and was the home of Albert Gallatin Jenkins. The addition at left was added after the war. — Courtesy: Emma Simms Maginnis

McCAUSLAND HOMESTEAD
General John McCausland's home on the Kanawha River in Mason County which he built in 1885. He lived there until his death in 1927.
— Courtesy: Stan Cohen

Lt. Col. John McCausland

Although Virginia had not yet seceded, the writing was clearly on the wall, so on April 29, 1861, Robert E. Lee, in charge of all Virginia state forces, commissioned John McCausland a lieutenant colonel of volunteers and put him in charge of the Kanawha situation. McCausland, later nicknamed "Tiger John," was a more than logical choice for the assignment, having been reared in the Kanawha Valley and having received his early education at the Buffalo Academy. He knew the people of the valley well and liked the area so much that after the war he built a home across the river from Buffalo (the house yet stands at McCausland Run), and lived out his remaining days there, which turned out to be quite a few. In addition to his familiarity with the land and its people, McCausland had a military background that included his being an 1857 graduate of V.M.I. and later serving as an assistant professor of mathematics at that institution. He organized the famous Rockbridge Artillery and was elected commander but turned that position over to another so that he could participate in the Kanawha campaign for obvious personal attachment. Yet his most striking quality was that he was so intensely devoted to the Southern cause that he later refused to surrender at Appomattox, and remained an "unreconstructed rebel" until his dying day. There was never any doubt of this man's loyalty,

GENERAL [then Lieutenant Colonel] JOHN McCAUSLAND
36th Virginia Infantry. — Courtesy: West Virginia State Archives

military knowledge or courage. Surely of all people in the Kanawha campaign, McCausland was the one probably most capable of leading the Kanawha to victory—but just as with Patton, and as with Jenkins who was also qualified as such, he was not given that all important position of full command. This was the type of man the Kanawha needed and it was apparently presumed that if anybody could lead the Kanawha volunteer forces, it was McCausland, so included with his commission were the orders to:

> *...proceed to the valley of the Kanawha and muster into the service of the State such volunteer companies (not exceeding ten) as may offer their services, in compliance with the call of the governor; take command of them, and direct military operations for the protection of that section of the country. Your policy will be strictly defensive, and you will endeavor to give quiet and assurance to the inhabitants. It has been reported that two companies are already found in Kanawha County, Captain Patton's and Captain Swann's, and that there are two in Putnam County, Captain Beckett's and Captain Fife's. It is supposed that others will offer their services. The number of enlisted men to a company, fixed by the Convention, is eighty-two. You will report the condition of arms, &c. of each company, and, to enable you to supply deficiencies, five hundred muskets, of the old pattern, will be sent. I regret to state that they are the only kind at present for issue. Four field pieces will also be sent you as soon as possible, for the service of which you are desired to organize a company of artillery. The position of companies at present is left to your judgement, and you are desired to report what points below Charleston will most effectually accomplish the objects in view....*[25]

Upon arriving in the Kanawha from Richmond, McCausland found the units of Patton, Swann, Fife, and Beckett ready to cooperate just as Lee had presumed. He immediately went to work, converting his old alma mater, the Buffalo Academy, into a recruiting station, and it's believed that the entire upper class volunteered and that the majority of them took part in the battle of Scary. As requested, the one artillery company was formed at Charleston, financed primarily by Dr. John Peter Hale who served as captain. Christened Hale's Battery, or the Kanawha Artillery, the group also included Lt. William Alexander Quarrier and young Lt. James C. Welch, with most of the members being drawn from the ranks of the Kanawha Riflemen. William Taylor Thayer and his brother, Otis A. Thayer, had established a foundry at Malden, where they made a ten-pound smooth bore iron cast cannon nicknamed the "Peacemaker," a piece which later purportedly turned the tide at Scary. This was probably the artillery section mentioned in the diary of Private William Clark Reynolds of the Kanawha Riflemen on May 3, 1861: "Went to Malden in the morning and to the foundry and saw the cannon."[26] Otis Thayer became a lieutenant in the state militia but never took part in active service, while William T. Thayer joined the Kanawha Riflemen and was later transferred, obviously enough, to Hale's Battery.

On April 30 the Confederate Ordnance Department was ordered to send to the Kanawha, in addition to the two hundred flint-lock muskets ordered (some 300 short of what Lee promised), four iron six-pounder cannon, dismounted, with twenty rounds of ammunition, and axles for the carriages.[27] It appears they were sent and received but despite this, and all other supplies sent, there was a sore lack of war materials for the Virginia volunteers. Worse yet, there was an even stronger shortage of volunteers. McCausland's efforts at recruitment had been valiant but fell far short of expectations. Possibly McCausland's hot temper and fiery personality discouraged some potential recruits, although it is unlikely, and didn't much matter anyway as the Virginia authorities sent someone else along to aid the Kanawha situation.

CAPT. JOHN PETER HALE
Kanawha Artillery. He became a noted author and historian after the war.
— Courtesy: West Virgina State Archives

WILLIAM T. THAYER
Kanawha Rifleman. He helped make the artillery piece that aided the Scary victory.
— Courtesy: Larry Legge and Charleston Newspapers.

Colonel Christopher Quarles Tompkins

A man of great charisma and extensive military training was needed. To this end the authorities looked toward another resident of the area, and on May 3, 1861, Adjutant General of Virginia Forces, R.S. Garnett, commissioned Christopher Quarles Tompkins a colonel of the Virginia volunteer forces in the Kanawha Valley, all this twenty-one days before Virginia voted to secede from the Union. Tompkins was also informed that McCausland would assist him.[28]

Tompkins was an even more logical choice than McCausland to command the forces of the Kanawha. He was a highly experienced military man and a well known and respected resident of the valley, owning a fine mansion three miles east of Gauley Bridge, and just outside the Kanawha Valley, known as "Gauley Mount." His home was a "veritable showplace, with slaves, a splendid library," a seventy foot long barn, and a vineyard of 800 vines.[29] There was a tutor present for his children and carriages were always available so that Tompkins, his wife and children could be transported to Richmond whenever they wished, and they so desired often, as Mrs. Tompkins was a "cultured Richmond belle." Col. Tompkins had originally lived in Richmond but had relocated at Gauley where he was Mining Agent and Superintendent of Colleries (coal mines) in Kanawha and Fayette counties, with particular interests at Paint Creek where he was Chief Agent of the Paint Creek Coal and Iron Manufacturing Company.

But Governor John Letcher of Virginia undoubtedly desired Tompkins due to his long and distinguished military career. He had served sixteen years in the United States Army, had graduated 27th in a class of 49 at West Point in 1836, and had served as an officer with various artillery units in the Florida Seminole War, the battle of Locha-Hatchee and, later, the Mexican War. He resigned from the army in 1841 having attained the rank of captain. He continued as a captain of the Virginia militia from 1848 to 1851, followed by a stint as a lieutenant colonel for the next two years. When war came to the Kanawha, Christopher Q. Tompkins was forty-three years old and probably would not have accepted his assignment had he not been under the impression that the war would be of a short duration. Although not in total agreement with the Southern cause, he went ahead and accepted his duties as offered with the necessary amount of fervor.[30] With the addition of Tompkins to the triumvirate of Patton, Jenkins, and McCausland, there was now a fourth man who had the ability and credentials to successfully lead the Kanawha if given full command, but as with the other three, Tompkins also did not receive that prestigious position.

With Tompkins and McCausland, at least temporarily, leading the way, events began to transpire rapidly, as there was no longer any doubt that Virginia would side with the Confederacy. On May 6 the *Kanawha Valley Star* printed orders for the Kanawha Riflemen to assemble for parade and inspection on May 11th, an obvious war preparation.[31] But before that ever took place, on the ninth of the month, the Kanawha Riflemen were officially mustered into the service of the State and "...escorted by the Sharpshooters, Capt. Swann, with flying banners and martial music, the tears and sobs and smiles and waving of hankerchiefs of the fair, the encouragement of the sterner sex and the blessings of all, they marched to the Methodist Camp Ground, which they speedily put in order and designated Camp Lee."[32]

COLONEL CHRISTOPHER QUARLES TOMPKINS
22nd Virginia Infantry. — Courtesy: Virginia State Library

The Training Camps

Camp Lee has often been confused with Camp Two Mile, one school of thought being that it was one and the same camp, the other it being a companion camp located near Camp Two Mile. Camp Two Mile itself was named after the small stream which entered the Kanawha River after flowing through the property of Adam Brown Dickinson Littlepage, who resided with his wife, Rebecca, and children, in a fine stone mansion there (the house stands there yet today and is presently the quarters of the Charleston Housing Authority). The military camp extended from the Kanawha to the junction of the Ripley-Ravenswood road with the Point Pleasant road (present Washington Street West), and many of the soldiers pitched their tents in the apple orchards surrounding Kanawha Two Mile (hence the modern day housing development Orchard Manor). Also, although at what exact date it was established is unknown, a fortification was built on the heights across Kanawha Two Mile, behind Orchard Manor area, known as Fort Fife, so named after Capt. William Fife of the Buffalo Blues.

On May 11, McCausland ran a "recruitment ad" in the *Kanawha Valley Star* directed at already existing and potential volunteer and militia groups in his area of command, which read:

> *I have arrived to take command of the Department (of the Kanawha). I have instructions to call into the field ten companies and one company of artillery. These troops will be encamped in the Kanawha Valley, near Buffalo, Putnam County. They are intended for the protection of the Department and I appeal to the citizens of the border counties to abstain from anything which will arouse the ill feeling on either side of the Ohio River. This Department is organized by the proper authority of the State and is provided with the credit to sustain itself, but for complete success I firmly rely on the friendly disposition of the people therein.*
>
> *The volunteer companies of the counties of Mason, Jackson, and Putnam will rendezvous at Buffalo, Putnam County.*
>
> *The volunteer companies of the counties of Cabell, Wayne, and Logan will rendezvous at Barboursville, Cabell County.*
>
> *The volunteer companies of the counties of Kanawha, Boone, Wyoming, Raleigh, Fayette, Nicholas, and Clay will rendezvous at Charleston, Kanawha County.*
>
> *The captains of the volunteer companies in the above counties will remain at their respective drill grounds until ordered to their rendezvous by the commandant of the Department. So soon as preparation to receive them can be made, the companies will be ordered to their respective rendezvous, mustered into the service of the State and ordered to the Camp of Instruction. No company will be mustered into service unless it has at least eighty-two men.*
>
> *The Captain will see that each man is provided with a uniform, one blanket and haversack, one extra pair of shoes, two flannel shirts (to be worn in the place of the ordinary shirts), one comb and brush, toothbrush, two pairs of drawers, four pairs of woolen socks, four hankerchiefs, two pairs of white gloves, one pair of rough pantaloons for fatigue duty, needles, thread, wax, buttons, secured in a small buckskin bag. The whole (excepting the blanket) will be placed in a bag, this will be placed on the blanket, rolled up, and secured to the back of each man by two straps.*

Actually, McCausland's "ad" was old news to most of the volunteer companies, who had already received the notice a number of days prior to its appearance in the *Star*. In fact, this was probably what prompted the Kanawha Riflemen and Swann's Sharpshooters to move to Camp Lee. And while few of the volunteers were actually provided with the items required by McCausland, particularly uniforms, war spirits were high and they came irregardless, including such volunteer companies as the one organized by John Swann's brother (law partners prior to the war) Capt. Thomas Belt Swann, an outspoken opponent of secession who preferred to fight for his native state, who brought the Elk River Tigers, composed of men from Kanawha and Clay counties, who, according to McCausland, "could fight like hell."[33] Logan County produced the Logan Volunteer Rifle Company (Logan Riflemen) led by Capt. Charles J. Stone; the Logan Wildcats of Capt. Henry M. Beckley; and the Chapmanville Daredevils. Boone County contributed Capt. James W. McSherry's Boone County Rangers. From Fayette County came the Fayetteville Rifles (Fayette Rifles/Riflemen) of Capt. Robert Augustus ('Gus') Bailey; Capt. Beuhring Jones' Dixie Rifles; the Mountain Cove Guard; and the Fayette Rangers of Capt. William Tyree. One cavalry company of especial note was the Sandy Rangers from Wayne County, led by Mexican War veteran Capt. James M. Corns, who were nicknamed the "Bloodtubs" because of their bright red flannel hunting shirts and caps. Their original membership was fifty-three but quickly rose to 110, probably having incorporated a number of men from the Fairview Riflemen, also of Wayne County, commanded by Capt. Milton Jamison Ferguson. There is some belief that "Devil" Anse Hatfield of post-war Hatfield-McCoy fueding fame served with the Sandy Rangers at Scary, although Confederate service records fail to bear this out.[34]

These volunteer forces were just a sampling; many others came, slowly building a competent fighting force of Virginia volunteers. They came from all walks of life—farmers, merchants, students, schoolteachers, lawyers—a vast variety of occupational backgrounds. Unfortunately, weapons and supplies continued to fail to equal their patriotism. Many of them had to provide their own weapons, which consisted of such pieces as "flint-lock

THE APPLE ORCHARD — CAMP TWO MILE — POSTWAR VIEW
Many Confederate soldiers pitched their tents in this area.
— Courtesy: Mrs. John T. Morgan

COLONEL [then Captain]
THOMAS BELT SWANN
Elk River Tigers.

REUNION OF THE LOGAN COUNTY WILDCATS
Co. D, 36th Virginia Infantry.

CAPTAIN WILLIAM TYREE
Fayette Rangers.
— Courtesy: Fayette County Historical Society

"DEVIL" ANSE HATFIELD
Famous feuder purported to have fought at Scary. — Courtesy: Library of Congress

muskets, smooth bore guns with ramrods and percussion caps, squirrel rifles, shotguns (many of the 'cornstock' variety), and other related firearms.''[35] Men without guns came with sharp pikes, butcher knives, and other assorted hand weapons. The cavalry, for the most part, had to provide their own mounts and usually had no weaponry beyond a sabre and a shotgun. The artillery, including that of Lt. James Welch, was composed of some iron and brass cannon. Uniforms, with the exception of the companies which made their own, were almost non-existent.

Regardless of the quality of their supplies the morale and spirit of the volunteers were high, and war preparations continued within the valley. During the early morning hours of May 13 the Kanawha Riflemen and Swann's Sharpshooters boarded the steamer *Julia Maffitt* en route for the camp of instruction at Buffalo, leaving the Charleston Home Guard of Capt. W.A. Jackson, a 100 man contingent, to protect the citizens of Charleston in their absence. Upon arrival at ''Camp Buffalo'' the two outfits joined with the Buffalo Blues who were already present and took up quarters in the Buffalo Academy, apparently quite a feat in itself considering the small size of the Academy.[36]

Typical of life at Camp Buffalo was the information relayed in the letter of May 15 written at the camp by Thomas Lee Broun to his sister Annie. Broun, Patton's law partner prior to the war, was an 1848 graduate of the University of Virginia, had taught school, and had studied law before succeeding William S. Rosecrans as President of the Coal River Navigation Company in 1858. The letter read:

> *I am getting somewhat accustomed to military life. On last Thursday we encamped near Charleston. On Sunday night last at midnight we were ordered off to this point, 35 miles below Charleston—we reached by steamboat but at 9 o'clock Monday morning. A great excitement prevailed in camp Monday night. Disaffected people living here and near the Ohio (Virginians too) ordered us to leave, gave us 24 hours to depart, otherwise they would compel us, etc. etc. These disaffected creatures are about like the Ragged mountain people (in Albermarle County). Designing persons had made them believe that we were sent here to compel them to vote for Secession, etc. etc. Our company (Kanawha Riflemen) numbers ninety good and true men. Amongst the most intelligent men in this part of the State, ten members of the Kanawha Bar, and my most intimate companions are of our number.*
>
> *Every man was on the qui vive Monday night, with his Bowie knife, revolver, and Harper's Ferry rifle. I was a sentinel and was thoroughly armed and wide awake for the issue. Our Company is the best drilled Company in Western Va. My old law partner, Mr. Patton, is our Commander. Troops are daily coming in to this point, and we shall soon muster 1000 strong—at this encampment.*
>
> *The exercise is very severe, drilling, drilling all the time, cleaning rifles, blackening our boots, cleaning up our rooms, washing clothes, etc. etc. to keep us actively and busily employed. It is too hard a life for some persons. I, however, am fattening on it, in fine spirits and excellent health. And now that our old glorious State is thoroughly aroused and armed to the teeth, heaven grant us a speedy and eternal separation from Yankeedom.*
>
> *...I have my Bible and prayer-book with me, and make it a duty to read them frequently...the Country people are all quieting down and there is no danger now of any conflict with them. Wednesday 12 o'clock...*[37]

The seventeen days spent at Camp Buffalo by the Kanawha Riflemen were not without moments of pleasure and relaxation, as indicated by Private William Clark Reynolds, who reported on one day that he ''Went over to Eighteen mile creek fishing with Cabel and Donnally. Caught forty three fish and drank two bottles of native Isabella.''[38] Even the attitude of

BUFFALO ACADEMY
Much as it looked during the war. — Courtesy: Emma Simms Maginnis

BUFFALO ACADEMY
As it looks today. — Courtesy: Gary Bays

THOMAS LEE BROUN
Kanawha Rifleman and Patton's law partner prior to the war. Later became a major in the 3rd Regiment, Wise Legion, 60th Virginia.
— Courtesy: West Virginia State Archives

the officer in charge at Camp Buffalo, Lt. Col. John McCausland, was very positive, although he was intelligent enough to realize his small and ill-equipped army was yet far short of being a combat force to be reckoned with. Taking note of this he wrote a letter on May 16 to V.M.I Superintendent Francis Smith:

> *I am in need of drill masters. Send me some. I am preparing rapidly. I sent to the Col. of Ordnance for 500 cartridge boxes, 500 bayonets, scabbards, if they have not been sent please send them & some fixed ammunition. Have you been watching the Wheeling Convention, they will apply to Lincoln for arms & men & will resist authority of the state. Enclosed I send a letter I received. I receive daily such letters and influential men tell me the same thing. The Ohio paper suggests that the men I now have should be captured, as the Missouri troops were. I have only to say they* can't *take one of us alive. Please send us tents as our present camp cannot be moved. I have not yet made my return to the Governor Inspector Genl. I will do it soon. I labor very hard and will try to give a good account of my conduct.*
> *Could we get 5000 foot troops as the war may begin here?*[39]

McCausland not only worried about supplies and a potential enemy approach, but also about keeping his soldiers well fed, writing on May 17 to Major Crenshaw in Richmond: "In the event we are not able to get groceries from Cincinnati when could they be furnished from Richmond?"[40] Indeed, all of his fears were justified. His force was increased on the same day he wrote Francis Smith by the arrival of the Border Guards of Capt. Albert J. Beckett, and on the 22nd of May by the Putnam County Border Riflemen (Rifles), led by Capt. (Dr.) Andrew Russell Barbee, a former practicing physician at Poca Bottom in Putnam County, who like Capt. T.B. Swann of the Elk River Tigers, opposed secession but remained loyal to Virginia. But while the forces at Camp Buffalo continued to grow, an event of far greater importance took place on the 22nd when some scouts under McCausland, operating near Gallipolis, Ohio, viewed Companies A and D of the 21st Ohio Volunteer Infantry gathering there, the first Federal troops to arrive for participation in the Kanawha campaign. Although the Yankee presence was taken into consideration, two companies of Federal infantry were nothing to be too worried about.

On May 23 Col. Christopher Q. Tompkins, who had apparently arrived at Camp Buffalo, reported his total strength there as "350 men comprising five companies" but felt he could raise fifteen or sixteen more companies within the next two to three weeks, and also reiterated the now well known fact of the complete lack of material for uniforms.[41] On the 25th Swann's Sharpshooters were officially mustered into the service of the state. The Rev. T.L. Smith performed a service for the Camp Buffalo volunteers at the Buffalo Presbyterian Church on the 26th, and that night there was a false alarm in camp caused by the unannounced arrival of Capt. James W. McSherry's Boone Rangers.

Yet despite all this activity, there was a definite problem in the Kanawha Valley. Union sentiment was much stronger than had been anticipated and as a result the expected overflow of secessionist volunteers never materialized. The Confederate government, still in its infancy, lacked appropriate military supplies and men, while the Virginia government was equally plagued. Even the constant fear throughout the valley that Northern soldiers, particularly those from Ohio, would soon invade the Kanawha failed to incite the desired Virginia patriotism.

Col. Tompkins, one of the most educated and level-headed of the Kanawha commanders, was well aware of the precarious position of the Virginia volunteers at Camp Buffalo. Realizing he would probably soon be outnumbered by a much better trained and equipped army, he hastened to Kanawha Falls, near Gauley Bridge, where he wrote an urgent appeal to the Adjutant General on May 27, the exact same day that the remainder of the 21st Ohio Volunteer Infantry arrived at Gallipolis:

> *I have this moment an express from Lieutenant-Colonel McCausland, at Buffalo, dated yesterday, stating, "The government has sent two hundred men to Gallipolis and will have six hundred more there today. We are informed they are intended to attack this camp. Send down all the troops you have. In addition to this, reliable information reaches me that large numbers of troops are concentrating at Oak Hill, twenty-three miles back of Gallipolis and also at other places along the border. My idea is that these troops have been thrown into the proximity in order to overawe the loyal citizens of that region. For further particulars I beg leave to refer you to the bearer of this, Mr. David Kirkpatrick, a resident of this valley, and a well-informed man.*[42]

Whatever the enemy's intentions were, before the stage transporting this

CAPTAIN [DR.] ANDREW RUSSELL BARBEE
Putnam County Border Riflemen Co. A, 22nd Virginia Infantry.

POSTWAR VIEW
Camp Buffalo. Buffalo Academy in middle — steeple of Presbyterian Church in background. The church in right foreground built after the war. — Courtesy: Emma Simms Maginnis

BUFFALO PRESBYTERIAN CHURCH
Today. — Courtesy: Gary Bays

dispatch to Richmond could depart, Tompkins decided upon an intended plan of action and sent it along with the prior message:

> *...I shall of course proceed to Buffalo as rapidly as possible. The idea is that the enemy intend crossing the Ohio River, to attack the camps at Buffalo. Unless they come in greatly superior force, we shall drive them back. On the other hand, if his numbers are large and the disaffection of the inhabitants strongly evinced, I shall take the most defensible position I may find, and rally the volunteers now in process of formation in the adjoining counties. Great excitement prevails in this region. The divided sentiment of the people adds to the confusion, and, except the few loyal companies now mustered into the service of the State, there are few of the people who sympathize with the secession policy.... It is very desirable that Mr. Kirkpatrick should be the purveyor of some supplies for the troops which cannot be procured here. I beg that the quartermaster may be instructed to forward by him materials for tents, three hundred blankets, five hundred cartridge-boxes (musket), and ten thousand percussion caps (rifle), &c....*[43]

There could no longer be any doubt that the situation had become critical, and Tompkins and McCausland knew it better than anybody else. More recruits were desperately needed to meet the impending Federal challenge. Various officers began to roam the adjacent Kanawha tributaries and "hollows" attempting to raise additional troops. McCausland plastered posters throughout the valley calling for enlistments, and at one time even proposed a draft, which was so unpopular with General Alfred Beckley that it almost cost Virginia a large number of volunteer companies under his command. 1st Lieutenant Leigh Wilbur Reid, Recruiting Officer, Virginia Forces, ran an ad in the May 28th issue of the *Kanawha Valley Star,* and a number of subsequent issues, calling for volunteers and promising the same pay as that of Federal soldiers: "...Monthly pay: Sergeants $17; Corporals $13; Privates $11; with liberal allowances for clothing and subsistence and medical attendance free of expense." On May 29 Edgar C. Phelps wrote a letter to Col. Tompkins requesting a military camp at Ripley in Jackson County:

> *...We now have a rifle company fully organized and I have 60 men in my cavalry company and will be able to get at least 20 more...for drill purposes this county is preferable to any place in my knowledge. Provisions are abundant and consequently cheap and if we can get a camp here we can raise one if not two more companies....*[44]

Great enthusiasm and valiant efforts were not enough, though, and the ranks failed to show any respectable increase. Although Col. Tompkins issued a persuasive appeal to the men of Kanawha and Virginia on May 30, he had finally come to realize that the "home grown" troops needed were not to be had. Help had to come from elsewhere. Since his continuous pleas to the Adjutant General had for the most part gone unheeded he decided to send McCausland to Richmond hoping to impress upon the Adjutant General the importance of his requests. It was McCausland's job to:

> *...inform...of the disaffection of...population and the difficulty of procuring reliable troops for the emergency. There can be no doubt that it is the intention of the enemy to occupy as much of this country as he may find open to invasion, and your attention is specially called to the necessity of sending, as early as practicable, a force at least sufficient to hold this valley in security. I have now under my command here three-hundred and forty men, and when the companies now in the process of formation in this valley shall have been completed it is probably their numbers will not exceed one thousand men. It is doubtful, in my mind, whether the militia will obey a call to the field. For these reasons it would seem proper that re-enforcements should be sent from such sources as you deem proper. I beg leave, respectfully, to urge the importance of sending us rifles, with suitable ammunition, and I again request that staff officers for this department may be drawn from the troops comprising this command.*[45]

Exactly as to when the Adjutant General received this message is not known but it apparently struck a positive chord. On May 31 the Adjutant General wrote to Col. W.B. Blair informing him that Col. Tompkins now had 500 men but needed 1600, and for Blair to raise those troops if possible and send them to the Kanawha.[46]

So as the month of May, for the year 1861, drew to a close, the Virginia volunteer forces retained full possession of the Kanawha Valley with a force somewhere between 340 and 500 in number, ill equipped with outdated weapons and meager supplies, few uniforms, and poorly trained, with a sprinkling of high calibre officers such as Patton, McCausland, Jenkins, and Tompkins; and the majority of the citizenry refusing to cooperate or participate. They were a rag-tag army at best. Yet they did have some advantages, such as being on familiar terrain protecting their homes and families, and the most important advantage, that of being able to pick the best possible position for defense against the Federal troops. It would not be necessary for them to take the offensive; the Yankees at Gallipolis would do that soon enough.

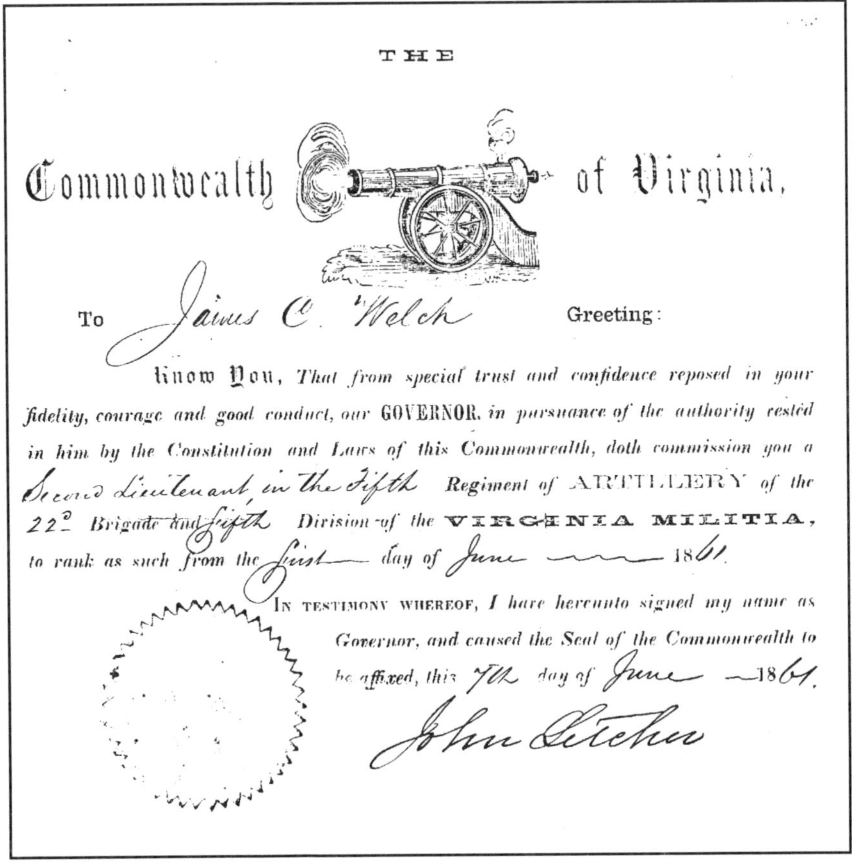

THE

Commonwealth of Virginia,

To James C. Welch Greeting:

Know You, *That from special trust and confidence reposed in your fidelity, courage and good conduct, our* GOVERNOR, *in pursuance of the authority vested in him by the Constitution and Laws of this Commonwealth, doth commission you a* Second Lieutenant, in the Fifth *Regiment of* ARTILLERY *of the* 22nd *Brigade* ~~and~~ fifth *Division of the* VIRGINIA MILITIA, *to rank as such from the* first *day of* June 1861.

IN TESTIMONY WHEREOF, *I have hereunto signed my name as Governor, and caused the Seal of the Commonwealth to be affixed, this* 7th *day of* June 1861.

John Letcher

JAMES C. WELCH'S PROMOTION PAPER

COLONEL JESSE S. NORTON
21st Ohio Volunteer Infantry. — From S.S. Canfield's "History of the 21st [Ohio] Regiment" — Courtesy: Ohio Historical Society

CHAPTER TWO

Reflections of Pvt. Elijah Beeman Company A, 12th Ohio Volunteer Infantry

The rebels across Scary Creek were on higher ground, well entrenched and difficult to view through the heavy foliage and dense woods. Yankee infantry wouldn't be able to get anywhere near the enemy artillery pieces in order to knock them out. Capt. Cotter's Ohio artillery would have to take care of that piece of business. Meanwhile, foot soldiers, such as Pvt. Elijah Beeman of Company A, 12th Ohio Volunteer Infantry, would have to make concentrated efforts elsewhere on the battlefield, possibly some sort of flanking movement. Beeman was obviously frightened, not thoroughly convinced of his presence at Scary Creek, but as with his opponent across Scary, Lt. James Welch, he would take advantage of the tense lull prior to the battle to ponder the circumstances that had brought him to this obscure little stream in (West)ern Virginia.

President Abraham Lincoln's initial call on April 15, 1861 for 75,000 three month's volunteers had met with overwhelming response, so much so that many of the men had to be sent back home or be kept in training camps in anticipation of a second call. Ohio had been one of the first states to answer the call thereby filling their quota much more rapidly than had been expected. As a result, the bulk of the Ohio boys sent to participate in the Kanawha campaign were taken from the second call although many had replied to the first. And as the second call was for three years service, as opposed to the earlier three months, some, such as the 12th Ohio, would enter the campaign with a three year commitment.

One of the earliest units to be involved in the Kanawha campaign was the 21st Ohio Volunteer Infantry, mostly farmers and their sons, organized at Camp Taylor near Cleveland and mustered in on April 27th. Under command of Col. Jesse S. Norton, of Perrysburg, Ohio, a man seemingly omnipresent in the Kanawha campaign, the 21st Ohio left Camp Taylor on May 23 and two companies, A and D, arrived on that date at Gallipolis, having been sent in advance of the main column on an earlier date and being the enemy that Lt. Col. John McCausland's scouts had viewed from across the Ohio River—the first Federal troops to officially enter the Kanawha campaign. Col. Norton and the remainder of the 21st Ohio joined the advance companies at Gallipolis on May 27, having received their arms at Columbus while en route, ineffective smooth bore muskets which reportedly later contributed to their loss at Scary Creek.[1]

Gallipolis itself was the perfect jumping off point for the Kanawha movement. Nicknamed Negropolis due to the large number of slaves who had escaped from the Kanawha and went there to live,[2] Gallipolis had "for many years before the war...been the depot of supplies for the entire Kanawha Valley, and at the inception of the rebellion the Confederates looked upon possession of (the Kanawha Valley) with a jealous eye."[3] Taking note of this fact the city prepared early by constructing extensive rifle-pits on the surrounding hills and forming the 77 man Gallia Guard led by Capt. Henry Graham. When the 21st Ohio arrived they received an extremely warm reception by the citizens and on May 29 they "went into camp in a wheatfield, on the Barlow farm, at the upper end of the city, naming it Camp Carrington."[4]

The second outfit to take a prominent position in the Kanawha campaign was the 11th Ohio Volunteer Infantry, first organized at Camp Jackson near Columbus in late April, but on May 1st they boarded a train on the Little Miami Railroad and moved to Camp Dennison near Cincinnati. Named after the governor of Ohio, Camp Dennison was one of the first training camps established for volunteers and eventually grew to rather large proportions, but in early May the 11th Ohio found it to be:

> *...a stubble field, of the muddiest description. Arriving at this future celebrated camp about nightfall there was "hurrying to and fro" to prepare quarters from the approaching storm. Plenty of pine boards were at hand, but they had to be carried from along the track of the Railroad a considerable distance through the mud to the place where the "shanties" were to be erected.... Huddled together under their partially erected "quarters," the rain coming down in torrents, with a steady drip, drip, drip through the many crevices in the boards, mud beneath and all around them, but few closed their eyes that night....*[5]

Ironically, rains would continually plague Ohio troops during the entire Kanawha and western Virginia campaigns. Fortunately, at Camp Dennison, a great many of the 11th Ohio were engineers and mechanics, particularly those in Company K of Capt. Philander Parmele Lane, and soon had their living conditions vastly improved. As for Lane, another invaluable figure in the Kanawha campaign, he was a thirty-nine year old family man and mechanic, who, through the urging of his comrades, organized and accepted leadership of the Union Rifles, a local militia unit which eventually became Company K of the 11th Ohio. Captain Lane proved to be one of the most sensible and competent officers in the Kanawha from the 11th Ohio, certainly more so than the bungling, egotistical, incompetent Col. Charles A. DeVilliers.[6]

DeVilliers had been quite conspicuous on the drill grounds of Camp Dennison, a man "foreign in appearance, of very dark complexion and sharp features, wore a smart red and gold cap, bright blue tight coat and red trousers, and was highly conceited in manner and talk."[7] Although a man of mystery, he was impressive in various military drills and claimed experience in the foreign military service, which helped to get him elected Colonel of the 11th Ohio when the position became open. While the 11th Ohio considered him a blessing at the time, once the Kanawha movement had been put into action it didn't take long for them to find out what a mistake DeVilliers was. Brigadier General Jacob Dolson Cox, later given command of the Ohio troops in the Kanawha, sarcastically referred to him after the war, as "my little Frenchman."[8]

Jacob Dolson Cox was just one of many men of political influence or impressive wealth bumbling about the grounds of Camp Dennison more

COLONEL [then Captain] PHILANDER PARMELE LANE
11th Ohio Volunteer Infantry. — Courtesy: Ohio Historical Society

or less just waiting for something of importance to happen to themselves. A Canadian by birth, and a lawyer prior to the war, Cox had no military training beyond some insignificant drilling with a militia group, of which he was oddly elected leader, undoubtedly due to his popularity rather than his military capability. During this period at Camp Dennison he took note of a William S. Rosecrans who was making quite an impression on his superiors as a drill instructor and, like Cox, biding his time for something more important. Neither would have to wait long—both would play an active part in driving the Confederates out of the Kanawha Valley.[9]

Certainly one of the most active outfits in the Kanawha campaign was the 12th Ohio Volunteer Infantry, to which Elijah Beeman belonged, organized at Camp Jackson on May 3, having elected fifty-one year old John W. Lowe of Xenia, a Mexican War veteran, as colonel; Jacob Ammen of Ripley as lieutenant colonel (promoted shortly thereafter to another regiment and replaced by Jonathan D. Hines); and thirty-eighty year old Carr B. White of Georgetown, also a Mexican War veteran, as major. It is also interesting to note that White was a boyhood friend of Ulysses S. Grant. While stationed at Camp Jackson the 12th Ohio encountered:

> *...rain, mud, and many other discouraging features. Sleeping accomodations were of the worst possible description, consisting of rough boards, with straw for those who were fortunte enough to steal it. Blankets were unknown, and many poor souls, who had never before attempted to sleep outside of a good feather bed, were indeed very uncomfortably situated.*[10]

As with so many other Ohio soldier boys, the 12th moved to Camp Dennison on May 6 where they received their basic training after having found their quarters "neatly constructed, and well adapted to secure health and comfort, being built of light, dry lumber, well ventilated, and affording every desirable facility for an easy living."[11] This was certainly quite a contrast to the conditions found by the 11th Ohio upon their arrival at Camp Dennison.

Also destined to play a dominant role in the Kanawha campaign, as well as the Scary battle, was Capt. Charles S. Cotter's Independent Battery Ohio Volunteer Artillery, a three month's service group recruited in Cleveland on April 25. Actually, the majority of the men, including Cotter, were from Ravenna, Portage County, Ohio, where Cotter had commanded a militia gun squad prior to the war, noted for their performances at holiday celebrations. In addition, Cotter carried on a silver and brass plating shop, together with a brass foundry. With such a background, when war came Cotter was already an accomplished artillerist. Cotter's men were moved to Camp Chase on July 2 where they were mustered in and moved to Gallipolis the next day, taking two field pieces in tow, later supplemented by two additional pieces "borrowed" from the city of Gallipolis.[12]

The 17th Ohio Volunteer Infantry, although they only participated indirectly in the Kanawha campaign, were organized at Lancaster on April 20 and soon afterward were sent to Jackson County in (West) Virginia to protect railroads and do guard duty against guerillas. Two companies were sent to garrison Ravenswood until July 10.[13]

Cavalry, often relegated to insignificant roles in the early stages of the war, was composed of Capt. John S. George's Independent Company Ohio Volunteer Cavalry, organized at Ironton as a three month's service outfit.

BRIGADIER GENERAL JACOB DOLSON COX
Courtesy: United States Army Military History Institute

COLONEL JAMES V. GUTHRIE
1st Kentucky Volunteer Infantry. — Courtesy: Library of Congress

During the forthcoming Kanawha campaign they would be used almost entirely as "orderlies, messengers, mounted scouts and videttes."[14]

Besides these Ohio military organizations a number of citizens fled neutral Kentucky and came to Ohio in order to form Federal Kentucky groups. One of the first such creations was the 1st Kentucky Volunteer Infantry, assembled at Camp Clay near Cincinnati by Col. James V. Guthrie.[15] Another such group was the 2nd Kentucky Volunteer Infantry, also formed at Camp Taylor and led by Mexican War veteran Col. William E. Woodruff, who had been busy aiding Lovell H. Rosseau in the defenses of Louisville, across the river at Camp Jo Holt in Indiana. When Woodruff went to Camp Taylor he took two companies with him which became the nucleus of the 2nd Kentucky.[16]

Although their role in the Kanawha campaign is sketchy at best, the 1st Kentucky Independent Battery, also known as Simmonds' Battery, commanded by Capt. Seth J. Simmonds, did participate. They were originally Company E of the 1st Kentucky Volunteer Infantry but were made into an artillery company early in the war.[17] Brigadier General Jacob D. Cox would later describe the men of these Kentucky units:

> *...made up chiefly of steamboat crews and longshore-men thrown out of employment by the stoppage of commerce on the river.... The colonels and part of the field officers were Kentuckians, but the organizations were Ohio regiments in nearly everything but the name. The men were mostly of a rough and reckless class, and gave a good deal of trouble by insubordination; but they did not lack courage, and after they had been under discipline for a while, became good fighting regiments....*[18]

Given overall command of these Ohio and Kentucky soldiers was Major General George Brinton McClellan, a former captain of artillery in the regular army who was engaged in the railroad business at the outbreak of the war. Indeed he later proved to be a better General on paper than in practice, but he did have enough foresight to realize the military strategicness of the Ohio River line and the Kanawha. He early "envisioned a quick drive up the Great Kanawha and on into the Valley of Virginia,"[19] eventually capturing Richmond. For various reasons he hesitated making such a move, primarily so as not to give off implications of aggression and instead turned his attention to the B & O Railroad which ran through the northern section of (West) Virginia. Undoubtedly, such an early move on the Kanawha would have brought it under Federal control with little, if any, resistance. But George McClellan was never one to make moves when the time was right.

For now, the raw Ohio and Kentucky soldiers continued to drill and train properly in preparation for the impending campaign, as well exemplified in a series of letters written by Pvt. Elijah Beeman of the 12th Ohio while stationed at Camp Dennison:

Camp Dennison
May 10th 1861

"I arrived at Camp in Due time and have been busy helping fix our quarters and leveling harred ground. Our quarters are Better than they was at Camp Jackson. We Recd. 60 Muskets Thursday evening for to practice with. I got the comfort the same day that I arrived here and it came in very good *play*. We have slept first rate since we came here. I was put upon guard Thursday at 8 o'clock and stood till eight the next morning. 16 out of 24 hours. The common time is 8 out of 24. The guard is regulated now so that we only have to stand 2 hours on and 4 off. We have a very pleasant Camp much more so than Camp Jackson. I don't know when I will come home. I expect to stay here 2 or 3 weeks. If I can get off I will be up to see the folks. We will get our uniforms next week. I guess we are all well and some of us are getting fat, Upon the food that we have. I tell you that ours is some pumpkin Meat potatoes coffee and bread are the principal things that we have to eat. We have seven or eight thousand encamped about us. 20,000 is the number that our camp is allowed to contain. We are not a going to get any Revolvers from the citizens. They have advanced in price so much that it would take over $2000 to amnest our citizens with them. I am a going to keep those that I have got. You must write and let me know how the folks are and how they talk about Shawhan and the rest of the Democrats. I guess the Morrow Company is considered about as good as any. Our Regiment is a rifle regiment. We rather have the promise of getting rifles. You must all write and let me know all of the news. I give my love to all of the folks and to *Ann*."

Direct your letters
E. Beeman
Camp Dennison
Care of Capt. Wallace[20]

Camp Dennison
May 15 1861

Dear father, I recd. the clothes as well as the letter you sent to me and was very glad to hear that you were all well. Our Camp is very pleasantly Situated upon the western side of the river hemmed in by lofty hills. The Camp is large enough to accomodate 25,000 men. There is only about 8,000 in Camp at present. Each of us recd. a musket apiece today for to train with. We will have rifles when we go into active service. I expect we will stay here several weeks yet. There is more probability of us being ordered to *Cairo* than anywhere else. Since Kentucky has decided to remain in the Union there is not So much fear of Cincinnati being attacked. A cannon came up on the cars from Cincinnati yesterday. They was a practicing with It. I expect you heard them firing. I was very glad to get my clothes and writing utensils. We get along pretty well down here much better than we did at Camp Jackson. We have our quarters assigned to us here. I and John *Kelly* are pardners in most everything. He got his trunk from home the other day and we put our things together. We have volunteered for three months. I expect we will be requested to stay 3 years or to the end of the War. When our time is out I expect some of the boys will get enough of It at the end of 3 months. There is some talk of about 50 *ladies* coming down here tomorrow. The best time for you folks to come down would be about friday week. When you write tell me if Ethels folks are well. We expect to get our Uniforms next week. They say we are learning pretty fast. Well I shall bring my letter to a close hoping that you are all well. I will try and come home if I can get off. I sent my Sachel and shirt home.

Elijah Beeman
12th Regiment Camp Dennison[21]

May 29th 1861

Dear Father. I recd. your letter a few minutes ago Stating that you were all well except your self. I am sorry to know that you are troubled by me volunteering for three years. I would have come home sooner but our company could not leave all at once. I have The promise of getting to go home for 5 or 6 days. I thought I would wait till I got my uniform before I came home. Captain went up to town yesterday to fill up the Company and We have to wait till he comes back before we can have our Election. Those that went home went on conditions. I was unconditional. Therefore I will have longer to stay at home. I expect. We will be sent to Western Virginia in less than three weeks. Give my love to all, Hope you will forgive the delay That has been keeping me back.

Your affectionate son
E. Beeman[22]

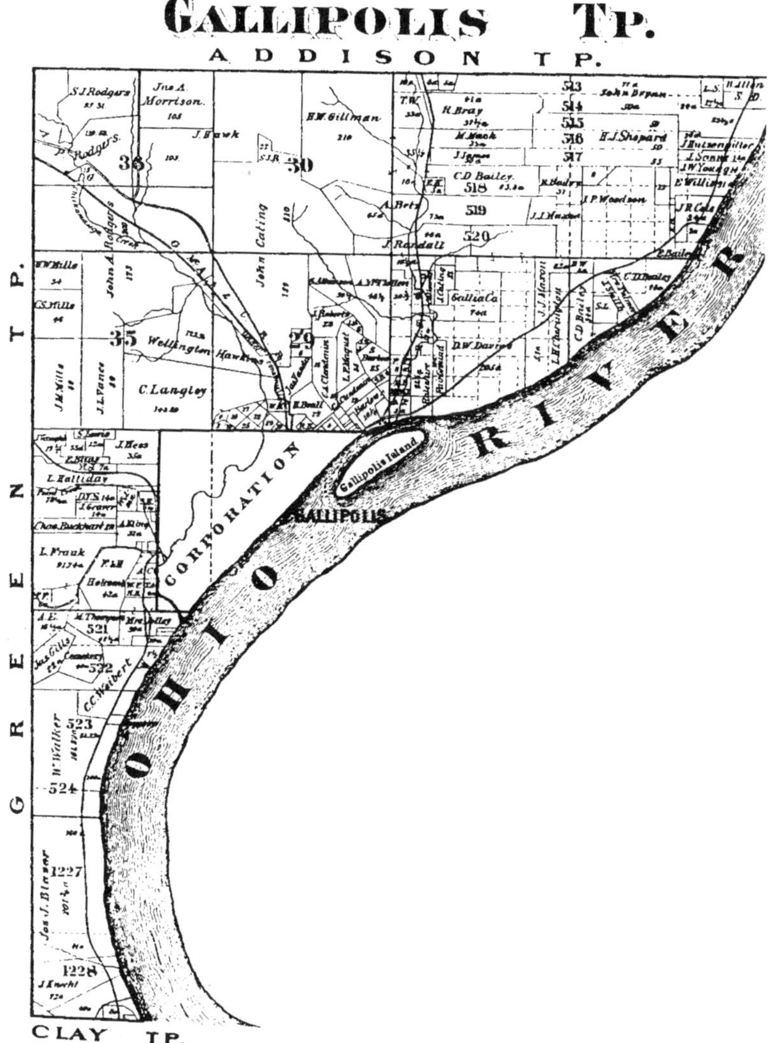

CAMP CARRINGTON

Located near the center of this map on the Barlow property. It served as the gathering point of Federal forces for the Kanawha campaign.

VALCOULON PLACE
Patton's headquarters at Camp Tompkins. — Courtesy: Garland Ellis

CHAPTER THREE

Campaigning in the Land of Milk and Honey

Although Capt. George S. Patton was against leaving Camp Buffalo, Col. Christopher Q. Tompkins ordered all units to depart on May 29 taking passage on two steamers, the *Julia Maffitt* and the *Kanawha Valley,* en route to Charleston where the soldiers quartered in Brooks Hall and performed obligatory guard duty until June 3rd, at which time they went to Coalsmouth and established Camp Tompkins on the farm of William and Beverly D. Tompkins, from whom the camp derived its name.[1] Col. Christopher Q. Tompkins, who was not related to the Tompkins family at Coalsmouth, selected the site because of its strategic location and to give reassurance to residents of the area by hindering Union sentiment there. Situated slightly west of the mouth of Coal River near Tackett's Creek and the community of Coalsmouth, this military camp became the hub of Virginia volunteer forces as recruits poured in on a near daily basis. Tompkins and Patton made their headquarters in "Valcoulon Place," an antebellum mansion on the estate composed of "a large and spacious three story brick house of colonial design, surrounded with gardens, beautiful grounds and well kept fields."[2]

The first three companies at Camp Tompkins were the Border Rifles, the Kanawha Riflemen, and one cavalry outfit, the Sandy Rangers. Within a matter of weeks the ranks swelled as numerous other companies arrived until there were seven infantry companies, four cavalry, and some artillery, all destined to play a crucial role in the Scary battle. Composing the infantry were to be found Patton's Kanawha Riflemen; John Swann's Kanawha Sharpshooters; Andrew Barbee's Border Rifles; a small infantry company from Wheeling under the command of Capt. James W. Sweeney, a man who had served under William Walker in Nicaragua; the Kanawha Militia (recruits) of Capt. B.S. Thompson; a Monroe County company under Captain James White; and the Fayetteville Rifles of Captain Robert Augustus Bailey.

There were four cavalry groups, all eventually placed under the command of Capt. Albert Gallatin Jenkins, including Jenkins' own Cabell County Border Rangers; Capt. James Corns' Sandy Rangers; the Fayette Rangers of Capt. William Tyree; and the Kanawha Rangers led by Capt. Charles Irvine Lewis, a doctor from Cannelton near Gauley Bridge.

There were two artillery pieces at Camp Tompkins, comprising the Kanawha Artillery, under the direction of Lt. James C. Welch and Lt. William A. Quarrier.

HUDSON M. DICKINSON
Enlisted in May, 1861, as a Private in the Kanawha Rangers. — From "Well Known Confederate Veterans and Their Records" by William E. Mickle

Although Col. Tompkins was in command of the Virginia volunteers, he was often absent in order to execute his official duties and, as a result, Patton actually became the officer in charge at Camp Tompkins. V.M.I. Cadet John Koontz Thompson, who did not arrive at Camp Tompkins until July 3, entered the Border Rifles and served as drill master and Assistant Officer in Charge at Camp Tompkins. Ironically, he was the eighteen year old son of Dr. John J. Thompson who claimed neutrality and on whose farm Federal soldiers encamped the night prior to the battle of Scary Creek.

The road to Camp Tompkins had not been a pleasant one for many of the companies, as typified by the experience of the Fayetteville Riflemen, who when first organized in Fayette County, had uniforms made that, if not practical, were certainly pleasant to look at. The "jackets were made of blue flannel with yellow stripes across the breast like the European hussars ...pants were of dark gray jeans with a wide yellow stripe on each leg." Later on their enemies would call them the "yellowjackets."[3] They left Fayetteville on June 3 and arrived in Charleston a few days later where they quartered in the Yankee Sawmill. Then arose the desperate problem of arming the men with proper weapons:

> *After a day or two, we marched to a store in the business part of town to receive our guns. We had been promised rifles, had volunteered as riflemen and had Fayetteville Rifles inscribed on our flag. Imagine our astonishment when they started to hand us smooth-bore muskets. Being the Orderly Sergeant, I was the first man to receive a gun. I was unwilling to start a mutiny and perhaps break up a fine company, but your Uncle Joel, the second sergeant, refused to take a gun and then the trouble began. We want rifles. Look at your flag. Rifles. Rifles. I never saw men so thoroughly exasperated. Some of the people told me that they were frightened. The men made a speech and a compromise was affected....*[4]

Within a few days, they were at Camp Tompkins, joining the other groups that would take part in the Scary Creek battle, but for now they drilled endlessly, so much so that many became agitated and desired a "day off to go fishing."[5] In order to break the monotony of Camp Tompkins, Col. Tompkins often sent men down the Kanawha to scout for approaching Federals, although there were not any yet to be found. Fayetteville Rifleman William Bahlmann recalled, "We had dress parade every afternoon at 4 o'clock. For this parade we wore white cotton gloves and blacked our shoes. Camp Tompkins was the only place I ever saw this done and not always there. The captain takes the company to the parade and the O.S. (Orderly Sergeant) brings it back."[6] In addition to all the other problems with camp life, there was only one well, whose water became 'ropy' from so much use, causing a slight spread of dysentery within the camp. Despite such hardships a formidable little army was beginning to evolve and on June 4th, Patton while modestly requesting a promotion at the same time, reported his total strength at Camp Tompkins as "about 850 men, which will be largely increased in the next few days."[7]

WILLIAM F. BAHLMANN
Fayette Rifles, 22nd Virginia Infantry. — Courtesy: Larry L. Legge

GENERAL HENRY ALEXANDER WISE
Courtesy: National Archives

The early days of June, 1861 were characterized by increasing activity from both the Virginians and the Ohioans. While Lt. Col. John McCausland was in Richmond attempting to convince authorities of the pressing situation on the Kanawha, General George McClellan had a meeting at Cincinnati with Judge L. Ruffner and Col. B.F. Smith, both of the Kanawha Valley, who managed to convince him to suspend his proposed movement on the Kanawha, instilling him with the belief that Union sentiment was strong enough there to resist any secessionist activity. McClellan, apparently believing such nonsense, then turned his attention to Grafton, Weston, and Elizabeth "in order to encourage the Union sentiment and to induce the Kanawha people to take a more decided course."[8] He felt they were "not yet fully up to the mark, and need careful nursing...."[9] McClellan apparently failed to recognize that an army of 850 or more secessionists, who were at least partially trained and armed, could be a thorn in the side of the Federal army.

This sudden 'holding pattern' of the Kanawha movement gave the Confederates the time they so direly needed. Persistent recruitment efforts continued to fall extremely short of expectations. At this point the Virginians could probably pester the Federal army with skirmishing and bushwacking but it's doubtful they could have won a battle. And during this time that McClellan failed to utilize his advantage, McCausland finally convinced the Richmond authorities of the necessity of troops and arms but, more importantly, the Virginia government decided what was really needed in the Kanawha military situation, since there was much doubt the state volunteer forces would prove an effective fighting force, was properly trained soldiers led by a man who could be popular with both the troops and the inhabitants of the area. So on June 6, one day prior to the day that Capt. John P. Hale of the Kanawha Artillery sent food and culinary supplies to Lt. James C. Welch at Camp Tompkins,[10] Adjutant and Inspector General of Virginia, Samuel Cooper, appointed ex-governor of Virginia, Henry Alexander Wise, a Brigadier General of Provisional Forces, and

"...Having been appointed brigadier-general of Provisional Forces, you will proceed, with the force placed at your disposal, by the most speedy route of communication, to the valley of the Kanawha. You will by such means and agencies as may be within your control, rally the people of that valley and the adjoining counties to resist and repel the invading army, which is reported to be on its march towards Lewisburg, which may as probably be directed towards the Virginia and Tennessee Railroad, by any of the various routes between that indicated in the valley of the Big Sandy River. You must rely upon the arms among the people to supply the requisite armament, and upon their valor and knowledge of the country as a substitute for organization and discipline. If there be any who have arms beyond their power or will to use, you can take them with such arrangement as the case may indicate for future settlement. As your transportation will of course be very limited, and the service of such character as will indicate the lightest practicable train, the troops must be taught to rely upon the supplies of the country, but not be permitted to take them except through officers authorized for that purpose, and they should be instructed always to make prompt payment, or to give such receipts as will insure early and adequate remuneration. All officers commanding separate parties should be instructed to unite with the greatest vigilance and closest scrutiny the highest regard for the personal and property rights of all with whom they may come in contact, save the common enemy of the State, towards whom the rules of war, as known to civilized nations, will be applied.

The imperfect information possessed of the force and objects of the enemy do not permit specific instructions either as to your line of operations or the movements to be made. You must exercise a sound discretion, so that all your efforts may tend to the

result of repelling the enemy if possible, and if not, of checking him as near the border of our territory as may be practicable. If the disparity of numbers should be very great, your defensive positions will for the present necessarily be retired to the mountain passes, and sorties against the enemy should always be so made as to embarrass and delay his movements without hazarding the loss of detachments from your command, teaching them to wait until you have the means to strike a blow which shall be effective. The several officers of experience who have been directed to report to you will be assigned by you to such duties as the necessities of the case may require.

General Floyd, who has been appointed a brigadier-general, has been specially charged with the protection of the line of the Tennessee and Virginia Railroad. It may well occur that a junction of your forces may become desirable, in which event each should exhibit his letters of instruction to the other, so that you may cordially co-operate to attain the common object of both. In the event of such a junction, and whilst serving together, General Floyd, being senior by commission, will, according to the Rules and Articles of War, command the whole.

June 10, 1861

P.S.—Such volunteers as may be engaged for your command and sent forward to Lewisburg within the next twenty days will there be mustered into service by companies and their transportation paid to that point, it being understood that these volunteers are not to be taken from any of the organized regiments or companies now in service of the Confederate States."[11]

The Confederate army in the Kanawha had needed a miracle in order to survive and it was thought that the arrival of Wise would indeed be that miracle. A figurehead of great charisma was required to rally the Kanawhans and Wise had all the credentials of such. Born at Drummondtown, Virginia, he was well educated, politically prominent, and had served as governor of Virginia prior to the war, during which time he had shown some favoritism to western Virginia, thereby inducing Virginia authorities to assume that he would be well accepted by the citizens of the Kanawha. Although he had no military training at all he did have "a remarkably correct apprehension of topography, and was quick to see the strategic value of positions."[12] But probably his most outstanding quality was his extreme adeptness at making long, "windbag," persuasive speeches.

On the surface he definitely appeared to be the man for the assignment, but what the authorities apparently failed to take into consideration, besides his total lack of military training, was his advanced age and poor health. Within a short matter of time he proved "erratic, impulsive, and thoroughly unpredictable,"[13] more of a hindrance than a help. If ever there was a man incapable of directing the Kanawha army to victory it was Henry A. Wise—most regretfully, he received that command. Even with that in mind, General Wise was being given a near impossible assignment to which he made absolutely no objection, at least not until his first major failure, and for that he must be duly credited.

The first military company to join the Wise Legion, also known as the Wise Brigade, was the time honored Richmond Light Infantry Blues, commanded by General Henry A. Wise's eldest son, Captain Obidiah Jennings Wise, better known as O. Jennings. When George S. Patton heard of this he must certainly have been elated, for the Blues were the same outfit he had watched in awe during his Richmond residency. On June 7 the Blues were stationed at Aquia Creek in Virginia where they received news of General Wise's appointment, provoking O. Jennings to leave for Richmond in order to secure permission for him and the Blues to accompany his father to western Virginia, the "land that is said to flow with milk and honey."

By the 9th of the month the Blues had received their tents, one of the few companies in the Kanawha campaign to be blessed with such, and O. Jennings had returned having been given official permission to join his father. (General Wise would also take along another son, Richard Alsop Wise, and give him a position in the Wise Legion.)[14] But while matters were improving for the Kanawha situation in Richmond, events were not going well at all in the valley itself. On June 9th Capt. George S. Patton wrote to Col. C.Q. Tompkins from Camp Tompkins expressing his particular views:

CAPTAIN OBIDIAH JENNINGS WISE
Richmond Light Infantry Blues. — Courtesy: Virginia State Library

Private and Confidential

Headquarters
Camp Tompkins
June 9th 1861

Col. C.Q. Tompkins,
Sir,

From all the information I can gather, the state of feeling through this section of country and below is very bad. In Wayne County especially as you will learn from Mr. Spurlock, the condition of things is horrible.

About Winfield also, matters have assumed a suspicious and serious character. As evidence of the fact, three men, whom I sent to that place, on yesterday, to arrest a supposed deserter from Capt. Barbee's company, were prohibited by *Penn Wright* and other citizens from making the arrest, although the man expressed an entire willingness to return to his company, but was not allowed to do so. Another circumstance of suspicous character, is the fact that within the past week a large supply of Coffee and Sugar has been landed at Winfield—a much larger supply than was ever know to be brought to that point, and entirely disproportionate to the demand for such articles at that point—they arrived there at the same time, with the visit of Miller, Waggoner, and Boreman, which renders the matter doubly suspicous. It is currently reported in the country that they are intended for the use of the Ohio troops in their passage up the Valley. This chimes in with an idea which you advanced in our conversation last night in relation to Winfield being probably made a depot of supplies for the enemy in their advance.

I am credibly informed that Dr. John J. Thompson, a member of the Virginia Legislature, is engaged in circulation for signature, petitions to the Governor of Va. to, not only, not send any more troops to this Valley but to disband those already raised. This information came through 1st Sergt. Dudding of Capt. Barbee's Company, one of the party whom I sent to Winfield to bring back the supposed deserter—he is an entirely reliable man.

The news from Wayne Co., in regard to prohibiting reinforcements coming to Capt. Corns' Company, is having a very depressing effect upon Capt. Corns and his men.

I would send, at once, a sufficiently strong force to bring back the man from Winfield, but that I have grave doubts whether the man was legally enlisted, and could be treated as a deserter.

Another fact that has come to my knowledge, illustrating the feeling of Winfield. One of Capt. Lewis' scouts passed over to Red House, and was notified by persons there "to leave at once or he would not be able to leave at all." This occured day before yesterday and has now just been reported to me by Capt. Lewis.

The various matters I have mentioned, although small in themselves, are, when taken together, of considerable importance and I have therefore, written them.

Yours respectfully
Geo. S. Patton
Capt. Commdg.[15]

With the entry of General Wise upon the Kanawha campaign the Confederate situation was now watched on two fronts, that of the volunteers already in the valley, and the movement of Wise and his ever increasing Legion from Richmond to Charleston.

As of June 13th the Richmond Light Infantry Blues were in Richmond, having arrived there on the 10th, and departed for the Kanawha Valley. General Wise had already left Richmond "without a man or a gun to accompany him" (although there has been much skepticism that the authorities would let a man of such military stature travel alone), and had been in the area east of Staunton attempting to drum up recruits.[16] The Blues arrived on the same day and joined General Wise in a splendid dinner prepared by the town ladies, after which they returned to the train and advanced to Goshorn, approximately twenty miles west of Staunton. Here the female citizens presented the General with a flag for the Legion, giving him an opportunity to give one of his characteristic speeches. Then the train moved on to Jackson's River where the soldiers debarked and boarded stages, arriving at Callahan's about midnight.[17]

Back on the Kanawha Capt. John Peter Hale of the Kanawha Artillery dispatched the following letter from Elk Bridge to Lt. James C. Welch at Camp Tompkins:

Elk Bridge
June 13, 1861

Lieut. J. Welch

Dear Sir

Learning today that you have one or two men off of duty and one short of force I have concluded to send you down three or four men by *Victor* in the morning. With the number of men you have I think you had better limit yourself to one sentinel on duty at a time. This, I think, would be sufficient and would relieve your men very much. I am sorry to learn that you have not gotten in your recruits from Coal. Hope you still get them. The Col. has given us 20 carbines: This is all there are. It is about one to every five of our company. I send you down 4 by the men. The Col. says we must distribute them among the officers of the company.

Please write me how you are situated and how you are getting on. The Col. talks of sending Charley Walker with anther squad and another gun down in a few days.

I enclose your commission which was handed me today. I hope you and your detachment are completely fixed and in good spirits.

Your Friend
J.P. Hale[18]

Capt. George S. Patton became worried on June 14th about the dredge boats on the Kanawha River and issued a special order to Lt. James C. Welch through his adjutant, D.L. Ruffner: "You will see to it that the dredge boats, now in Kanawha River, be not taken away; they must not be allowed to pass down, and if it will be necessary, you must use your gun to stop them. P.S.—Keep a bright lookout for them tonight."[19]

On that same day the Richmond Blues continued past White Sulphur Springs and went into camp on the Fairgrounds at Lewisburg, where they would remain for four days. During their stay at Lewisburg they would be introduced to Capt. Jacob N. Taylor's Greenbrier Riflemen (Bruce Rifles), the first (West)ern Virginia volunteers to join the Legion, although they would not be incorporated into the Legion officially until a much later date.

A confident General Wise wrote Richmond on June 16 requesting artillery for his command, while back at Camp Tompkins Capt. Patton had apparently dropped his fears of the dredge boats on the Kanawha, as he wrote Lt. James C. Welch: "If the dredge boats come down the river tonight or today you will not interfere with them but allow them to pass. Have your guard heard any firing of guns or cannon during the night?"[20] But the true fear of war was expressed in the letter to Lt. Welch written to him by a young lady, possibly his wife, that same Sunday day:

"Meredith tells me he will leave in a few minutes for Coal in a skiff. Mr. Quarrier gave me a band for your cannon and some papers for you. I expected to have gone over to Coal last Friday by the way of the Mouth. Mr. Q. has not come yet. I fear you will want them. We heard last night that we shall be invaded in a few days. Mr. R. and family will leave Tuesday morning for the mountains. I shall keep house. I heard you had lost your uniform—As the boat was detained I found just enough flannel in town to make you a jacket. I shall make it tomorrow and send it down with your pants. I should have done it sooner but they told me I would have to get some flannel dyed first. If the report of the invasion is true (May God in Heaven protect you)."[21]

Her projected date of the Federal invasion of the Kanawha Valley was off some twenty or more days, but the invasion would indeed come and Lt. Welch would be one of its first fatalities.

The next seven days involved the movement of General Wise and his Legion from Lewisburg to Gauley Bridge, and to Charleston; the numbers and conditions of troops; and the watchful eye kept by the soldiers at Camp Tompkins on the Federals at Gallipolis; all detailed in the following collection of letters:

Lewisburg, Va.
June 17th, 1861

To Col. C.Q. Tompkins
Col. & c, & c

Sir,

Rec. ? your dispatches last night at 10½ o'clock and forwarded immediately to Adjt. Genl. Cooper. Here there are two efficient companies, Capt. Wise's and Capt. Caskie's, the Blues of Richmond 98 men, and cavalry 60 men, and 2 pieces of field artillery without a mustered company under Capt. Buckholtz. In addition there are two companies of green recruits, one from Greenbrier and one from Monroe, which I will endeavor to get ready by tomorrow to go on with Wise's & Caskie's companies, and the artillery. They will, in all say 298 men, start tomorrow morning, and be at Gauley Bridge Thursday evening next. There they will post themselves at Gauley Bridge, and the falls, sending a detachment up to Twenty Mile Creek, and guarding the Gauley road, and the road leading from Twenty Mile Creek to the Ka Valley at Hughes Creek about 15 miles below the Bridge. At that point, Hughes Creek, you will post a small guard at Twenty Mile Creek, and in scouring that road & neighborhood with orders to sieze the persons, arms, ammunition, horses, cattles, hogs, sheep & provisons & forage of all traitorous and suspected persons. That disposition you will maintain at these points, strengthening them with adequate force if necessary and to be shared, until I reach Gauley Bridge. You will cover and guard the road from Parkersburg to Charleston at the gorges of the Pocatalico with as strong forces as you can distribute to the points on that creek, scouring the surrounding countryside as far as your force will allow, and siezing, and making prisoners all resident enemies, with their arms & c as above ordered.

You will in like manner strongly post, and guard the Guyandotte Road where it enters the Ka Valley at the most defensible points, securing the country around and seizing, and disarming all suspicious persons as above ordered.... And if possible you will occupy the mouth of Ka, guarding the pass from Letart falls into...the Ka Valley, treating as enemies, in like manner all suspected persons in that region. There must be no hesitation in the most rigid treatment of all known or justly suspected traitors, taking their arms, provisions, & forage for our own subsistence, & making them prisoners of war. If taken in any considerable numbers, they must be moved back up the Valley, even as high as Fayetteville if necessary, or to any other sound locality where they can be guarded. As to the details and distribution of forces, you must exercise a sound discretion, supplying as well as you can any omissions, and extending the orders and their application as far as your forces will permit. The main point is to be strictly guarded on the left bank of the Ka in the Coal river pass of the Guyandotte road; and the points to be strictly guarded on the right bank are the passes of the Letart Falls road & of the Parkersburg road and the Pocatalico.

If the mouth of the Ka can not be guarded, and held so as to check the enemy without risking too much danger of being cut off, you will restrict yourself to guarding the passes on both sides of the Ka Valley.

You will send a small force, with provisions & forage to meet Capt. Wise at the Falls of Ka, & order report to be made to him there. I will remain here a day or two to bring up troops in the rear, to raise more troops, & to forward them with arms as fast as possible. Wage the war vigorously on all traitors & check the invaders as near as you can to the border.

Respectfully
Henry A. Wise
Brig. Genl.[22]

June 17, 1861

Friend Goshorn -

This will be handed you by Judge Morehead in whom you can strictly rely. I will now make a few statements of matters here for the consideration as soon as a sufficient number of regiments are concentrated here, to move up Kanawha. There is no doubt of this. It may be ten days or more before the movement is made & I would advise a thorough system of defense on your part, & as great an accumulation of artillery as you can command. The officers & c xxx

Gen. H.A. Wise
Sir

The above is an abstract from a letter received here today by private hands from a citizen of Gallipolis, Ohio, near Point Pleasant, who is well known and highly esteemed by many of the best citizens of this place - it may be received with entire confidence. I will add that it...repetition of what reaches me frequently day after day & sometimes again & again the same day. I send it to you as an illustration of the circumstances which have & will continue to dictate my disposition of the forces under my command.

The instructions of yours of the 17th Inst. recieved by...requiring a reinforcement for Capt. Wise at Gauley Bridge here has been complied with. A company formed at that point has been ordered to report for duty to Capt. Wise. A depot of provisions has been established at Hughes' Creek & Capt. Wise notified of the fact.

Very respectfully
C.Q. Tompkins
Col. Va. Vols.[23]

Artillery Detachment
Headquarters Camp Tompkins
June 17th 1861

Capt. J.P. Hale
Dr. Sir

You will please send by the first opportunity the clothing & cap of Patrick Burns. He wanted to go up after them. I think it would be as well to examine them and see that they are all right.

LETTER TORN - from Welch

Kan. C.H. June 17th 1861

Lt. J.C. Welch
Dear Sir

Your note in relation to Patrick's "Dudds" is recieved. I will send them first opportunity. Could have sent yesterday if I had known the *Maffitt* was going down. Also have more guns (muskets) to send you. Also haversacks. I regret to have to say to your men that it has been impossible so far to get material for uniforms. We tryed several persons going & sending down to get material anywhere it could be found from Gallipolis to Cinn. least all efforts have failed so far. It is now impossible, as you know, to get anything from tailors. We are now trying to get it from the East. Hope we may succeed. Please explain to your men fully the reasons why the uniforms have not been forthcoming, as they may without explanation think we have neglected the matter or are not trying to get it.

You should have 4 horses to your gun with harness - all complete. You should latch up once or twice a day to practice the horses and men. If you have not the horses & harness let me know & I will see that they are sent down to you. We have had lent 2 to each gun here. lent experiments have proved conclusively that we must have 4. They are now getting in the 4 to each gun.

Respectfully
J.P. Hale
Capt. Kan. Artillery[25]

Lewisburg, Va.
June 19th, 1861

To Col. C.Q. Tompkins
Col. Vols. Commdg.

Sir

Mr. Thayer handed your letter at 10 A.M. today. Capts. Caskie & Buckholtz move this mg for Gauley Bridge with 2000 stands of flint muskets & 2 six pounder field pieces, ammunition for and will reach there probably on Friday next. The arms must not be distributed to the militia en masse, lest they fall into the hands of some traitors. My son Capt. Wise will reach Gauley Bridge probably tonight with 220 infantry & by Friday next you will have there about 300 reinforcements, to be followed as early as possible by volunteers from Monroe & Rockingham say 300 men. You will approach the mouth of the Ka river as near as you can safely, arrest all suspicous persons or known traitors & enemies, retire them up the valley, seizing their arms & munitions, and driving to your camp all their provisions, horses, cattle & stock of every kind. Guard every road and gorge you can, and observe previous general orders according to your own sound discretion. As soon as I get to the Valley the militia shall be called out to test the men, to disarm all suspected, and to arm as well as can be done all true citizens and especially those who will volunteer & enter the service for not less than one year.

Respectfully
Henry A. Wise
Brig. Genl.

P.S. - I leave here tomorrow for Gauley Bridge with my staff - commissary & ... only behind to forward men, ammunition and provisions.[26]

Headquarters
Camp Tompkins
June 19 1861

Col. C.Q. Tompkins
Commanding

Colonel:

This letter will be handed you by Messrs. Moorehead and Myers, residents of Gallipolis - who were stopped, and sent to me by my outposts this morning. Myers is well known in the community, and is now in the employ of Clement Smith Esq. of Peytona - his business, he says, is with Mr. Smith.

Joseph Moorehead, as he is called, is a Virginian by birth and has resided in Louisiana until 1854 since which time he has lived in Gallipolis. His own account is that he left Galliplois on account of persecution because of his opinions. He is the bearer of a letter...from H.M. Onderisk (whom I believe to be a true man) of Gallipolis to Alvin Goshorn, which letter I opened and read. You had better see it. Mr. G. will of course hand it to you. Both these men were stopped and searched - but Moorehead had the precaution of...the letter in advance. They are both communicative, and I am inclined to have some belief in Moorehead, who is a reliable man apparently. A courier from me will reach you before they do.

Yours respectfully
Geo. S. Patton
Commdg.[27]

Hd. Qrs.
Kanawha C.H., Va.
June 21, 1861

Gen. H.A. Wise

Sir

I deem it my duty to keep you apprised of the intelligence that reaches me disclosing the movement of the Enemy. Each day brings a confirmation of their intention to invade the valley & attack my command at no distant period. I send you the latest paper, containing the announcement of their programme, every word of which has been corraborated by private communications from Guyandotte, Point Pleasant, & Parkersburg. I think there can be no doubt about the destination of these troops for whose transportation the enumerated boats have been engaged & if there has been no interruption of their plans it cannot be long before they are upon us from at least two, & it may be three directions viz Guyandotte, Parkersburg & Pt. Pleasant. I do not think it necessary to detail the news embodied in the...paper, but will say that the corraboration of its correctness impels me to suggest that unless events surrounding you necessitates the use of your forces at some point above this, it would be judicious to reinforce me without delay - it can do no harm even if subsequent developments should falsify the intelligence upon which my suggestion is founded.

(unsigned - but undoubtedly
from Col. C.Q. Tompkins)[28]

Charleston Kan.
June 21st, 1861

General

Some doubt as to your movement in this direction relayed in answer to your first letter from Lewisburg. As it is anticipating your arrival in the valley within a few days & beg leave to submit to your consideration the views that have influenced my policy up to this moment & if you will permit me to add my opinions as to future events.

When I took command of the troops in this department they numbered about 300 all told - of those half were drilled & well armed, the remainder raw volunteers & badly equipped. Three companies were at Buffalo in accordance with the programme directing volunteers to rendezvous at that place. An examination of the position satisfied me that it was entirely unsuited to the purpose as it was manifestly necessary to keep the troops together in the presence of four times their number of the enemy. I retired them to the number of Coal & this place.

In the meantime the disaffection of the population along the Ohio & especially in Mason County because...citizens were threatened & whole neighborhoods kept in consternation. The leading citizens of the county were apalled at the prospect of civil war in their very midst & often request, full...with all whom I could meet it was asked to adopt a concilitory policy & to send influential persons through the disturbed districts for the purpose of tranquilizing the people.

(unsigned - but undoubtedly
from Col. C.Q. Tompkins)[29]

Headquarters Camp Tompkins
June 22, 1861

Col. C.Q. Tompkins

Sir,

Your form of this date is to hand. I have myself very little doubt but that the enemy have crossed the river, and are now, at all events, in Point Pleasant and if not in other places on the river. I am in hopes that I will obtain reliable information from there tonight, at all events, I certainly will tomorrow. I have a very reliable man now on his way down the river on this side, who is provided with a relay of horses, and who will bring me accurate news - of course it will be communicated to you as soon as recieved.

I doubt very much whether one steamer would be sufficient to transport the garrison here up the river - it might assist in ferrying us over - but would be of little use for cavalry. In a letter just recieved from Mr. T. Smith, he suggests a bridge of boats. I have little doubt but that such a scheme would be entirly practicable, if furnished with the boats, had time to tie them securely together and ready. I would also have to be furnished with two cables at least 800 feet long. With these conditions fulfilled I think a bridge might be thrown across in about an hour, but you are well aware of the unexpected difficulties which may arise, when there is no regular army corps of engineers, and laborers. To prevent any accident I would suggest that both a steamboat, and flat-boats be furnished me.

Be so kind as to indicate more explicitly the plan you desire me to pursue. Suppose, for instance, that a column of the enemy is attacking you, and another threatening me, but not so closely, as to prevent my crossing the river. Am I to abandon this position and fall back on that of Two Mile and then give and thereby, the possession of the commanding hills opposite Charleston or would it be better for me to retreat on this side the river, and hold the hills myself. I merely throw out these hints for your consideration. If they do attack at 2 Mile and not here should I endeavor to avoid them, and join the column in front? If possible, I will come up to Charleston, on tomorrow, for a short interview -unless something should occur tonight.

I have arrested Lt. Moore, and directed him to report at Headquarters. he did not come into quarters until a late hour this evening, and his absence from quarters last night without leave is unexplained except by the fact that his horses were used by Capt. Lewis, to bring me dispatches last night. I regret exceedingly to report, that I have been informed that he fired his revolver three or four times into a steamboat on Coal River, to the great alarm, and danger of wife and family of the owner. I direct him to report at Headquarters - he had much better be in Charleston than here. I have cautioned him that he will be under arrest until relieved by you and that he must keep to his quarters there. He speaks something of resigning and I hope for his own sake that that or some other views may save him the exposure of a trial by Court Martial. Another reason for sending him away is that if there is a Court Martial, it will be at Head Qtrs., I suppose, and he ought to be there - it would be exceedingly disagreeable to be here -and under all the circumstances I have adopted the plan which I hope will be acceptable to you. The arrest is forwarded in your letter, and his subsequent conduct.

I remain sir, Yours Truly
Geo. S. Patton
Capt. Commdg.

P.S. - Be so kind as to say to Mr. Smith that I would like to have 500 new Harper's Ferry cartridges - I enclose receipts for the musket powder. The expedition to Red House have not yet returned. 4 P.M.[30]

Gauley Bridge
June 23rd, 1861

To Col. C.Q. Tompkins
Commdg.

Sir

I arrived here at 6 P.M. yesterday. On the way, yesterday, Mr. Kirkpatrick handed me two dispatches from you of the 17th & 19th and later I met Mr. Williams who handed me yours to Capt. Wise accompanied by yours to me all of the 21st insts. I find here today 275 men mustered in my Legion, and a Fayette company not mustered into service, in all about 340 men, besides a few unorganized men who are with Capt. Buckholtz's artillery. By the evening Capt. Brock's cavalry of about 90 men will be here and tomorrow mg the whole force will be about 430 men. I will leave two untrained companies here, say 130, with Capt. Buckholtz to be drilled in infantry and artillery practice and to guard the Gauley Bridge, and will take on with me tomorrow two of the infantry and two of the cavalry companies of my Legion to Charleston, say 300 efficient men, well armed. When I see you I will be happy to interchange views upon all the topics of this command. I am now hurried by the messenger, Mr. Tompkins, who will take this. Saw your sons yesterday who report all well at Gauley Mtn., & vic.? a kind note from your good lady which I shall be glad to avail myself of as I can, to make your home my home in this neighborhood. I ought to add that I am expecting some six to ten companies here from the East by the last of next week.

Very respectfully
Henry A. Wise
Brig. Genl.[31]

Kanawha Court House Va.
June 23, 1861

Colonel:

I came up this morning to see you, and regret that your absence deprived me of the opportunity. I hope...that your numerous engagements will not prevent you from paying my post a visit at the earliest opportunity.

In consequence of being deprived of the services of Mr. Moore, by his arrest and probably permanent disconnection with my company. I have now only one commissioned officer attached to my company which is utterly insufficient of course. I can have but little to do with the immediate command of the Riflemen. For this reason, and because I think Mr. Fitzhugh is placed in a position which seperates him from his company, without any corresponding advantages to himself. I must respectfully ask you to relieve him from special duty, and order him to report to me. Only one other alternative remains if you cannot relieve Mr. Fitzhugh, and that is, to relieve me from the command of the post at Coalsmouth so that I may take command of my company. For Mr. Fitzhugh's own sake I think he ought to be sent to his company, for in case of...by the election of a successor...in cse he should not return, he would not prominently before the company and might be passd over. If it is possible therefore I by leave must...insist upon his being ordered to his company.

I regret very much that you have found it necessary to think of taking Mr. Is. Smith away from me. He is on my little staff, and his valuable aid would be much missed. I do not know where I can find any one to fill his place. Certainly I can take no one from my already reduced company. I have only him and Mr. Ruffner a small enough force for the necessary rank of my headquarters and I shall be a good deal embarrassed by his removal. I say nothing about the detaching of Dr. Patrick but yield to your desire with regret that the necessities of the service should require the constant deterioration of a company, in which I took so much pride and pleasure.

You will excuse the above remarks but I feel very deeply on this subject, especially in connection with recruitments.

I have arrested a member of Capt. Barbee's company reported for being asleep on post at the picket guard. Should I send him up for trial before the General Court Martial for Wednesday.

I will try and see you again in some important matters this week. I am compelled to return this evening.

Very Respectfully Yours
Geo. S. Patton[32]

Col. C.Q. Tompkins
Cmmdg.

H.Q. Camp Tompkins
June 23, 1861

Colonel:

I send you the Cincinnati Gazette of Friday the 21st which is perhaps later than any you have seen. By an article from the Wheeling Intelligencer it would seem that some persons think the Bellair expedition destined for Cairo. This however may be intended as a blind.

You have doubtless seen Lewis Wilson, who left the Point at 10 o'clock yesterday morning. No troops there then, but great anticipation of them.

No troops at Guyandotte at 4 P.M. yesterday. Three gentlemen from Cabell rode over to bring me the newspaper and information of the movement at Bellair. They are reliable these men and promise to forward information continually. They say that the country people in the Guyandotte road are ready to join us at the first approach of the enemy and are getting their arms and ammunition ready.

I will probably have late news from Point Pleasant sometime this evening, if so, I will at once communicate it.

I have arrested and confined to his quarters Lieut. J.R. Miller of the Wayne company for unofficially and ungentleman like conduct. He, by fraud and deceit, practiced in the Arsenal of the Guard, became possessed of the countersign, and then used it to pass himself, and five or six privates of the company out of the line of sentinels and carried them up the road indirectly on the way to a grocery at the Bridge. I had taken tea at a friends and went there on their way on my return. I immediately sent a guard after them, but they endeavored to slip back. I had put the sentinels on the alert however and they were captured. Miller has been reportedly elected, has acted as a Lieutenant, and is so borne on the Muster Roll, but has never been commissioned. I presume that he will have to be treated as an officer, and tried as such. He had better be included in the order for a General Court Martial. He told I am informed several distinct falsehoods, and ought to be tried.

I remain sir
Very Respectfully
Geo. S. Patton
Capt. Commdg.[33]

June 23, 1861

Mr. Welch:
Dear Sir—

I am making out my muster roll and want you to send me a list of the names of your men with the age of each man, the time that he was enrolled and when he was mustered into service annexed to his name. Please attend to this immediately and let me hear from you the very first opportunity. If the enemy should come upon you let there be no loading by detail.

Yours Truly
P.C. Eastham
1st. Sergt.[34]

On June 21st the Confederate authorities at Richmond had confirmed sending a field piece and ammunition, with the promise of an artillery company to soon follow when conditions permitted, responding to General Wise's request of June 16th.[35] And as noted, Wise arrived at Gauley Bridge on the evening of the 22nd (oddly enough this was the same day his Federal counterpart, Jacob D. Cox, received his commission as a Brigadier General), mounted on "Legion," a famous charger presented to him at Staunton, preceded a few days by his son O. Jennings riding his "exquisite chestnut thoroughbred filly."[36] At Gauley Bridge, the headwaters of the Kanawha, they would remain two days.

Defensive preparations were quickly enacted at Gauley with the establishment of seven posts, all under the command of Major Bradfute Warwick, and most of them manned by the Dixie Rifles of Capt. Beuhring H. Jones, composed of men from Fayette and surrounding counties. One post was located "up New River; two up Gauley River; a fourth up Scrabble Creek; another near the top of the precipitous mountain overlooking Gauley Bridge; the sixth near the Falls; and the final one on the small island in the river, opposite the guard house and artillery camp."[37]

As the Wise Legion left Gauley for Charleston on the 25th a dispatch was sent to the Adjutant General of Virginia from Raleigh Court House (Beckley) by Brigadier General Alfred Beckley, for whom the city of Beckley is named, of the Virginia Militia. He reported "that he had just visited the base of six regiments and that twelve companies of militia had been mustered into service in Nicholas, Fayette, Logan, Boone, Wyoming and Raleigh Counties."[38] Wise gradually added these to his command and shortly thereafter dispersed various elements to strategic positions between Summersville and Elk River. On that same day the Kanawha Artillery reported their condition in a letter to Lt. James C. Welch from Capt. John P. Hale:

"Your note by Patrick just received. I am sorry he was under the necessity of coming up for his clothes. I ordered them sent to him by the first opportunity after he left here. Learning that they had not gone, a day or two after I repeated the order with emphasis. And I supposed they had gone and he had them long since. They were left at the lower camp and Jno. Porter was to ship them. I note what you say about the saddles. Hope you will soon get your horses all broken as to be able to spare them and send them up—but until you can spare them, keep them. We have lent 2 saddles to 8 horses. The boys have been riding bareback—which is not pleasant. Lt. Walker with 15 men has gone to 2 Mile. We have had several recruits here. The whole number in all our company now is 87. We are expecting several more. Sorry your Coal men came in so slowly. Hope you are getting along comfortably."[39]

Needless to say, Charleston was the scene of much anticipation at this time. So far Wise had shown little evidence of his incompetence and soldiers were seemingly proud to join up and follow him. It appeared that the citizens of the Kanawha were about to get the man they felt would be their saviour, and on Wednesday, June 26, the same day that Capt. J.P. Hale appointed officers of the Kanawha Artillery,[40] their waiting was over, as reported by the Richmond Light Infantry Blues:

"....This morning we changed our mode of travel from the march by land to that of steam on the Kanawha River. We had a delightful passage down the river. When we arrived at Malden we found a number of ladies saluting us with flags and the waving of handkerchiefs. We landed and presented arms to the Ladies. They then persuaded Captain Wise to let his company remain and take dinner, which was agreed to, and in a few hours they had a sumptous meal prepared for us, to which we did ample justice, our appetites having been whetted by a long fast. After dinner we bade our fair entertainers good bye and steamed away for Charleston, at which place we arrived at 4 P.M. and were stationed at the Court House...."[41]

A number of units accompanied General Wise into Charleston besides the Blues, including the Greenbrier Riflemen; the Pig Run (River) Invincibles from Pittsylvania County, Virginia; and Jackson's Invincibles from the old town of Alexandria; as well as the cavalry company of Capt. John P. Brock, known as either the Valley Rangers or Rockingham Cavalry. And there was

BRIGADIER GENERAL ALFRED BECKLEY
27th Brigade Virginia Militia. "McCausland's draft plan infuriated him."
— Courtesy: Mrs. M.M. (Lucille) Ralsten, Beckley, WV

the personal staff of Wise, which included two men of noted military ability: Col. Charles Frederick Henningsen, later to command the 2nd Regiment Infantry of the Wise Legion, noted for his "ruthless destruction of Granada" in Latin America; and Col. Frank Anderson, best remembered for leading "the military forces in the filibustering expediton of William Walker in Nicaragua."[42] It's believed that Wise established his headquarters in the Kanawha House, a hotel operated by John Wright, at the corner of Front and Summers Street.

After a few days in Charleston, Wise moved his troops to the site of Camp Two Mile (Camp Lee) located on the west side farm of Adam Brown Dickinson Littlepage and his wife, Rebecca. Wise immediately employed his knowledge of topography and had extensive breastworks built, including a 100 foot square fort on the steep rise behind the Littlepage home, breastworks to guard the chute at the mouth of Elk River, and, later, breastworks on nearby Tyler Mountain. But his primary interest at this time seemed to be his desire to use the Littlepage house as his own personal headquarters, something the Littlepage's didn't approve of.

Reportedly Wise was already angry at Adam Littlepage for refusing to join his Legion, although it must be noted that Adam was a wealthy Southern sympathizer, owned a number of slaves, and later gave his life while in service of the Confederate Army. History has not made it clear as to whether or not Adam was present at the time Wise attempted to enter the house, but there is no doubt that his fiesty wife Rebecca was there. Easily Wise's equal

COLONEL CHARLES FREDERICK HENNINGSEN
Elite member of Wise's staff. — From "The Story of the Filibusters" by J.J. Roche

THE LITTLEPAGE STONE MANSION — CAMP TWO MILE — POSTWAR VIEW
Courtesy: Mrs. John T. Morgan

THE LITTLEPAGE STONE MANSION — CAMP TWO MILE — POSTWAR VIEW
Courtesy: Mrs. John T. Morgan

THE LITTLEPAGE STONE MANSION
Today. — Photo by the author

in stubbornness and temperament, she reportedly gathered her seven children about her and stood in front of the door refusing to admit the agitated General. Wise was furious and ordered six cannon trained on the house in order to blow it to bits, as well as anyone who stood in the way. He then ordered his aide-de-camp to command the artillerists to commence firing, an order the aide-de-camp flatly refused to obey. Wise was now at the boiling point and personally gave the order to fire, but not a single soldier responded. Disgusted by the entire affair Wise retreated to his tent and reportedly never did enter the Littlepage house during his entire tenure in the Kanawha. But the story does not end there. There was much refute of the incident after the war, particularly when James L. Capston, who served as orderly sergeant of Caskies Rangers at the time of the purported incident, read a story about it in an 1886 issue of *The Philadelphia Times* and doubted its authenticity. As he was responsible for the carrying out of details under General Wise he felt he would have known of such an affair, and after conferring with some old war-time buddies, he decided the whole story was a big hoax.

Hoping to finally end the dispute, Charles F. Littlepage, one of seven children present at the time of the purported confrontation, stated that events did indeed transpire as told except:

> *"Force was not used to compel mother to comply. Guns were not ordered to be loaded and fired at our home, nor did anyone except mother refuse to obey the order of Gen. Wise. But the conversation referred to certainly did take place between Gen. Wise, my father, and my now gray-haired mother."*[43]

In addition, Charles mentioned that when Gen. Wise later retreated from the Kanawha he took with him everything movable from the Littlepage house, which would mean that Wise obviously entered the house, or at least his soldiers did. Regardless of Charles Littlepage's revelations, some Littlepage descendants hold to the original story, which could yet be true, because Charles was only ten years old at the time of the incident and may not have comprehended the events properly.

The 'Littlepage Incident,' though, was only the beginning of a near 'reign of terror' under which General Wise placed the Kanawha. Because of the strongly divided sentiment in the area he was suspicious of everybody, and hunted down those he felt were relaying information to the Federal soldiers. It was said that he cussed everybody, and when nobody else was

REBECCA LITTLEPAGE
In her later years. She dared to defy General Wise.
— Courtesy: Mrs. John T. Morgan

around to cuss, he would cuss his son, O. Jennings. He often complained of the "domestic enemies" and said that "rigid and harsh discipline of traitors in the Kanawha Valley and adjacent counties would fill all the jails of the trans-Allegheny."[44] Many citizens who lived near Camp Two Mile fled their homes and there was rumor amongst Wise's soldiers that the people had poisoned their wells when they departed, and as a result the soldiers went to the Absalom Bowen Tavern (Six-Mile House) at Tyler Mountain where they knew the well water was clean. It was said that "the entire force from Wise's camp gathered round the well, drank as much as they could hold, and filled their canteens until all the water was gone."[45] It was also a practice of Wise to visit area farms and confiscate horses, and it was during such a visit to the McCown farm on Tyler Mountain that Tobias Marianni, an Italian who could not speak English, was taken prisoner for hiding horses. Whatever hopes the Confederate authorities had in relation to Wise raising a large army were soon lost, as the most ardent secessionists began to regret his appearance, so much so that he soon found himself nicknamed "Old" Wise.

An editorial would appear after Wise's departure from the valley in the November 29, 1861 issue of the *Wheeling Intelligencer* which purportedly gave an accurate, although obviously biased, view of Wise's time spent in the Kanawha and his attitude toward the people, particularly the Unionists:

> *"Since early in the summer, the valley has been the scene of warfare. Wise came among the people as a besom of devastation. He literally laid bare the country all around him. His worthless promises to pay are left widespread among the people; but their corn, their wheat, their oats, their hay, their bacon—their all—is gone, to be heard of no more. He took horses, mules, wagons, and impressed them in his service, both as he came and as he left. He paid for nothing the whole time. His cavalry, sustained themselves by depredating first upon one farm and then upon another. They roved from field to field, from locality to locality, like droves of grasshoppers. They let down fences, entered and fed their horses from grain in the shock. They took corn and oats from the barns. They quartered themselves at the tables of the farmers like so many brigands and footpads, never even giving so much as a slip of Wise's script in return. Their trail was desolation everywhere. The infantry were provided for by the script system. Foragers stay and make valuation on farm products, to store houses of provisions, etc., and give the owners certificates therefor. If the owners objected, the property was considered sold in spite of the objections, and was transferred to the wagons just as though it had been paid for in gold. Nothing was allowed to interfere. In like manner clothing and everything else that was of value was taken.*
>
> *In the town of Charleston, the case of two young Jews, clothes dealers, afforded a distressing example of Wise's brutalism. He got hold of a letter which one of them had written to a dealer in the East, at the bottom of which was a note indicating his sympathy with the Union. Wise had him and his brother arrested and thrown into prison; and on being visited by a lawyer on their behalf, revealed a depth of devilish brutality that astounded his visitor beyond belief. He said he intended to have these Jews shot unless they made over their stock of goods to him; that if they would assign the goods, he would not shoot them; but that he wanted it understood that either through blood or an instrument of writing he intended to have the goods. The lawyers (from whose own lips we have these facts) went back to the poor fellows and told them the sorry tale. He left them in prison in tears. The sequel was that Wise took the property and carried them away captive with him.*
>
> *"The old demon used to curse frightfully. His profanity was most disgusting.... His whole bearing was that of maniac devil—seemingly let loose to fill a portion of the unexpired term of Satan himself. Never did a people more rejoice to see a pestilence leave their midst than the people of Kanawha to see Wise compelled to make off. The feeling was not confined to Union men; it was general."*

THE BOWEN TAVERN (SIX-MILE HOUSE)
Much as it looked during the war. — Courtesy: Bowen heirs and Gary Bays

THE BOWEN TAVERN (SIX-MILE HOUSE)
Today. — Courtesy: Gary Bays

In any event, Wise didn't much care whether or not he was liked, and proceeded to go about his official duties. Major C.B. Duffield was delegated to try the prisoners. Col. Adler, a native of Hungary, was brought in as an engineer, and Professor Thomas I.L. Snead of William and Mary, and Lt. J.B. Harvie of the Provisional Army were employed as scientific explorers. And on June 27th Lt. James Welch received instructions on how to make lacquer for his artillery:

Charleston
Thursday night June 27, 1861

Dear Jim—

I told you last night I would send you directions for lacquer iron ordnance which is as follows.

Black lead, pulverized, 12 parts
Litharge—5 parts
Linseed Oil—66 parts
Red lead—12 parts
Lampblack—5 parts

Boil it gently for about twenty minutes stirring it constantly during that time (according to Haswell)

This lacker is as good for iron work as for ordnance. Don't use anything but this lacker as this is the best and as cheap as any other. Scrape the guns clean before using the lacquer.

Yours
Henry D. Baines

Col. McCausland, obviously a bit perturbed by Wise, as well as being a bit skeptical of his military ability, wrote the following letter to V.M.I. Superintendent Francis Smith on June 28:

"'....I am in hope that you will be able to send me 10 cadets soon. If you could only see our soldiers—rough—undisciplined—and badly uniformed—in fact, with their every-day clothes, amounting to nothing at all. You would be surprised that we have been able to hold this region. Genl. Wise has commenced pursuing traitors, he hunts them down and gives them a severe trial. I am anxious about the result. I fear that we have not force enough to carry out his extensive plans. I expect to lead a Regiment to the Ohio very soon. It is the intention of Genl. Wise to advance one Regt. to Point Pleasant but I also fear that we may have to fall back. If we can occupy it for a short time without a fight, the position can be fortified and soon made strong.

Disaffection is declining and soon the state laws can be well executed.... I work day and night. I am called upon from every side, but endeavor to satisfy all.

....We now have 1500 volunteers from this region and Wise has only *300 in his* Legion....'"[47]

Captain Assistant Adjutant General of the Wise Brigade (or Legion), E.J. Harvie, reported the command's condition on the 29th, stating, "There are at present 30 companies including the Va. volunteers and those belonging to the Wise Brigade...."[48]

While McCausland was busy filing justifiable complaints, Capt. Albert Gallatin Jenkins was taking visible action against the enemy. Sometime during the latter part of June, on a Saturday night, he led a raiding party of about fifty mounted men from Charleston to Point Pleasant, taking a number of prominent Union men prisoner. Col. Jesse S. Norton, at Gallipolis with the 21st Ohio, led an unsuccessful attempt to capture the raiders. After "scouring the countryside" a few miles east of the mouth of the Kanawha, Norton and his 100 man force gave up pursuit and took thirty prominent secessionists prisoner, to be used as hostages and to insure fair treatment of Jenkins' prisoners. Among those Norton took were James Clark, J.F. Dintz, A.B. Dorst, J.W. Echard, A.E. Eastman, H.J. Fisher, Benjamin Franklin, R.B. Hackney, S. Hargiss, James Johnson, Jacob C. Kline, T.B. Kline, R. Knupp, David Long, Alexander McCausland, J.N. McMullen, Robert Mitchell, E.J. Ransom, Frank Ransom, A. Roseberry, W.O. Roseberry, O.H.B. Sebrill, and G.D. Slaughter. By July 5th these men had arrived at Camp Chase near Columbus, giving them the distinction of being the first prisoners to enter that noted prison camp. Their stay was short, though, as they were released a few days later.[49]

At about this same time late June or early July, Norton led a raid, with Capt. George F. Walker of Company F and Lt. Arnold McMahon of Company C, on the Jenkins home at Greenbottom, where they destroyed

COLONEL [then Lieutenant] ARNOLD McMAHAN
Company C — 21st Ohio Volunteer Infantry. Assisted Colonel Norton's raid on Greenbottom. — From S.S. Canfield's "History of the 21st Ohio"; Courtesy: Library of Congress.

the crops and fields and captured a steamboat load of cattle, corn, horses, and other supplies, which they took with them as they returned to Gallipolis. Norton also mentioned at this time that there were then 3,500 of the enemy at Charleston, although his source of information was probably questionable.[50] Norton belatedly reported the expedition to Governor Dennison on July 7: "Have captured four horses, two mules, sixteen head fat cattle from the notorious A.G. Jenkins, Captain Company Virginia Border Rangers. Expected to meet him but he could not be found. He has ten thousand (10,000) bushels corn which will go to the rebel camp unless it is taken. Shall I appropriate, if answer quick. Shall I order the cattle killed for the use of the army?"[51]

General McClellan had certainly not been blind to all this secessionist activity. He was just a bit slow to respond, as became his custom throughout his Civil War career. As noted, he postponed the Kanawha movement on June 1 after conferring with some prominent men of the Kanawha, yet on June 11th he postponed it again, "...I have been obliged to defer the Kanawha movement for a few days. I hope before I am ready to make it to have received authority to muster in Virginia troops for the defense of that valley...."[52] On June 12 Winfield Scott cleared McClellan to use loyal Virginia men as requested but by the 19th McClellan remained more concerned with affairs elsewhere in his command: "...Movement on Grafton appears more important than that in the valley of the Kanawha. Had arranged to reach Kanawha tomorrow. Will now defer it...."[53] And on June 23 McClellan avoided the Kanawha Valley for a fourth time, "....As soon as practicable, I intend to clean out the valley of the Kanawha...."[54] His original deferment of movement was prompted by the belief that too early an invasion of the Kanawha might aggravate loyal Unionists there, but now McClellan was missing opportune moments. And with the arrival of General Wise in Charleston on the 26th the taking of the Kanawha would no longer be such an easy chore. So on June 27th McClellan initiated his coup of the campaign, the employment of Alan Pinkerton's (founder of the Pinkerton Detective Agency) first rate spy, Pryce Lewis.[55]

Pryce Lewis (or Price as Pinkerton called him) and his adventures as a Federal spy behind the Confederate lines receives minimal attention here for two basic reasons, one being that his story has been told in detail by himself as well as by Pinkerton in other available sources, and secondly, because for all his accomplishments while in the capacity of a spy, there were actually very little, if any, positive results. He returned to friendly lines too late to be of consequence to the Scary Creek battle, and Cox, prodded by McClellan and then Rosecrans, probably would have moved on Charleston without the information Lewis brought. Afterall, Cox didn't even believe Lewis at first, and seemingly continued to have doubts.

In short, Lewis was already an accomplished Pinkerton operative when McClellan asked for assistance from Pinkerton to obtain information from Confederate territory. Lewis was a natural for Pinkerton's plan to send someone who would attract so much attention that no one would ever believe he was a spy. The idea was to dress Lewis up in the fanciest of English wear, including a stove-pipe hat and the use of Pinkerton's gold watch and diamond ring, provide him with a finely crafted carriage stocked with some fine wine, and send him into western Virginia in the guise of an

PRYCE LEWIS
Pinkerton spy in the Kanawha. — Photo by O.F. Weaver, Chicago, in the Mary Lewis collection

English tourist, easily perpetrated by Lewis who had been reared in England and had read extensively of the Crimean War, an intriguing subject to the noveau Confederate soldiers. Another Pinkerton operative, Sam Bridgeman, a fifty-year old Virginia native, went along as Lewis' driver and footman. Two other Pinkerton men, completely independent of Lewis and Bridgeman, were sent disguised as common laborers to Point Pleasant and worked their way up the Kanawha Valley in conjunction with Lewis' trip.

Lewis and Bridgeman left Cincinnati on June 27th, landed at Guyandotte on the following day, and took the "main road away from the river into the country," made friends with a staunch Southern sympathizing farmer along the way, finally encountering Confederate cavalry pickets near Camp Tompkins. They were soon afterward brought to an old stone farmhouse with a broad verandah on the porch (Valcoulon Place) and met with and made good friends of Col. Patton in his office on the second floor. The day was spent exchanging light conversation, consumption of Lewis' wine, talk of the Crimean War, and Patton's boast that at Camp Tompkins he had "fortifications here that with 600 Confederate soldiers I can defend against 10,000 Yankees for ten years." By this time Lewis could no longer have any doubt about the validity of his disguise. Here was one of the brighter Confederate officers in the Kanawha Valley being the best of friends with him and even offering to give him a tour of the camp and its fortifications.

During the latter part of the day Patton gave Lewis a pass to Charleston which the two operatives hastily used after bidding Patton a fond farewell. Somewhere between Camp Tompkins and Charleston the two encountered a runaway horse bearing the daughter of a Judge Beveridge, a rather prominent man of the valley. They rescued her and became good friends with her as well as three Confederate recruiting officers that were with her. Lewis and Bridgeman finally reached Charleston late in the evening and took up quarters in the hotel of John Wright, the Kanawha House, where they would have to obtain a pass to Richmond from Gen. Henry A. Wise, not at all a friendly sort such as Patton. In fact, when they did manage to meet with Wise he flatly refused to give them a pass, causing Lewis to become verbally agitated with the General and to make threats that he would get permission from the English consul in Richmond. Wise was certainly not a man to argue with, and Lewis was well aware of his fiery nature, yet he persisted in his guise as a very irritated English gentleman tourist. To make matters worse for Lewis, Bridgeman was becoming a bit loose lipped from the intake of alcohol while patronizing the Charleston saloons. Time was running out for the two spies. Lewis knew the ruse could only work for a few more days at most. Then, if caught in the hands of Gen. Wise, their fate would probably be death.

Lewis yet managed to make more soldier friends while seeking an escape route, and even got a tour of Wise's main camp, probably Camp Two Mile, "about two miles out of town on the Charleston Fair Grounds," where he observed battalion drill, met with the commanding officer (probably McCausland), and learned from the Commissary that 3,500 rations were issued that day. Of the rebel soldiers Lewis said, "considering the lack of uniformity in their dress, made a very creditable appearance. Very few in the ranks were well dressed, the majority were like farmers or laborers." And once again the spirits of alcohol nearly caused Lewis to be exposed

MEETING AT VALCOULON — CAMP TOMPKINS
Left to right: Sam Bridgeman, assistant to Lewis, Pryce Lewis, Pinkerton spy, Captain George S. Patton.
— From Alan Pinkerton's "Spy of The Rebellion"

through Bridgeman.

Luck had indeed been a major part of Lewis' success so far, no matter how well he performed his part of the disguise, and luck came again the night that Wise left Charleston for Ripley leaving Col. C.Q. Tompkins in command. Tompkins, a friendly sort such as Patton, told Lewis that Wise must have misunderstood him, that no passes were necessary for the roads were open to Richmond. Quick to seize the opportunity, Lewis and Bridgeman departed soon after, went to Brownstown (Marmet), cut across country hoping to get back to Ohio, and blundered into more Confederates at Logan. Once again Lewis employed his great acting skills and deceived the soldiers there, finally making his way back to Cincinnati after spending nineteen harrowing days in enemy country, gathering enough accurate information on Confederate strength and fortifications to make Cox's drive up the Kanawha an easy chore, with little or no loss of men. But when Lewis left Cincinnati on July 20 to meet Cox on the Kanawha he was too late. The Scary battle had already been fought.

CHAPTER FOUR

Defensive and Diversionary Tactics

General Wise's military movements and the reasoning behind them for the early part of July remain shrouded in a cloud of mystery. By June 29 it was quite clear that, as McCausland had seemingly feared, Wise had "eyes bigger than his stomach." With barely enough men to hold the Kanawha Valley alone, he envisioned a far larger area for his military command—the entire country between the Great Kanawha River and the Little Kanawha River. Whatever possessed the man to believe that he could accomplish such a task will probably never be known but the obvious detrimental effect it could have on his position at Charleston failed to cause any hesitation by him at all. Within a matter of days he had forces in Ripley in Jackson County and at Glenville in Gilmer County. Certainly not to be overlooked is the fact that Wise's comrades, who were operating against McClellan in northwestern Virginia, began requesting such diversionary tactics and movements as of July 1st, but since Wise apparently began his movement to Ripley a day prior to that the operation must be credited to him. Probably, as his later letters from Ripley indicated, Wise felt it was essential to hold Ripley in his line of defense of the Kanawha, fearing Federal troops at Parkersburg or Ravenswood would soon invade the Kanawha via that route.

The Ripley force, composed of the Richmond Light Infantry Blues under Capt. O. Jennings Wise, and Capt. George S. Patton with his Kanawha Riflemen, comprising a total force of 800 men, departed Camp Two Mile at 9 P.M. on the 29th, and marched throughout the night, causing many to become tired and footsore. But on the 30th the cavalry company of Capt. John P. Brock (Company H, 10th Virginia Cavalry) arrived from Two Mile and presented horses to the weary foot soldiers to use on their forty mile trip.

The Virginians knew their task would not be easy. The 17th Ohio Volunteer Infantry was already at work against guerrillas in Jackson County and it was known that two companies, possibly later increased to four, were stationed at Ravenswood only 11 miles from Ripley. In addition, word had reached the local citizenry of the approaching Confederates, provoking many of the loyal Unionists to flee across the Ohio River as well as to other safe places. In fact, when O. Jennings and Patton arrived at Ripley they found that any soldiers that may have previously been there had apparently fallen back to Ravenswood, leaving behind nothing more than a relieved secessionist townfolk. With no enemy to be found the Virginians spent the night in the court house.

Rest was of a short duration. July 1st found the Confederates mounted, put under the command of Patton, and sent three miles west toward the Ohio River to Cottage Mills (Cottageville) where the enemy was purported to be entrenched. Taking an old road (which is now State Rt. 33) the soldiers passed the farm of George and Susanna Horton Crow at Angerona, where they left a contingent of horses to be watched by a few soldiers and the Crow's son, George Burton. After arriving at Cottageville the Virginians "dismounted and formed in line of battle for an attack," but once again the enemy was nowhere to be found.[1] Moving back to Ripley they encountered a Unionist militia of Cottageville home guards led by Capt. Hopkins (probably James T. Hopkins, a 57 year old area blacksmith). Lying in ambush on the top of Antil(l) Hill, now known as either Coonrod or Conrad Hill, the militia fired one hasty, ineffective volley at the Confederates, who immediately returned the fire. Capt. Hopkins, a man of stuttered speech, later told of the episode to George Crow, who, after the war related it to a reunion of veterans just as it was told to him: "....when the rebels appeared ...and fired one volley, his (Hopkins') force dropped to their hands and knees and started on all fours in the opposite direction down the hill and on coming to a new rail fence they were afraid to arise but 'bu-bu-butted the bo-bo-bottom rail out' and went on down the hill, and scarcely dared to stand erect until they had crossed the Ohio River...."[2]

By this time General McClellan had become well aware of the enemy movements about Ripley. He immediately ordered Col. Jesse S. Norton of the 21st Ohio Volunteer Infantry, with a 1200 man force, to depart Gallipolis and give support to the 17th Ohio at Ravenswood. The Federal force arrived by steamer at Letarts (Letartsville) at 2 P.M. on July 3, and departed their boats at 11 P.M. at Ravenswood, from which point they proceeded to march upon Ripley.[3] Some sources, including McClellan, have indicated that Norton's men drove the enemy out of Ripley, but records clearly show that the Confederates had already departed on a march back to Charleston, camping at Scofford (probably a prominent farm) on Grass Lick that night and continuing to Sissonville the next day.[4] At this stage of events General Wise, apparently perturbed by the retreat and prompted on by his peers, decided to personally join the Ripley force and left Camp Two Mile, placing a justifiably paranoid Col. Tompkins in charge in his absence. On July 4 the General joined the "Ripley task force" at Sissonville, bringing with him his full staff and reinforcements.[5] Feeling Ripley must be held, he decided to renew the advance upon Ravenswood, although he had already lost any element of surprise, and began the march back to Ripley the next day, an event recorded in the diary of Joab (or Joel) Smith, a member of Capt. William E. Lipscomb's Jackson County Border Rifles: "....a tedious journey through the rain...spent another night at Scofford, or rather from two in the morning until daylight...lay down on the wet ground, where I was nearly devoured by fleas...rose at daylight after two hours of restless slumber...without breakfast reached Ripley at 11 A.M...."[6] A fight with Col. Norton had been anticipated, but the Federals had apparently withdrawn from Ripley and returned to Ravenswood.

The incidents of the next few days have become a blur on history. Numerous sources have indicated that, once in Ripley, General Wise decided to attack Ravenswood in force, changed his mind at the last minute for some unknown reason, and began his return to Charleston on July 5, accompanied by the Richmond Light Infantry Blues, while leaving a small defensive force at Ripley. This is just not possible in light of the fact that Gen. Wise wrote a number of letters and dispatches from Ripley after July 5. In them he continued to hold to his belief that Ripley had to be defended, although Col. Tompkins totally disagreed and pleaded with Wise to return to Charleston where the Federals at Gallipolis posed a much more serious threat to the Kanawha Valley.

The next few days found the Confederate force at Ripley plagued by a number of false alarms, yet some of the soldiers did manage the pleasure of a bath in Mill Creek.[7] On July 6, Wise issued a proclamation to the citizens of Ripley calling for their assistance,[8] and began correspondence to Col. Tompkins defending his movements:

Headquarters Ripley Va.
July 6, 1861

Colonel:

Yours respecting the three Regiments from Cincinnati; received tonight at 2 o'clock. If, by "your (my) early return" you mean the forces here under command I have but to repeat, what I forwarded today, that their presence here, is absolutely required in order to prevent entire occupation of this road, (which we came), and the roads Eastward, by the enemy, both from Ravenswood and Parkersburg. A retrograde movement from here will have a bad effect, and in my opinion, will hasten and aid the attack upon the Valley. A few works here will enable a much smaller force to hold the place, with more effect than the number of men now here could, without them, and the place (Ripley) itself, is a far more important position than I deemed it before coming here.

As soon as these works are completed I can return some of the companies and as soon as I give particular directions about there, I will in person return to "Two Mile"—considering this road there to a part of our line of defense.

Yours Respectfully
Henry A. Wise
Brig. Genl.
Commanding the Valley &
adjacent counties of Kanawha

To. Col. C.Q. Tompkins)
Charleston)

P.S. Before leaving here at all, it is important to obstruct, and if possible render impassible the road leading to this place from Parkersburg, Ravenswood, and that from the Ohio, via Mill Creek. There is not a mattock, spade, or pick axe to be got here. If, to be got at Charleston send a few to Ripley immediately.[9]

Ripley July 6th, 1861
Saturday

To Col. Tompkins
Commdg. & c & c

Sir

You dated yours "Saturday the 6th 1 A.M."—it reached me here on my arrival at 10 A.M.—It confirms the note I sent yesterday morning. My movement will be made to meet this combined operation against us. They can't cut me off. We have three good roads of retreat—the one we came, the one by Little Sandy creek & the California or Suttonsville road. I fear more the ascent of the Kan. as to much that I remain here to take a deliberate reconnoisance of

Ravenswood & Mill Creek and will send back to you the most efficient forces here upon the earliest intelligence of the enemy approach upon you, and I start immediately orders to Col. Richardson at Gauley Bridge to forward to you all the men, guns & ammunition he can spare from that point. If they make no attack or approach from Ravenswood or Mill Creek I think of making a sudden & rapid move down Mill Creek to Letarts Falls and swinging across & up the Kanawha Valley—to gain the rear of any force attacking you, or to scour Mason & if you are not attacked, and take Col. McCausland's intended position at & below Buffalo. My remaining here awhile will retard or prevent this invasion, I think, from either point & strengthens us in all this region. The men get on very well & we will have forage aplenty, but the literal sacking of this place makes immediate supplies of bacon scarce. I would attack Ravenswood at once, but reliable information that the enemy have heavy guns on the opposite shore restrains me. I must reconoiter. We have every road under our command & scouts are sent far out in every direction obstructing all information to and from this town. There is no doubt it was Norton's force from Gallipolis that sacked this town. It was riddled,—the house I am in has every piece of furniture showing the effectiveness of the force.

Please tell my son Richard to send up to me immediately his valis, with three shirts, ½ doz. collars, a pair of drawers, my flannel under waistcoat & flannel undershirt & one pair of socks, my blue sack coat, my black thick pants, the gray summer coat in the box of things I bought from Jew ships stock, and some two twists of tobacco & also my boots and leggings. Mr. Duffield knows about the Jew box.

Very respectfully & truly
Henry A. Wise

P.S. TELL HIM TO SEND ME SOME MONEY.[10]

Ripley July 7th 1861

To Col. Tompkins
Commdg.

Sir:

Sent dispatches by Surgeon Pallen. Detained your messenger to give you news of Middle of the day—now 2 P.M.—alarm sounded this morning & the troops were promptly at posts pointed out to them at sundown. Scouts saw two of the enemies' picket guard who ran. After going the rounds of posts, the men were retired for breakfast. No alarm since. Caught two spies last night, our own citizens, one from Wirt & the other from Jackson, Sargent & Ball—examined them thoroughly & with aid from Mr. Geo. A. Fitzhugh got from each a full confession—their watchword was "Chippewa." We got two good horses from them & two pistols—young men. From them I infer about 800 men at Ravenswood, but a Mr. Haynes, much relied on, says less than 500 at Ravenswood—450 at Murraysville and 250 at Flisher?, 13 & 5 miles off. The artillery at Ravenswood,a barrel cannonade only. I think of an attack on into the night. Respectfully,

Henry A. Wise
Brig. Genl.[11]

Hd. Qrs. Va. Vol.
Kanawha C.H. Va.
July 7, 1861

Sir:

Your letter of 7th and Mr. Fitzhugh's of this date are just received (7½ P.M.) Their contents impress me with the fact that you do not fully appreciate the information which I have communicated to you three times within the last 3 hours & I am impelled, in spite of your evident determination to continue your present occupation, to repeat again those & cumulative circumstances which if true render your situation perilous, & seems to establish the necessity of concentrating all your forces at their respective garrisons to insure a successful defense or a strong move down the river. The information that the demonstrations in the direction of Ravenswood were intended as a ruse to "bag" you & to diminish our strength here has been again confirmed...& in addition intelligence reaches here this evening that a courier has been dispatched to Hurricane Bridge & its vicinity by Col. Norton announced to the citizens that he would occupy it tonight & inviting them to turn out & join him. In consideration of this evidence, & the fact that you are more remote from us than the enemy will be at "Buffalo," or Thirteen," I most respectfully repeat the suggestion that self-preservation & success in the event of an engagement demand your return with all...of your command. It comprises the most efficient men in the Department. Nevertheless, if you are not brought to my conclusions, any order for reinforcements will be promptly complied...with.

In my letter this morning I omitted to report that Gen. Cox in his address vowed that Gen. McClellan would make a movement down Gauley simultaneously with his approach up the Valley.

I reinforced Coal this morning with Capt. Chandler's company of 90 men, which makes the strength of that post 330 infantry & 130 cavalry.

C.Q. Tompkins
Col. Commdg.[12]

Brig. Gen.
H.A. Wise
Commdg.

Col. Tompkins' pleas finally paid off and on the morning of July 8, following another false alarm, the Ripley force began the march back to Charleston under a blazing hot sun. They reached Sissonville that night, where Kanawha Rifleman William Clark Reynolds recorded: "traveled 24 miles and slept in the dog fennel—minus dinner and supper." Finally, on July 10th, after marching "through a drenching rain" the Ripley force returned to Camp Two Mile.[13] General McClellan, due to the forfeit of Ripley and Ravenswood by General Wise, managed to claim a Union victory.

The Confederate excursion into Gilmer County didn't fare any better. Capt. Robert A. Caskie took a cavalry task force of about 160 men, apparently his own Mounted Rangers and Biernes' Sharpshooters, to Glenville, the county seat, via Spencer and Arnoldsburg, and arrived on Sunday, July 7 only to find a battalion of the 17th Ohio Volunteer Infantry, commanded by Lt. Col. Francis B. Pond, occupying the town. Caskie's men drove the Union pickets in under a heavy fire, and a good deal of gunfire was exchanged on the outskirts of town, but once Lt. Col. Pond drew his men into a line of battle at the court house, Caskie's soldiers made no further attempt to attack them, although desultory firing continued throughout the night. It was reported that early the next morning "both sides were firing like hell," with the Federals holding their position, yet Caskie realized the situation was futile and began his return to Charleston on that Monday morning. Since there were no casualties in the battle the only accomplishment of the Confederates was that they had temporarily taken a small amount of pressure off the Confederates fighting McClellan's soldiers.[14]

In retrospect, the Ripley-Glenville maneuvers didn't accomplish much. General Wise did get to flaunt his underestimated military mite a bit and his willingness to fight, but there were no casualties on either Antil(l) Hill or Glenville, both minor skirmishes which certainly did not prove an army's fighting ability. In addition, the two movements helped to deplete the already meager Confederate supplies and weapons, not to mention the wear and tear on the soldiers involved. But most important of all, General Wise failed to obtain his objective—the area between the two Kanawhas. Needless to say, he would have been much better off, as Col. Tompkins implied, to have remained at Charleston strengthening its defenses and keeping supplies intact and horses and men well rested and ready for the impending Federal invasion. Of course, Wise can't be criticized too harshly for believing Ripley would be the primary route of Federal invasion, because when the invasion did come Ripley was one of the three avenues used, although it proved the least threatening of the group.

One bright aspect of the Ripley jaunts was the addition of a number of Jackson County militia units to the army of Wise, including the Jackson County Border Rifles, led by young Ripley lawyer Capt. William H. Lipscomb; the Jackson County Rangers of Capt. M.S. Kirtley; and the Western Riflemen under Capt. Franklin P. Turner.[15] Of even greater importance, though, was that the Confederate situation had continued to improve at Charleston during the Ripley-Glenville maneuvers. On July 1st, while still at Two Mile, General Wise had received a dispatch from Adjutant and Inspector General Samuel Cooper which informed him that the volunteer forces under Col. Tompkins did not necessarily have to be added to the Wise Legion in order for Wise to command them, a problem of command which had plagued him since his arrival in the Kanawha. The dispatch also promised, "Several companies, both horse and foot, have been sent to you from this quarter. Among them is a company of artillery, with a battery consisting of two 6-pounder guns and two 12-pounder howitzers, which with the two 6-pounders previously sent to you will complete the full battery originally intended for you. Every effort is being made to send forward the troops for your command as fast as they can be raised."[16]

Despite such promises, not much in the way of ordnance supplies was ever seen as the situation continued to grow worse. On July 2 Col. Tompkins reported, "We have entirely exhausted our stock of Rifle Powder—there being in the hands of the men not more than 20-30 charges for their pieces. As rifles are the predominating arms in the hands of these troops it is all important that a supply of rifle powder should be forwarded immediately. The General requests that this matter will receive the prompt attention of the authorities in Richmond as his movements are almost wholly dependent upon it."[17] On the same day, Gen. Wise wrote Richmond enforcing the same viewpoint, "I represent to you emphatically again that the army here is chiefly composed of Riflemen and there is no Rifle Powder here. With an army in front of the enemy most of our men will be raw, without bayonets and without powder."[18] Col. John McCausland even got into the picture when, on July 3, he wrote V.M.I. Superintendent Francis Smith: "Please send as many cartridges for flint muskets as you can spare. Powder is very scarce and difficult to get. Cadet Thompson arrived today, much obliged to you for him...."[19] As the Ordnance problem grew worse, so did control of his soldiers, with the threat of insubordination arising at Camp Tompkins, as illustrated in the July 3 letter from Major Issac Noyes Smith to Lt. James C. Welch:

Headquarters
Camp Tompkins
July 3rd, 1861

Lieut. Welch—
Sir—

Sergt. Holcomb of Capt. Lewis' company reports to me that several of his men have expressed a determination to leave their quarters tomorrow morning and join Capt. Lewis, wherever he may be, contrary to Capt. L's own orders; saying at the same time that they would ask leave from no one—I have ordered Sergt. Holcomb to forbid them going & prevent them, if they attempt it, and have authorized him to call upon you for assistance in carrying out orders. You will have your whole detachment ready to render him that assistance when he calls upon you, and if you are compelled to use force to restrain them from doing it, use it prudently but firmly, and bring the insubordinate men to the guard house under arrest.

By order of Maj. Smith
Commdg.
D.L. Ruffner
Adjt.[20]

Undoubtedly this tedious situation with weapons and men was intensified by the constant rumors of the impending Federal invasion of the Kanawha. One such, only six days before the drive did transpire, was elicited in a letter from E.J. Harvie, Captain Assistant Adjutant General of the Wise Legion at Charleston, written on July 6th to Col. J.H. Richardson, who had recently arrived from Richmond to Gauley Bridge and had assumed command there. Although tagged on to some standard military orders, the message was quite clear and bore consideration: "....I have just learned from information, which appears to be authentic, that Genl. Cox proposes to leave Cincinnati on Thursday next in command of three Regiments. His purpose is, as I understand it, the invasion of the Kanawha Valley with the view of eventually falling upon you at Gauley Bridge. This may be nothing, than a mere idle rumor but I have thought it advisable to apprise you of it and put you on your guard...."[21] For once the loose talk was well founded, giving Col. Tompkins good reason to want General Wise to return from Ripley at that time. Whenever Wise did receive this news there was no way he could treat Cox's presence at Point Pleasant as an idle threat or as a bluff to the Kanawha.

Robert E. Lee ordered Patton to report for official duty under General Wise on the following day, a somewhat token move, as Patton was already serving under Wise at Ripley. And on July 7 Patton received a dose of good news for himself—he was elected a lieutenant colonel, although he often continued to refer to himself as 'Captain Patton.' His subordinate, Lt. James Welch, also received a message containing some pleasant news:

Charleston July 7, 1861

Lieutenant J.C. Welch—

Dear Sir. I have just seen Capt. J.P. Hale. he has an old rig of a Work Horse for me. he told me to place this horse in the team & take one out to ride. he says you will have to furnish your own horse. If Geo. does not get the horse you expected him to get Capt. Hale says for you to get a good stout work horse & put it in the team & for me & you to take out the mare horse & the Little mare for our own use. I write you this because I heard you say that you had 5 or 6 horses at home. I think perhaps you may have one that will suit the wagon. If you concluded to do this you can have your choice between the two. I write this thinking you would rather do this than to buy a horse. If you have the chance to write to me to let me know what is going on.

Your friend
A.J. Jarrell[22]

Actually, Patton's advance in rank and Welch's horse offer for his artillery team was about the only good news at all for the Confederates. Most of their news was bad and the worst of it came on July 8 when E.J. Harvie submitted the official status of Wise's army in the Kanawha as of that date to the General. It was discouraging to say the least. The total number of soldiers under Wise's command was listed at 2,863 and some of those were not yet present for duty. The report went on to say that the men were entirely destitute of all the essentials necessary to make soldiers effective combatants—weapons, uniforms, knapsacks, tents, blankets, and so forth—and led by incompetent officers, resulting in a near total lack of discipline and training. Harvie concluded that "....In their present condition, untrained and awkward as many of them are in the use of arms, but little is to be expected from them and whenever brought into collision with a disciplined force it were unwise to rely upon them for attack or defense...." But he did close with a somewhat bright outlook, "....They furnish the material for an army of hardy and capable soldiers, but much labor must be expended on them to make them such...."[23] But there was no such time available with Cox's invasion only four days away. (For full particulars of the July 8 status report, see Appendix.) Troop strength did apparently continue to increase as evidenced in E.J. Harvie's communication of July 9 to Capt. L.V. Bucholtz, Ordnance Officer for the Wise Brigade stationed at Gauley Bridge, stating, "The forces now Commd. by Genl. Wise amount in all to about 3500—they will from time to time be increasing in numbers...." but, as usual, the weapon situation was bleak, reporting, "Most of the troops, as you know, are armed with rifles & we have little or no ammunition on hand for them."[13] In essence, General Wise was having not so much trouble as to recruiting men as he was to arming those men. Thirty-five hundred soldiers, if properly armed, could indeed be an effective fighting army.

CHAPTER FIVE

Advance Movement

While the Ripley and Glenville maneuvers had no particular positive effect for General Wise, it certainly worked to the betterment of the Federals. No longer could McClellan take the secessionists of the Kanawha lightly, something had to be done and be done soon. The fear of another, more effective, show of force by Wise began to spread. Although General McClellan desired to lead the entrance of Federals into the Kanawha, it was not possible as he had his hands full with the enemy in front of him in northwestern Virginia. Responsibility for the Kanawha had to be relegated to someone else, and that someone was Jacob Dolson Cox, a pre-war lawyer who had received his commission as a Brigadier General on June 22. On July 2 McClellan ordered Cox to:

> *"....assume command of the First and Second Kentucky Regiments and the Twelfth Ohio. Call upon Governor Dennison to supply you with one company of cavalry and six guns. Captain Kingsbury probably has State guns enough to give you.*
>
> *You will expedite the equipment of those regiments, and move them at once to Gallipolis, via Hamden and Portland, hiring teams for the supplies of the troops between Portland and Gallipolis, sending to the quartermaster in advance to have teams ready. With the regiment first ready to move proceed to Gallipolis and assume command of the Twenty-first. Cross the river and occupy Point Pleasant. With the regiment that next arrives occupy Letart's Falls, and then move the other two regiments to the mouth of Ten-Mile Creek, or the point in rear of your line of defense. Intrench two guns at Letart's and four at your advanced position on the Kanawha. Remain on the defensive, and endeavor to keep the rebels near Charleston until I can cut off their retreat by movement from Beverly. Should you receive certain intelligence that I am hard pressed, seek to relieve me by a rapid advance on Charleston, but place no credit in rumors, for I shall be successful. Use your cavalry as pickets, not exposing them. Punish Ripley, if you can. Repress any outbreaks that may occur at Guyandotte or Barboursville.*
>
> *Remember, my plan is to cut them off, and do all you can to assist that object. Always keep two or three boats on hand. Call on Capt. W.J. Kountz, at Marietta or Ripley, to supply boats from his fleet. If the two companies of Seventeenth Ohio are still at Ravenswood when you reach Gallipolis, order them to rejoin their regiment, via Parkersburg or Webster. Communicate frequently. A telegraph line follows me out...."*[1]

All did not go well for Cox. Although Governor Dennison wished them well and promised the necessary supplies, the "guns for the (artillery) battery were not to be had, and a section of two bronze guns (six-pounder smoothbores rifled) was the only artillery" Cox had. In addition, problems with the railroad company plagued the movement of Cox's troops, with the first ones departing on July 6, and Cox himself leaving on the 7th with seven companies of the 11th Ohio that he had managed to have added to his command.[2]

Cox reached Gallipolis on the 9th, the same day that hostile forces lured a boat to shore near Gallipolis and took boxes containing a few pistols and sabres belonging to private citizens (this is almost undoubtedly the same incident recorded in the "Diary of a Border Ranger" by James Sedinger and purported to have taken place on July 19, and so presented in this account based upon the fact that Sedinger, being an actual participant to the event, should have known when the deed transpired, although Cox's letter of July 14 to McClellan would seem to indicate Sedinger's memory was a bit fuzzy when he wrote his "diary"), and the Ohio units were united on the 10th and moved to Point Pleasant, the movements of General Wise about Ravenswood and Ripley had given Francis H. Pierpont, of the Commonwealth government of Virginia, a good scare. On July 3 he wrote to McClellan:

> *"...I propose that we occupy Point Pleasant. There are 3,500 secession troops at Charleston, fifty-two miles from Point Pleasant. Can we not take the regiment from Gallipolis and send him some other forces, and let them intrench themselves at Point Pleasant, if necessary? I have received intelligence in the last few days that they can raise a regiment in that neighborhood of Virginia troops if they had a rallying point...."*[3]

Pierpont also made reference to a regiment from Pittsburg that was ready and willing to take part in that movement. He also felt that the Ripley and Ravenswood maneuvers of Wise were an attempt by the enemy to "make a dash at the Northwestern Virginia Railroad and burn up the bridges, by dashing at different points with his cavalry...."[4] He made possibly correct assumptions, because as early as July 1 Brigadier General R.S. Garrett, commanding Confederate forces operating against McClellan near Laurel Hill, wrote: "...Unless I have been misinformed as to the state of feeling among the people and the condition of things in the Kanawha Valley it is my opinion that General Wise's command could be of more service to the cause by operating in the direction of Parkersburg and the Northwestern Railroad. It would produce a very effective diversion in favor of the operations from this point."[5] And on July 6 he wrote to Lt. Col. George Deas, Assistant Adjutant and Inspector General, once again that Pittsburg troops had indeed landed at Parkersburg and would soon prove a threat to him. He felt the Kanawha Valley was "comparatively loyal" to the secessionist cause and Wise could be more useful elsewhere, but not to move directly on Parkersburg which would prompt more Ohio troops to land there. He felt Wise should threaten Weston and Buckhannon so that pressure would be taken off him.[6]

But all was for naught. General Wise didn't receive the dispatch until July 11 by which time he had his hands full with the Federal buildup at Gallipolis and Point Pleasant. General Floyd's troops had yet to arrive in the Kanawha, so that by abandoning the Kanawha at this juncture would mean giving the valley to the Federals without a fight, and although lacking military knowledge, Wise was not about to hand over his territory without a fight. General Wise knew Cox was going to move on Charleston soon and began preparing proper defense, sending men to Poca to burn the bridge spanning the mouth of the Pocataligo (Poca) River and fortifying his camp at Two-Mile. On what later became Lower Kanawha Street, just below the old mill at Clendenin Street, he erected a breastwork out of oak timber in order to prevent steamboats with troops from passing through Elk chute.

And Cox was preparing equally fast. When he arived at Gallipolis he found McClellan had made some changes in his orders, instructing him to abandon defensive measures and advance on Charleston and Gauley Bridge, to place a regiment at Ripley, and to "beat up Barboursville, Guyandotte, etc., so that the entire course of the Ohio may be secured for us." Most importantly, to "Drive Wise out and catch him if you can. If you do catch him, send him to Columbus penitentiary."[7] There could no longer be any doubt. The lines were now drawn and a clash was inevitable in the Kanawha. It would be Cox versus Wise, Ohio men versus Virginians, but where that encounter was to take place was yet unknown. But it was going to happen and happen soon; everyone involved in the Kanawha campaign knew that.

So by July 11th it was quite obvious to Wise that some sort of effort should be made to repel Cox before he got any where near Charleston. Orders went out to occupy and defend Buffalo, which was rather pointless as Buffalo had already been determined undefensible. E.J. Harvie wrote Col. Adler of the Legion:

> *"The General requests that you will join the expedition to be sent down the Kanawha River under Col. McCausland, with the view of selecting the most suitable location for a military post.*
>
> *After aiding him in this matter you will please give the proper instructions for the construction of the necessary defenses of the position that may be selected and then return to the HD Quarters for further orders.*
>
> *Professor Snead will superintend the completion of the works already laid out by yourself in the vicinity of Two Mile Camp and Lt. Harvie will be left in charge of those to be constructed at the post that may be selected for the command of Col. McCausland."*[8]

And at Camp Tompkins Lt. William A Quarrier and Lt. James C. Welch received similar orders from Capt. Hale of the Kanawha Artillery:

> *"I have just received an order to have one gun & 15 men ready to go to Buffalo tomorrow. Haven't had time to decide who will go. Please hold yourself in readiness so that either one of you can go, most likely Lieut. Welch, if either of you. Matter waiting."*[9]

Whether or not these men made it to Buffalo, and it's doubtful that they did, is irrelevant because on this same day General Wise's greatest fear came true—General Cox, with all men and materials necessary at Point Pleasant began his three-pronged invasion of the Kanawha.

Cox's movement was quite simple in military terms. An advance guard, along with the cavalry in use as messengers, marched on roads on both sides of the river, while the bulk of the infantry, many weary from the twenty-five mile march from Hampden Station to Gallipolis, remained on the four light-draught steamboats: the *Economy, Mary Cook, Matamora,* and *Silver Lake.* In charge of the boats was Capt. A.J. Kountz, a man of considerable river experience. The First Kentucky, under Col. James V. Guthrie, had already been sent by boat to Ravenswood, and the Second Kentucky, under Col. William E. Woodruff, purportedly along with a small portion of Ohio militia, was also already enroute by boat to Guyandotte.[10]

The military strategy behind this maneuver was quite simple. The Federal force under Cox on the river was protected on the distant flanks by the Kentucky units, while the cavalry and advance guard gave protection to both the supply wagon column on the roads and the immediate flanks of the boats. And the steamers could quickly race to either shore to give support wherever necessary.

But while the plan had its advantages it also perilously split Cox's total force into three separate units, particularly endangering the Kentucky boys.

Wise could, and did, engage the distant flankers but only presented continual bushwhacking activity against the boats. Quite possibly, a large organized force under Wise could have taken advantage of the situation and easily have defeated any of the three approaching columns, but such was not the case.

Cox, aboard the lead ship, carefully surveyed the surrounding territory, giving reports that sounded more like a tourist than an officer engaged in war:

> *"Our first day's sail was thirteen miles up the river, and it was the very romance of campaigning. I took my station on top of the pilot-house of the lead boat, so that I might see over the banks of the stream and across the bottom-lands which bounded the valley. The afternoon was a lovely one. Summer clouds lazily drifted across the sky, the boats were dressed in their colors, and swarmed with men as a hive with bees. The bands played national tunes, and as we passed the houses of Union citizens, the inmates would wave their hankerchiefs to us and were answered by cheers from the troops. The scenery was picturesque, the gently winding river making beautiful reaches that opened new scenes upon us at every turn. On either side the advance-guard could be seen in the distance, the main body in the road, with skirmishers exploring the way in front and flankers on the sides. Now and then a horseman would bring some messages to the shore from the front, and a small boat would be sent to retrieve it, giving us the rumor with which the country was rife, and which gave just enough excitement and of the spice of possible danger to make this our first day in the enemy's country key everybody to a pitch that doubled the vividness of every sensation. The landscape seemed more beautiful, the sunshine more bright, and exhilaration of outdoor life more joyous than any we had ever known before."*[11]

The scene was not quite as appealing to the common foot soldier, many of whom were still recovering from the previous night when they had attempted to sleep in erect positions on the crowded boats while under a heavy morning dew. But one soldier of the 11th Ohio did report:

> *"The valley of the Kanawha, at almost any time of the year, is one of the utmost beauty, and is deeply interesting to the student of nature.... The river itself...is navigable nearly its entire length, or to the falls of Gauley. The bluffs at 'Red House' and 'Tyler Shoals,' are the pallisades of this noble little stream.... The tillable land on either side of the river is but a narrow strip, yet for productiveness can not be excelled...."*[12]

The first night's encampment was at the mouth of Thirteen Mile Creek, thirteen miles from Point Pleasant, on the northern bank of the Kanawha in the vicinity of present day Leon. Cotter's artillery was placed atop the ridge while the main camp ran from the top of the ridge to the river. Guards were appropriately posted, including pickets on the south side of the river. But late at night the peaceful serenity of camp life came to an abrupt halt.[13]

A terrified citizen rode into camp and told General Cox that General Wise was then approaching with 4000 men.[14] Another account says that he reported a battalion of cavalry under Captain Albert G. Jenkins was going to burn the bridge over Eighteen Mile Creek which was about five miles above camp.[15] Major Jonathon D. Hines of the 12th Ohio was ordered to investigate the position, but either word had leaked out to the enemy or the alarm had been entirely false, as the bridge was not burned nor the position attacked. Hines and his men, returning the next morning, reported a few enemy on horseback had come within shouting distance and taunted them with boasts on what General Wise would do to them. The Federals under Hines had departed camp minus their blankets in expectation of action and, once again, had spent the night under an extremely heavy dew.

The next day, July 12, proved a day of rest and preparation for most of the men with Cox. The steamers were sent back to Point Pleasant to secure additional men, probably more companies of the 11th Ohio, and returned during the night. One group of men that did not get to rest, however, were those serving under Captain Wallace of Company A, 12th Ohio, Elijah Berman's group, who had expressed interest in reported enemy activity at Buffalo about four miles distant. Major Hines received permission from Cox to check out the rumors and the necessary units advanced. At Buffalo, though, the only persons to be found were the apprehensive citizenry composed entirely of hard core secessionists. The men decided to camp about two miles above Buffalo in "some old quarters which had been abandoned by the rebel cavalry only the day before."[16] But as there were only a few houses many of the men had to sleep outdoors under a drenching rain, minus their blankets which they had left behind in the supply wagons. Needless to say, many of the Ohio boys were beginning to realize the importance of their blankets.

Meanwhile, General Wise received a letter from Adjutant and Inspector General Samuel Cooper informing him of the limitations of numbers permissible in the Legion and a promise that more men were on their way from Richmond, under Col. J. Lucius Davis, and that "a supply of rifle powder was sent" and "the Ordnance Department is ordered to increase the quantity."

On July 13th Cox was on the move again. But so was Wise. In an attempt to locate Federals, Wise ordered Lt. N.B. Bowyer to lead a scouting party consisting of William Alexander Burdette and Jack Hite of Beckett's cavalry company and Kanawha Riflemen Henry McFarland and Joel Lewis. They proceeded down the north side of the Kanawha to Red House, crossed the river to Winfield, and went to Vintroux's Landing across from Buffalo.[17] Little did they know that during their excursion Companies A and F of the 11th Ohio, under Lt. Solomon Teverbaugh, serving as Cox's advance guard, entered Buffalo and caught sight of the Confederate scouting party across the river. The Rebels opened fire and a short exchange of gunfire ensued, but the width of the river undoubtedly made it near impossible for the opposing forces to inflict any damage. With no casualties to be had the mounted Confederates, obviously outnumbered, quickly departed the scene. The 11th Ohio considered this incident as the first shots fired at them by rebels in the war.[18] Patton sent a report of the encounter to Col. Tompkins:

Headquarters Camp Tompkins
July 13, 1861

Colonel—

Two of my men whom I sent down as scouts last night, have just returned—they kept on this side of the river, and when about Wm. Alexander's, saw a portion of the enemy on the road on the other side, first two men on horseback in uniform who upon seeing our men, and four of Beckett's men, who were also there, galloped back. In a few moments the enemy appeared to the number of from 75 to 100. Shots were exchanged across the river and then our party came off—as they retreated they heard four distinct reports of cannon—evidently close at hand. This was about seven miles below Winfield and about 10 o'clock this morning. It is also stated that Lewis E. Ventroux, who was on a reconnoisance, saw the smoke of two steamboats ascending the river. I deem this of sufficient importance to dispatch it to you. There were no troops on this side of the river.

Capt. Sweeney, and three men have just gone down to Winfield and will bring late news.

You may rely upon the above, Joel Lewis & McFarland were the scouts from my company.

Very respectfully
George S. Patton
Major & C.

P.S. —No further word from Jenkins.[19]

HENRY D. McFARLAND
Kanawha Rifleman. He encountered the 11th Ohio during a scouting expedition near Buffalo. — From "Well Known Confederate Veterans and Their Records" by William E. Mickle

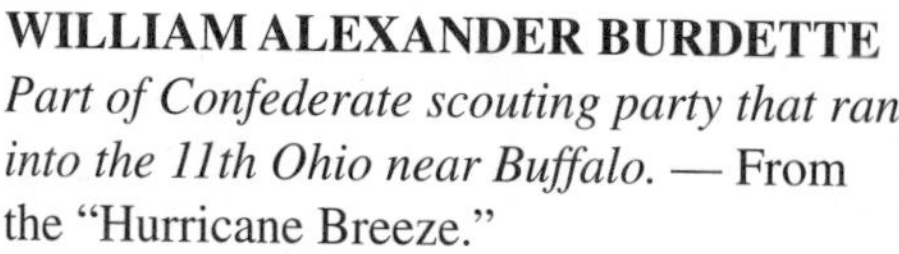

WILLIAM ALEXANDER BURDETTE
Part of Confederate scouting party that ran into the 11th Ohio near Buffalo. — From the "Hurricane Breeze."

Soon afterwards, word came into the Federal camp that the Confederates, some 600 to 800 strong, were waiting in ambush further up the river. Four companies of the 11th Ohio debarked from the boats and marched to Winfield in order to give attack but surprisingly found the village deserted. Later, the frightened citizenry, but no soldiers, were located hiding in the nearby woods. Finally, at 4 p.m., General Cox and his men arrived at Red House and set up camp.[20]

Elsewhere, Major General George McClellan, encouraged by his own successes in the northern section of western Virginia, was displaying over-confidence in the Kanawha campaign. On July 10 he had written, "The companies at Glenville are safe, and favorable chance of cutting off O.J. Wise."[21] O. Jennings, of course, returned to Charleston unmolested. On the 12th McClellan wrote, "....and the Gauley Bridge held, as it probably is by this time, by General Cox...."[22] And on July 13 it was "....I hope that General Cox has by this time driven Wise out of the Kanawha Valley...."[23] McClellan's expectations of immediate victories from his subordinates was nothing unusual, it became another of his many characteristics he carried throughout his military career.

General Wise, on the other hand, with but little interference from his superiors, continued to keep a cautious watch on Cox's movements. He had previously sent guerrilla parties down as far as to the Ohio, had already burned the bridge at the mouth of Poca River, and had kept his bushwhackers continually harrassing Cox's men. Patton's letter from Camp Tompkins to Col. Tompkins on July 13 well exemplified the Confederate defensive preparations:

> *"Nothing new to report since my dispatches of last night. As you have doubtless heard—the advance guard of the enemy, to the number of some hundred or more are above Buffalo occupying the camp built there by Col. McCausland. W. Clarkson fell in with one of their pickets on yesterday.*
>
> *I have scouts out on the Guyandotte road as far down as Winfield on this side of the river, as well as on the old Gallipolis road, and also have first rate men on the other side of the river in the road who will try to get as far as Buffalo, they started about 7 o'clock last night...."*[24]

Patton also proposed a plan, which apparently wasn't used, to engage Col. Jesse S. Norton at Buffalo and made reference that the "Scary bridge was effectually destroyed last night (July 12) and in case will prove a formidable obstacle to the enemy...."[25]

At Camp Lee orders were received by O. Jennings Wise, and possibly another company, to take defensive measures at Tyler Mountain:

> *"Col. Adler having determined to erect defenses at Tyler Mountain on the Mt. Pleasant road, and suggested the necessity of immediate stationing a company there provided with tents. You will therefore please remove your company to that place on receipt of this. The place selected by Col. Adler is about five miles from here at, or near the point where the road turns off from the Kanawha River. It is important for you to remove at once...."*[26]

And another message, also sent on July 13, although to whom it was directed is unknown, informed the officer:

> *"You will take your company to Tyler Mountain on the Point Pleasant Road and quarter them in the two vacant houses at that place. You will keep out the necessary scouts, day and night between 5 & ten miles below that point and give timely notice of any approach on the part of the enemy."*[27]

Meanwhile, General Wise had moved to Gauley Bridge in an attempt to secure more men and supplies for the impending crisis, and wrote to Col. Tompkins giving rather bleak results:

Gauley Bridge
July 13th 1861
3 A.M.

To Col. C.Q. Tompkins
Commdg.

Sir

I have ordered the disposition of forces here as well as I can, and find two companies, and part of another of infantry and a detachment of artillery, with one piece—a brass 6 pounder—is the utmost forces can be spared from this post. Indeed the want of drill and equipment make the companies just arrived unfit for service at once. I take this force, with all the arms & ammunition to be spared here on with me immediately. Could you meet us with a boat—do so, if possible. I send 1300 rounds ball cartridges—some cartridge boxes & cap boxes; and have sent to Lewisburg & Fayette C.H. for all the powder I can know of. Shall move in a few hours. Saw your son this mg. all well at your home. Had you not better move all the prisoners from in the jail and march them under guard to...

Col. Croghan could get no cannister shot.

Respectfully yours
Henry A. Wise
Brig. Genl.

Col. Anderson, of Nicaragua fame, takes command of the reinforcement & will, in place of Col. J. Lucius Davis until his arrival, command the Companies of the Legion at the lower posts of the valley. He has his written orders and will report to you at Charleston.[28]

Wise's defensive preparations were fine, but his finest weapon at this point was having instilled the citizen population of the Kanawha Valley with such a fear of the Yankees that Cox continually had his men assuring the citizenry that they were not going to cause destruction of property, rape the women, and steal the slaves. Approaching Federals often caught sight of citizens fleeing their homes and running to the nearest mountains or forest in order to escape the Yankee "butchers." Wise had finally put his flair at persuasive speechmaking to work, propaganda that it was.

Battle of Barboursville (Mud River)

It was only a matter of time until one of Cox's advancing forces would come into contact with hostile forces. And that encounter was to take place at Barboursville in Cabell County. At midnight, July 13, companies A, B, D, F, and K of the 2nd Kentucky,[29] under the command of Col. William E. Woodruff, while encamped at Guyandotte (near where the International Nickel Plant was later built), following their earlier arrival by boat, were awakened and given a stirring speech by Col. Woodruff who then placed them under the command of Lt. Col. George Neff, who had apparently been encamped at the Jenkins' farm at Greenbottom earlier, where he reportedly told Mrs. Jenkins that if he ever caught up with her husband he would hang him from the nearest tree. She said that her husband, if they should ever meet, would treat Neff as a gentleman and officer. With but a day's rations in their haversacks they proceeded to column march to a spot near Barboursville, then the county seat, where a hostile force of Virginians awaited their advance.

Anticipating the arrival of this blue column were perhaps as many as 600 Confederates,[30] including a party of Jenkins' Border Rangers led by Captain Milton Jamison (James) Ferguson, who was an attorney from Wayne County;[31] the Sandy Rangers of Captain James Corns, and a hastily gathered local militia made up of men from Wayne, Cabell, and Lincoln counties, under the leadership of Colonel J.J. Mansfield. Captain Ferguson was apparently in charge of the entire command.

BREVET BRIGADIER GENERAL [then Lieutenant Colonel] GEORGE W. NEFF

2nd Kentucky Volunteer Infantry. Victor at Barboursville — captured at Scary.
— Courtesy: Library of Congress

Fearing the worst, most of the women and children of Barboursville had left town and were at the nearby residence of Grandmother Blake, a kindly old woman who had always watched after the people of Barboursville.[32] Most of the men remained in town and debated amongst themselves on whether or not to participate in the impending battle. One such man was James Reynolds, an old gray haired Cabell farmer originally from Milton, who sat at his breakfast table with his two sons and William Clendenin Miller, a Barboursville businessman and property owner. Miller pleaded with Reynolds not to get involved but Reynolds countered, "Now, Mr. Miller, I am in this thing to the finish. My two boys and I are going out there on that ridge and put up a fight. I believe we are right about this thing and I believe we'll win."[33]

The ridge Reynolds spoke of was the Confederate defensive position, a high ridge, later known as Fortification Hill, that overlooked the confluence of the Mud and Guyandotte rivers where a covered bridge spanned the mouth of the Mud. From the top of the hill could be seen a distance of some two miles in all directions, while the hill was nearly inaccessible from all sides, as well as providing a buffer between the Mud River and Barboursville. To complete the picture, to the immediate right of the defenders was a "cut" in the ridge caused by the unfinished Chesapeake and Ohio railroad, with bluffs 45 feet high on each side of the "cut." All in all it was a perfect defensive position, providing the right calibre of soldier was stationed there.

The defending Confederates, although purported to be entrenched, probably were not in such a position. They were, for the most part, raw recruits

SITE OF THE BARBOURSVILLE BATTLE
The Confederates were on top of the hill — the Federals were in the foreground area. — Courtesy: Gary Bays

with "flintlock, muzzle-loading rifles which were loaded with one ball and three buckshot."[34] Some "came with shotguns, blunderbuses, squirrel rifles, and double barrel pistols."[35] The bulk of the men were untrained and, the militia in particular, had no intention of engaging in any warfare beyond defending their own homes and Barboursville.

The secessionist force, while preparing their defense, sent a Mr. Chapman, a young Lincoln County farmer, along the riverbanks to scout ahead and warn of the enemy advance. Five miles to the west, at Guyandotte, the Federal column led by Dr. Litch, a Barboursville man of Union sentiment who had been driven from his home weeks before, began their near silent march in the early morning darkness of Sunday, July 14. Scouting parties were sent out, only to discover that any further advance on the road before daylight would prove disastrous.

Unfortunately their wait did not help. Upon the first glimmer of sunlight that morning the Federals found that to get to Barboursville they had to advance directly through the Confederate position, which involved crossing the Mud River via the wooden bridge, putting them clearly within rifle range of the lurking enemy. And to make matters worse, the Confederates had removed the planks from the far side of the bridge, leaving gaping holes in the bed of the bridge.

Whether out of sheer ignorance, stupidity, or jut bad planning is not known, but the Yankees continued to advance into the obvious, catching sight of enemy cavalry retreating and dividing at the base of the hill as they approached. Once upon the bridge the Confederates fired upon them with a deadly volley. Immediately the soldiers in blue sought protection inside and under the bridge, upon the banks of the two rivers, and behind some abandoned brick kilns located nearby. Yet the initial enemy barrage had already taken its toll, killing one Kentucky soldier instantly and wounding a number of others.

Dr. Litch, who had held the advance of the column, found himself hanging to the remaining structural timbers of the bridge as the mule or horse which he had been riding fell through one of the gaps in the bridge floor. It was not the fault of the beast or rider, but was caused by the panic stricken soldiers plunging enmasse into the covered bridge seeking refuge, leaving Dr. Litch nowhere else to go but forward.

Taking note of their terror filled quarry, the Virginians became over-confident, yelling and cheering, some even venturing to the edge of the bridge so as to fire directly into the disorganized Federals. A better trained force could probably have won an easy victory at this point, but as events proved, the better trained men were the rugged soldiers of the 2nd Kentucky who apparently, like a cornered wild animal, sensed a "do or die" situation. The result was a fanatical charge across the bridge at the Confederates. The newly inspired Federals, "yelling and leaping like madmen," were led by Company A under Captain Alfred J.M. Brown(e), followed by Company D (the Woodward Guards) and the remainder of the Federal forces. The Confederates attempted an unsuccessful flanking attack to counter this latest and unexpected development, but soon found themselves retreating back to their position on the hill.[36]

With the tide of battle turning in their favor, the frenzied Federals fixed bayonets and began a wild charge up the steep slope. Confederate recruit

BARBOURSVILLE
Much as it looked during the battle. To the far right is the rear of Fortification Hill. — Courtesy: Barboursville Chapter D.A.R.

"Lucky" Savage, who had been on outpost duty earlier in the day, later remarked, "The guns of the Federals were equipped with bayonets that glistened in the (July) sun." As bayonets were a new commodity to many of the Confederates they thought the Federals were shooting knives at them. Savage, who mentioned that the Union charge looked more like a division than five companies, said, "I don't mind fighting with bullets, but when it comes to shooting butcher knives, I don't have anything with which to load my gun."[37]

Blue uniforms soon reached the crest of the hill, driving the Confederates into a disorganized retreat, led by the "green" militiamen, and were able to escape only because the men of the 2nd Kentucky were too winded from climbing the hill to give pursuit. However, they did continue firing at the rebels and in the course of action managed to hit Colonel J.J. Mansfield and knock him from his horse, although his men retrieved him.

One Confederate farmer, who had tied his horse to a sycamore tree in the ravine back of the ridge prior to the engagement, leapt onto his horse in the retreat and nearly beat it to death before he realized he had failed to untie it. And as for the scout, Mr. Chapman, who had found himself encircled by Union soldiers before he could return to the hill, he quickly departed his temporary hiding place and caught up with his comrades even though they had a hundred yards headstart on him.[38]

Reportedly, the Fairview Riflemen, with one artillery piece, were dispatched from Camp Tompkins "but arrived only in time to cover the retreat." It was also reported that Company H of the 12th Ohio was dispatched to aid the Federals but apparently never arrived in time to take part, if they even arrived at all.

Hearing the sounds of battle was sixteen year old John William ("Billy") Miller, who has also been at the breakfast table of James Reynolds earlier in the day, who ran from his home toward the formerly held rebel hill:

> *"My father didn't want me to join the army because I was so young. However, when I found out that there would probably be a battle within sight of our house, I took a little double-barreled pistol I owned and started toward the probable battlefield. Sometimes you could pull one trigger of the pistol and both barrels would go off, and sometimes you could pull both triggers and neither barrel would fire. Anyway, I felt that there was not a man in either army armed as well as I. I would, I firmly believed, take this deadly weapon and go out and put an end to this war. Just before I reached the field of battle, I met the Confederates coming back—fast. I fell in line without firing a shot—and the war went on four long years."*[39]

The first man "Billy" Miller met in the retreat was young Absolom Ballenger (or Ballengee) of Wayne County, who was wounded in the retreat when he fell over the precipice in the ridge created by the C&O "cut." As a result, Absolom sustained a broken leg and had to use his rifle as a crutch, eventually finding his way back to his comrades. "Billy" Miller recalled:

> *"He was the worse 'stove up' man I ever saw. He had a little muzzle loading shotgun. It shot what looked to be number eight birdshot.... I asked him if he thought he had got any of the Union men. He replied, 'I don't think so; I don't think I could quite reach them.' "*[40]

"Billy" then assisted Ballenger to Grandmother Blake's where she nursed his wound until nightfall, at which time she put him on a horse and took him three miles through the back country to a ferry over the Guyandotte situated near the historic Dusenberry mill. From this point he continued on his own and "hitch hiked" his way to safety.

Ironically, the only Confederate casualty was James Reynolds, whom the Virginians left upon the battlefield. He was recovered by the Federals, moved to the courthouse, and nursed to no avail, passing away either that afternoon or the following day. There were also some three to five Confederates who were slightly wounded.

In comparison, the 2nd Kentucky was not nearly so lucky, with five killed and eighteen wounded. (See Appendix.) But due to the victory their morale ran high and the boys of the 2nd moved on to Barboursville where the Woodland Guard planted their flag on the courthouse as banners flew and bands played, much to the disgust of the remaining townsfolk. Major General McClellan was extremely pleased with the affair and made an official report of it to Colonel E.D. Townshend on July 19: "One of Cox's regiments,

2nd Kentucky, defeated and drove 600 of Wise's men out of Barboursville, Cabell County, on 16th."[41]

Although the local Confederate militia men returned to their homes the actual Confederate fighting force continued to retreat all the way to the top of Coal Mountain where they took up defensive position. The 2nd Kentucky proceeded to follow, marching up the Teays Valley route, halting at Hurricane Bridge where they learned from a Union sympathizer of the intended ambush by the Ranger units on Coal Mountain. Attempting to out-maneuver the Rangers the 2nd Kentucky cut across country until they arrived at Winfield on the Kanawha River. Dispatched from Camp Tompkins, some scouts from the Border Rangers spotted the advance unit of the 2nd Kentucky on the Winfield Road and reported it to Camp Tompkins, where commanders utilized the information and ordered the scouts down the Kanawha three miles to keep a watch on both the River Road and Bill's Creek Road.

The Federals later crossed the river and rejoined Cox's command on the night of July 16.

The First Clash at Scary Creek

The small engagement at Barboursville was not the only clash between opposing forces on July 14. Cox had sent orders ahead to Col. Jesse S. Norton instructing him to make a reconnaissance of the enemy positions above Winfield and Red House Shoals. Norton advanced early in the morning with three companies of the 21st Ohio: Company F under Captain George F. Walker; Company G of Captain R. Henry Lovell; and Company H led by Captain A.M. Blackman. Possibly a portion of Captain George's cavalry also accompanied Norton. Following an approximate eight mile march the Federals encountered Rebel pickets and an artillery piece at the mouth of Scary Creek. There followed a small exchange of gunfire but Norton's men fell back once the Confederate artillery opened upon them. George S. Patton later recalled the incident:

> *"On Sunday the 14th July, a reconoitering party of two or three companies was sent up the south side of the Kanawha.... This party was led by Col. Jesse S. Norton of the 21st Ohio Regt. When it searched the hills near the creek they were opened upon, by two six pounder in the bush. This "masked battery" enforced them not a little, and they beat a precipitate retreat...."*[42]

Another witness to the event was Pvt. William Clark Reynolds of the Kanawha Riflemen who recorded in his diary: "July 14—First battle of Scarey. Our company with Barber (Barbee) and Bailey and a detachment of artillery went to Scarey Creek. Barber and the artillery fired on an approaching column of the enemy which retreated instantly. Later another column fled at the sight of our flag."[43]

At 9 P.M. General Cox dispatched Lieutenant Colonel David Enyart with his half of the First Kentucky Volunteer Infantry to support Norton. While crossing the Kanawha River in the darkness an order was misinterpreted which caused one tense soldier to accidentally fire his gun. The rest of the men began firing helter skelter and before the situation was corrected two soldiers were dead and several wounded. The tragedy was blamed on the darkness and the rawness of the men, yet that could not compensate for the demoralizing effect it had on the soldiers involved.

Norton's men fell back two miles from Scary Creek where they met Lieutenant Colonel Enyart with the First Kentucky. The combined forces decided not to pursue the enemy position, Norton having found it too strong to assault, and to await the arrival of General Cox and the main column. General Wise, quick to seize an opportunity for glory, immediately filed a report of the affair, writing:

> *"For the past two days troops from Ohio have been advancing up the valley, attended by three steamboats. Their object seemed to be to get possession of this town (Charleston). They were repulsed this afternoon by the troops under the command of Capt. Patton, stationed at the mouth of Coal River, a tributary of the Kanawha, but with what loss to the enemy is not yet ascertained. We did not lose a man in the engagement. The enemy ingloriously fled after our fire was opened upon them, leaving Capt. Patton's troops in possession of the field. Whether they will renew their attempt to approach this town remains to be seen. I presume they must have greatly underestimated our forces, or they would not have made the attempt to invade this valley by the River without having a force greatly superior to ours...."*[44]

Such an event finally, and possibly for the first time, caused Wise to have confidence in his soldiers and to take a new attitude toward their abilities, adding to the report: "....even in their present condition, untrained as they are, I feel confident of their being able successfully to meet an equal number of the enemy."[45]

Another event which took place on the 14th involved some men in Cox's main column. Two loyal citizens had informed the Federals then at Buffalo that a detachment of enemy cavalry would congregate at a location about five miles from town that night in order to acquire some supplies. Company F of the 11th Ohio was given the task of interfering with the rebel cavalry and left camp after sunset with the two citizens as guides. After marching single file over extremely rough, mountainous terrain they arrived at the supposed rendevous, consisting of three houses. Lt. Solomon Teverbaugh and Capt. Stephen Johnson, with sixty men, descended upon the house where the cavalry were supposed to be, but found only a few old women and a young baby.

Lt. A.H. Horton, with eight men and Sergeant Charley Achuff, closed in on the house of 'Squire' Thomas, an old man who was rumored to be dangerous, and another house in which lived the Squire's tenant. Thomas greeted the group with a rifle, but after some persuasion by Sergeant Achuff, laid his weapon down, although he made an unsuccessful attempt immediately afterward to go after Horton with an axe. All was soon resolved, though, and Thomas was given the oath of allegiance and permitted to go. The group of Federals, having found no rebels at all, returned to Buffalo as the sun began to rise, "tired, hungry, and considerably disgusted with the trip."[46]

Sometime during the 14th, General Cox sat down and wrote General McClellan a brief summary of the events up to that point:

HEADQUARTERS DISTRICT OF THE KANAWHA,
Red House, July 14, 1861

Maj. Gen. G.B. McClellan,
Camp near Buckhannon, Va.:

GENERAL: We reached this place yesterday about 4 p.m., and I am waiting here to receive news of the advance of the Kentuckians along the route from Guyandotte and Ripley to concentrate on Charleston as I have ordered. My own advance has, I am sure, made theirs entirely safe, and I have great pleasure in assuring you that we have already greatly relieved all the country behind us from a reign of terror which was driving men from their pursuits and from the country. We have met no resistance worth mentioning thus far. The enemy's forces have retreated as we have advanced, and we have exchanged a few shots with their scouts, nothing more. Your letter directed to Gallipolis giving me your first instructions did not reach me till yesterday, which was several days after I had ordered a regiment to Guyandotte. The reason for doing so was that armed parties were along the river between Guyandotte and Point Pleasant, and the very night of my arrival in Gallipolis they brought to a boat a few miles above Guyandotte and took from her a box of pistols and one of sabers belonging to private parties at Gallipolis. Knowing that we had considerable shipments of U.S. stores on the river, and that the river commerce should be secure, I was unwilling to leave that part of the country exposed, and thought it my duty to protect it, even at the expense of a temporary scattering of forces. I find that it has had no bad effect thus far. The rebels believed, as I am well informed, that my force in this valley is as great as the whole will be when concentrated, and suppose the Guyandotte force to be an additional column advancing, and I am confident of effecting the concentration in time for any necessity I may have, with the additional advantage of having produced a good moral effect upon the lower counties by the march of troops that way. My advance is steady, but not rapid. I scout the country ahead a day's march in advance, and then move with a good advance guard on each side of the river, sending out skirmishers, the steamers following with the baggage and a regiment which can be thrown upon either side at need. At Knob Shoals, a couple of miles above Buffalo, and here at Red House are very difficult places in the navigation of the river. One of our boats grounded at Knob Shoals, and was in some danger of being injured or wrecked, but got off again without damage. I have two boats above the obstructions placed here by the enemy, which, although they make the passage difficult and a little dangerous, have not totally stopped the channel. The Kentucky regiments have found some impediments in the lack of tents, which were a little behind, and in the enormous quantity of their baggage, which has hindered their fully performing their part of my plan, and my arrival at Charleston may be a day later than I advised you in my last dispatch. I have issued a peremptory order to reduce the baggage to the regulation weight. The Eleventh Regiment are yet without tents. I have half of them quartered at Point Pleasant as a guard there and the rest here. No more artillery has arrived. Only thirty-eight of my horsemen have saddles, and the rest of the troop are waiting at Gallipolis for their equipments. My force here now is as follows: Four companies of Eleventh Regiment, the whole of Twelfth, whole of Twenty-first, two rifle cannon, with forty-nine men, two smooth-bore cannon without caissons or cannoneers. In the course of twenty-four hours I shall expect to be joined by half the First Kentucky Regiment, leaving the other half at Ripley, and in two or three days to be joined by the whole of the Second Kentucky. If my reconnaissance is satisfactory, I shall not wait for the latter short of Charleston.

Meanwhile I remain, general, truly and respectfully, your obedient servant,

J.D. COX,
Brigadier-General, Commanding District of Kanawha[4]

General Cox was still at Winfield on the 15th of the month although McClellan probably had assumed that he had progressed a bit more rapidly, reporting, "....I am in constant expectation of hearing from General Cox that his efforts to drive the Wises out of the Kanawha Valley and occupy the Gauley Bridge have been crowned with success...."[48] Cox had his camp placed on the north side of the river, opposite Winfield, but detailed guards along the south bank.

For Wise, arms and ordnance continued to be his major problem. He had enough men to counter Cox, since the terrain gave him a material strength four times that of Cox, despite the General's doubts that his soldiers were willing and able to fight. Yet the best of soldiers can't fight if not properly armed. Captain Assistant Adjutant General E.J. Harvie dispatched a last minute plea to Adjutant & Inspector General Cooper:

Head Quarters Wise Brigade
Kanawha C.H. July 15, 1861

Sir,

I beg leave to call your attention to the very great want of all kinds of ordnance, but especially of cartridge boxes, cap pouches, bayonet scabbards, cartridges for old flint lock and smooth bore percussion muskets, sabres and cartridges for some Harpers Ferry Rifles, which a portion of my command use and caps for the muskets. All these things are very much needed. There is now under my command of my own Brigade and Vol. forces of Va. about four thousand men, and in the course of the next ten days this number will probably be increased to five thousand. I feel that I cannot too strongly represent to you the very great need of ordnance.

Powder is not only very scarce, but owing to the fact that very few of my men have cartridge boxes, whatever ammunition they may carry with them on march is liable from various causes to get spoiled.

If a full supply of the necessary articles cannot be sent at once, whatever quantity can be furnished will prove most acceptable.

The enemy is reported as being a few miles below in large force. The probabilities of a speedy general engagement are increasing.

You will also confer a favor by sending at your earliest convenience the laws of the Conf. States as passed by the Congress and whatever rules and regulations may have promulgated for the organization and government of the army.

I am, General
With much respect
Signed E.J. Harvie
Capt. A.A. Adjt. Genl.[49]

Wise himself followed up the initial report with another reporting the disastrous condition of his artillery units:

"Since writing to you this morning soliciting immediate supplies of ordnance, a report has been laid before me showing that we are entirely destitute of powder and ball for the cannon we have.

Our guns are all six pounders and to make them effective in the field it is important to supply us at an early day with the proper ammunition.

Both ball and grape with an ample supply of cannon powder should be sent."[50]

Ironically, the same day these messages were sent out, George Deas wrote Colonel Tompkins informing him that numerous military supplies that General Wise had previously ordered were being sent, and the appointment of officers in the Army of the Kanawha, as Wise's command was known,

SITE OF CAMP POCA
Today. — Courtesy: Gary Bays

would be conducted as soon as Governor John Letcher returned to Richmond. Of course it is doubtful any of the promised ammunition arrived in time for the battle of Scary Creek.

On July 16 Cox and his main column finally made it to the west side of the mouth of the Pocataligo (Poca) River, near the present site of Raymond City at Poca (or Pokey as the residents call it), and proceeded to establish Camp Poco in a cornfield there. The day was to bring on one of the strangest events of the entire campaign, the Poca River Skirmish, which apparently involved some of Cox's advance units at Poca prior to his arrival. With the Federals behind hastily built breastworks, and in possession of two six pounder cannon, Wise apparently felt the time was right to strike a blow. About 120 of Brock's and Beckett's cavalry outfits, led by Col. John Clarkson, were ordered to attack Poca where Wise later reported they "...thrashed about two hundred of their infantry, charging them up the mountainside to its top, driving them into their cannon, and killing eight known, with the loss of one horse only killed..."[51] What is unusual about this is that for many years it was felt that Wise's report was a fabrication, made only to make a favorable reflection upon himself, since no other reports, Union or Confederate, were known to exist, and Union casualty lists failed to support Wise's claim. But recently Capt. John Brock's report of the event was located in the National Archives Confederate Service Records and it states "...I proceeded to the hill near the mouth of Poca Creek, by order of Gen. Wise, and then came into contact with some three hundred of the enemy which we charged with success killing eight of the enemy...and routing the remainder driving them to their camp without any loss to my command, save one horse killed, one horse slightly wounded and one private wounded in the hand..." So it would appear that the Poca River Skirmish did indeed transpire although it remains doubtful that Cox suffered eight casualties.

General Cox, one of the best sources of the period, never made any mention of the skirmish on his July 16th report of his movements to McClellan:

HEADQUARTERS DISTRICT OF THE KANAWHA,
Mouth of Pocotaligo, July 16, 1861.

Maj. Gen. G.B. McClellan,
Commanding Department of the Ohio:

Sir: At Red House I was joined by half the First Kentucky Regiment, under Lieutenant-Colonel Enyart. I ordered him to join me, for two reasons: First, because my advance beyond Ripley was such that I felt assured that there was no danger of its being attacked by any considerable force, and second, because our wagon train was not sufficient to allow to Colonel Guthrie transportation enough for a whole regiment. I am now waiting at this point, which I reached last night, for the advance of the Second Kentucky from Guyandotte to Coalsmouth, and the half of the First Kentucky (if Colonel Guthrie finds it safe to do so) from Ripley to Sissonville. I shall then have my whole force, except part of the Eleventh (three companies), which is guarding stores at Point Pleasant, concentrating at three points upon a line of twenty miles long, commanding all the roads converging at Charleston from Parkersburg to Guyandotte. I have not yet received the remainder of my artillery, and the necessity of sending a strong detachment to communicate with the Second Kentucky has used all the horsemen who are equipped, except half a dozen. I look for both artillery and cavalry daily. The progress thus far has been steady, but for the last day it has been in the face of constant skirmishing. Small bodies of riflemen occupy the hills, and do not leave them till driven out by our skirmishers, who, being armed with altered muskets, are at a disadvantage as to the range of their pieces. We have, however, had but one man seriously hurt, and he, I think, will recover. The best information I can now get puts the force at Charleston superior to my own in numbers and in artillery. It is said they have so weakened the suspension bridge that it can be let fall at a moment's warning; that their battery of some eight cannon is strongly intrenched, and that Wise is determined to make a strong stand there. If so, he certainly has a position it will be difficult to take or turn from this side. The Elk is not fordable for some distance up, and the ford neither good nor easily held by the advancing party. These reports have had an appearance of truth, which has made it seem necessary to be cautious, and I shall remain here a day or two till I can get my force well together, and by means of cavalry scout and reconnoiter to better advantage. Meanwhile I would suggest such a demonstration in the direction of the Gauley from your side, if possible, as would cut off retreat. I have made a respectable advance every day but one since leaving Camp Dennison, and think we have gone as fast as is prudent. I am sorry to have to report an accident by which two men were killed and another badly wounded. The half of the Kentucky regiment were marching on Sunday evening last to join Colonel Norton, who had moved in advance from Red House. They were out after night-fall, not starting till about 9 o'clock. As they marched, the captain of the rear guard, to correct some irregularity in marching, commanded "steady," which the men mistook for "ready," when one of the guns in the rear going off by reason of the nervousness or carelessness of the man holding it, a portion of the company imagined they were attacked, and without waiting for orders fired in the direction of the shot. The above is the account given by the officers of the regiment. I should have said that I had sent Colonel Norton in advance to reconnoiter for our next day's march, and learning that he was in the vicinity of a considerable force with a small battery of artillery, I sent the re-enforcement after receiving the news. The difficulty of taking our artillery across the river has prevented me since last evening from making an attack, as the position is reported by Colonel Norton to be a very strong one naturally, being on a narrow hill difficult of access. I expect Colonel Woodruff to be in their rear before to-morrow, and will by that time have examined the ground and made arrangements for driving the enemy out.

Meanwhile, I remain, general, your obedient servant,

J.D. COX
Brigadier-General; Commanding

P.S.—I inclose a ticket torn from a musket-box found in the store-house of a secessionist named Barber, who lived a little above this point. It may seem to prove where the arms of some of Wise's troops were got and how issued.

J.D.C.[52]

The 16th had certainly been a day of intense preparation for battle by both armies. But the evacuation of innocent civilians was most important. Reportedly, high ranking officers from both armies met at the Robert Marshall Simms house, exchanged a smoke and a drink or two, and agreed to postpone the imminent battle until all civilians had been moved to safety. It was merely a verbal agreement, after which they shook hands and saluted as they parted. Just who these officers were is not known, but Patton and Norton would have been the obvious choices. Later that night fifty-eight civilians, including eighteen slaves and Mr. Simms, crossed the Kanawha by boat to a point of safety.[53]

At 7 P.M. a Federal scout reported the Rebels erecting fortifications on the right bank of Scary Creek, and indeed Patton had dispatched Captain A.R. Barbee to Scary because he and his men were from the vicinity and "knew every path and grapevine along the river."[54] At 11 P.M. the remainder of Cox's army arrived by steamer at Poca, but Cox did not feel an attack was feasible, "with General Wise but twelve miles away on one side, and Camp Tompkins on the other, any further advance was certain to result in a clash or arms."[55] Since his wagons had yet to arrive, he set up camps on both sides of the river, deploying two steamboats on each side. Desultory gunfire would continue through the night but nothing of importance transpired.

As the Federal soldiers settled in for the night, E.S. Godfrey of the 21st Ohio sat down to write his father a letter which closely resembled the dispatch sent by Cox to McClellan:

15 miles
Camp Poco July 16, 1861

Dear Father

I take this opportunity to write to you again. We left Pt. Pleasant at 10 o'clock & arrived at Pt. 13, 13 miles above Pt. Pleasant & encamped for the night. We left Pt. 13 at 10 next day & marched to Buffalo & encamped for the night & were reinforced by Col. DeVilliers. We started for Red House next day & got there safe & sound & pitched our tents & staid all night & next day till evening when we heard that Col. Norton & 3 of our Companies were surrounded by the enemy. I don't believe we were more than 30 minutes a getting everything on the Boat & ready to cross the river. We crossed over when a Gun went off accidentally in one of the Kentucky Regt's & they thought it was an attacked from the enemy & commenced firing & killed two of their own men & mortally wounded 3 others. We marched three miles & was met by Col. Norton & we laid down for the night. In the afternoon Col. Norton was attacked by the rebels & he retreated about 3 miles. They said the bullets whistled about them like hail. We have had several skirmishes with them since we have been here. I am not very well today. Charley has been a little sick for 2 or 3 days but is getting better. I think we will leave for Charleston in a day or two. No more at present.

Yours Truly
E.S. Godfrey

P.S.—I have not received any word from you since we left Gallipolis. Charley got one from you of the 9th & one from Carrie yesterday.

E.S.G.[56]

Most unusual at this point in affairs, since Wise's soldiers had already scored small victories at Scary Creek, and possibly Poca, was that the General once again began casting serious doubts on his military situation, writing the Confederate Secretary of War:

> *"....Our force here is entirely inadequate for the defense of this Valley. It would not be sufficient if this whole section of the country were loyal, but with a large part of it seriously disaffected, it is very clear that we have not enough for defense, much less for any advance movement. It has been reported to these Hd. Quarters that the enemy is advancing up this Valley with forces from two to four thousand on the other side and are but a few miles from this place. Our whole strength at this point with which to meet them, including the Vol. Forces of Va. does not exceed twenty five hundred. If attacked we intend to stand fast and make a desperate resistance...."*[57]

Indeed, with the arrival of morning, Wise's soldiers would make such a "desperate resistance" at Scary Creek, and evolve from the battle victorious, much to the great surprise of everyone involved, especially General Wise.

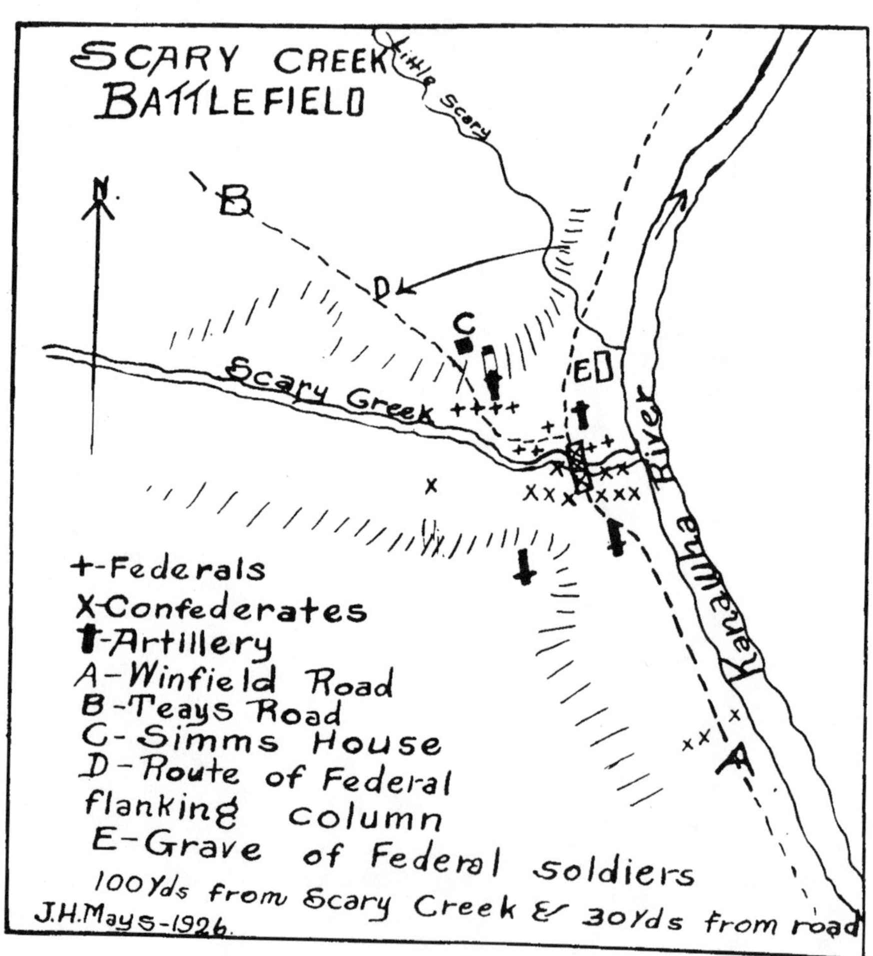

SCARY CREEK BATTLEFIELD MAP
As drawn by Confederate veteran James H. Mays in 1926.

CHAPTER SIX

A Day at Scary Creek

Scary Creek. The name itself conjures up images of mystery and fear. And well that it should, for in its relatively brief known history it has been the scene of numerous tragedies, from the Civil War battle discussed herein, to the death of a well-known railroad man within more recent years. Many people approach the place with caution, while some of the more superstitious avoid the place altogether. In reality, the place is nothing more than a harmless little country stream which empties into the south side of the Kanawhá River. Although not fordable at its mouth, it is generally not very deep or wide and extends to its headwaters on the slopes of nearby Coal Mountain. After having passed into and across the lower end of Teays Valley it proceeds to empty into the Kanawha through a deep channel bounded by steep banks. Just a few hundred feet upstream from the mouth of Scary can be found the concrete bridge of State Route 17 traversing the creek, and a few yards onward the bridge and tracks of the C&O Railroad also spanning the stream. The eastern side of Scary is bounded by a steep ridge that peaks at approximately 900 feet, while the western side is characterized by a bluff which slopes back from the Kanawha, and Scary, eventually rising to 600 feet before tapering off into the level lands of Teays Valley.

Traveling west over the Scary bridge on State Route 17 (the Winfield Road) the Teays Valley Road can be found branching off to the left, while the main road continues on and through Winfield and eventually arrives at the mouth of the Kanawha at far distant Henderson, across the Kanawha from Point Pleasant. Hooking left off the Teays Valley Road, near Scary, is the paved but extremely narrow Big Scary Creek Road, which continues to inch along the western bank for a few miles. A few hundred yards to the west of the mouth of Scary is Little Scary Creek, obviously so named to distinguish it from Big Scary, while a short distance further to the west is the Interstate Highway 64 bridge which spans the Kanawha between Scary and the town of Nitro.

One the eastern bank of Scary can be found Vintroux Road, a poor grade dirt road which snakes along for a short distance past some rural homes. A few miles to the east of the mouth of Scary is Coal River and the city of St. Albans.

The present settlement of Scary Creek covers less than 40 acres and has never had a population exceeding 100, although during the post-Civil War period a post office named Mouth of Scary was established at the junction of the Winfield and Teays Valley Road, which served a rural population covering an area of several miles, extending out Teays Valley, around by

THE SECOND SCARY CREEK BRIDGE
Built in 1890. — Courtesy: Emma Simms Maginnis

THE SCARY CREEK BRIDGE
Today. — Photo by the author

Bills Creek, outward to the Kanawha. The eastern boundary extended upriver to the Kanawha County line at the mouth of Gallatin Creek. While that particular post office no longer exists, Scary Creek yet retains a number of residents as well as a number of commercial business properties. But a large portion of the area remains forest land, particularly the eastern side of the creek.

There is little physical evidence today to indicate that there was any Civil War action at Scary. A state historical highway marker rests at the mouth, as does a small monument erected by the St. Albans Chapter of the United Daughters of the Confederacy, but that's the extent of obvious evidence of conflict, although Confederate trenches were visible until recent years and the State Historical Society had expressed an interest in establishing a park there as early as the 1920's (recently some possible remains of Confederate trenches were located). Some relics of the conflict can still be found on what is referred to as Simms Hill, or Scary Hill by older area residents, the bluff situated between the Teays Valley Road and State Route 17. In the location of the original walnut log church is Scary Creek Freewill Baptist Church Annex, formally St. John's of the Valley Episcopal Church, which was built by the Simms family, as was the original church. Beside the church is the original Simms family cemetery, existing at the time of the battle and presently containing the grave of Henry Edmund Simms, who served with Andrew Barbee's Putnam County Border Riflemen. Across the Teays Valley Road from the church is the original location of the Robert Marshall Simms house, but the only indication is an old abandoned brick well, which may or may not be part of the original estate. Often mistaken for the Simms home is the brick foundation of the John Kirtley home which was built long after

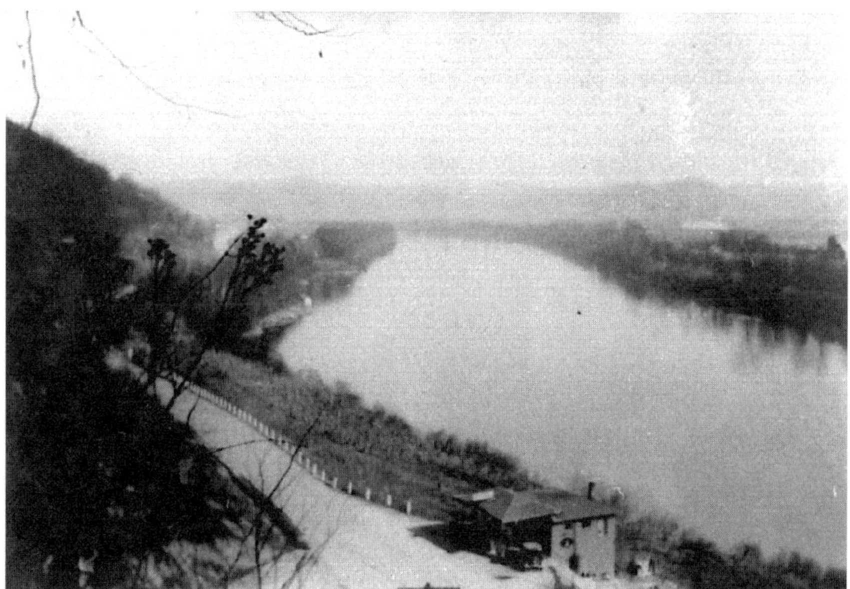

WESTERN VIEW FROM SIMMS HILL
Circa 1930. Mouth of Little Scary at left riverbend in foreground.
— Courtesy: Emma Simms Maginnis

ST. JOHN'S OF THE VALLEY EPISCOPAL CHURCH
About 1950. Scary Creek Battlefield. — Courtesy: Emma Simms Maginnis

the war but like the Simms home also fell victim to fire. About two miles downriver from the mouth of Scary, on the banks of the Kanawha, is the Emma Simms Maginnis farm, the original location of the Mary Ann Simms farm, but the only original structure remaining is the black servant's log kitchen cabin, which in itself has been moved a few hundred yards from its original position.[1]

The terrain and landscape of Scary Creek in 1861 was, needless to say, quite different from today. There was no Interstate Highway, no railroad, no paved road or concrete bridge, no modern housing or business property. There was no Vintroux Road or Scary Creek Road. The Winfield Road (also known then as either the County Road or the River Road) and the Teays Valley Road were but mere dusty wagon trails. There was a bridge across Scary but it was an extremely crude, wooden structure. Saint Albans was known as Coalsmouth, and the town of Nitro didn't even exist, being a town created out of the industrial needs of World War I. While on the Kanawha, about 100 yards below the mouth of Scary was located Johnson's Shoals, the horrendous system of rapids that had plagued boaters from the earliest of times. On the southern edge of the shoals, where Scary empties into the Kanawha, was a natural chute for boats. Alongside the chute was anchored Dudding's Mill, a floating tub mill built by Anderson Dudding. Situated on the western ridge of Scary Creek was the Robert Marshall Simms (or Sims) house, a walnut log church which also doubled as a schoolhouse, and the Simms family cemetery. Near the junction of the Winfield and Teays Valley roads were a number of wooden houses. Lt. Col. George S. Patton vividly described the area in a letter written to his brother during the war:

"About 2½ miles below the mouth of Coal River—Scary Creek empties into the Kanawha on the South side. It is a small mountain stream which as it approaches the river runs a bold range of hills—forming rugged and precipitous banks...there was a bridge over the ravine just at its mouth. The hills approach the river closely being only a narrow strip of bottom, and a cleared...knob on either side of the Creek. Its banks were slightly wooded with small trees...affording some shelter and at the end of the bridge were several farms and log houses used for a...shop, country store, dwelling and slaves...."[2]

HENRY EDMUND SIMMS
Member of the Putnam County Riflemen — he is buried in Simms Cemetery at Scary. — Courtesy: Emma Simms Maginnis

SCARY CREEK BATTLEFIELD MONUMENT
Erected by St. Albans Chapter U.D.C. — Courtesy: Gary Bays

ST. JOHN'S OF THE VALLEY EPISCOPAL CHURCH AND SIMMS FAMILY CEMETERY
At Scary. — Courtesy: Emma Simms Maginnis

This was the physical and geographical appearance of Scary Creek in Putnam County, (West)ern Virginia as the Civil War erupted in the country in 1861. Many later descriptions of the battle made reference to places that were built following the war, causing much confusion among historians, places such as the Vintroux church, home, and store; the John Kirtley home and store; the Scary Post Office and train depot; and the Meadows home, which was the Vintroux place remodeled.

The origination of the name Scary Creek remains unknown. Presumably the name had Indian origins as Scary was located on the northeastern boundary of the Cherokees, although the Iroquois and Shawnee also claimed the region. One legend states that two bands of Indians had a bloody encounter at Scary Creek and the victors taunted their opponent with an Indian term meaning "Scary."[3]

Border heroine Mrs. Mary Draper Ingles passed over Scary Creek in 1755 during her 700 mile escape route from an Indian camp near Louisville, Kentucky, but she had no part in the naming of the creek. The same applies to the Morris family who reportedly explored the region about 1774.

The earliest possible mention of Scary was in October of 1774 when the troops of Colonel Andres Lewis were en route through the Kanawha Valley to enter into what became known as the battle of Point Pleasant. One soldier's orderly book noted:

> *"Camp Near Mouth of Cole River*
>
> *....A sutler's canoe overset, two guns were lost and some baggage. Two canoes were overset that were fastened together and 27 bags of flour were floated. They were all recovered but two or three much wet. The men had two days' flour served out."*[4]

Although Scary is not specifically mentioned it is very probable that the treacherous Johnson's Shoals near the mouth of Scary provoked the incident. In fact, Johnson's Shoals continued to be a menace to boaters until 1898 when the first lock and dam system was complete.

Another legend states that Thomas Teays, pioneer hunter and surveyor, and for whom Teays Valley is named, was taken prisoner in 1782 by the Indians and held in captivity for seven years. Condemned to be burned at the stake, Teays was rescued by an Indian chief he had become friends with in earlier days by sharing a handful of salt. Teays was tracked by his former captors to the mouth of Big Scary Creek, where he hid in a hollow log and escaped his foes, although they passed directly over the log. Teays was so frightened that he christened the place Scary.[5]

For some time it was believed that, in 1785, Albert Gallatin had spent an uncomfortable night at Scary. In his journal he stated:

> *"While traveling at night on the Kanawha, to escape the notice of unfriendly Indians, our craft grounded on a bar at the mouth of a small stream, below Coal River."*[6]

Researchers at first thought Gallatin's location to be Scary but later concluded it was Gallatin's Branch (named after Gallatin), a small stream which empties into the Kanawha slightly east of the mouth of Scary. Fifteen years later Gallatin became Secretary of the Treasury under Thomas Jefferson. It is also interesting to note that Albert Gallatin Jenkins, a namesake of Gallatin's, was a commanding officer in the Civil War action at Scary.

Another story has it that, between 1800 and 1850, Johnson's Shoals proved such a hazard to salt boats that the rivermen nicknamed the place

SERVANTS' CABIN

Black servants' cabin on the Mary Ann Simms farm near Scary. — Courtesy: Emma Simms Maginnis

SCARY BATTLEFIELD

Today. Intersection of the Teays Valley and Winfield roads — Simms Hill in the background. — Photo by the author

THE VENTROUX HOME
It was built in the postwar period at the mouth of Scary Creek. — Courtesy: Emma Simms Maginnis

"Scary" Creek. While the actual origins of the name Scary will remain an unsolved mystery, what transpired at Scary Creek on July 17, 1861 is loosely documented history.

During the Federal occupation of Charleston one Union soldier was heard to remark, "I have talked with several concerning the battle at Scary, but I could not learn anything I had not heard before."[7] No statement could better characterize the battle of Scary Creek than this. With the passing of years the affair has become a collage of contradictory accounts, highly inaccurate information, exaggerated memoirs, and outright false statements. Whether it be from official reports made at the time or from participants, historians, and enthusiasts who later wrote of the engagements, the information that has been left behind has made an exact reconstruction of the battle impossible. For example, the personal correspondence of Patton, McCausland, and Pvt. J.H. Collins, raises doubt as to whether there was actually a bridge across Scary at the time of the battle, as they all refer to the bridge as having been effectively burned prior to the engagement. A number of 'facts' relating to Scary are easily confirmed, the rest can only be assumed by weighing the available evidence.

By July 17 there was no longer any question that a battle of some sort was going to take place at the mouth of Scary Creek. The uneasiness felt in the opposing camps the night of the 16th undoubtedly increased tenfold by daybreak. Capt. A.R. Barbee's Putnam County Border Riflemen were already well entrenched at Scary as the 'comedy of errors' began to unfold. General Wise had ordered Patton to fall back to Bunker Hill near the mouth of Upton Creek and make a stand if possible but Patton, with his military education, knew such a move was impractical. At Scary he had the advantage of holding a strong defensive position, reinforcements close at hand, and a better familiarity with the terrain than the enemy. Certainly these were important factors, considering the Federals outnumbered them, were better trained and armed (with the possible exception of some of their rifles), and also had reinforcements within hearing distance of the impending fight.

Before committing himself to a general engagement, Gen. Cox sought more information on troop strength at Scary by sending Lt. Col. Carr B. White of the 12th Ohio, with a detachment of that unit, to probe the enemy position. At about 9:00 A.M. White and his men were ferried across the Kanawha from Camp Poco to the small Federal outpost on the farms of John Morgan, a previous member of Barbee's Virginians who had had to return home for personal reasons, and the farm of Dr. John J. Thompson, an ex-member of Congress who claimed neutrality but whose son, John, was Assistant Officer in Charge at Camp Tompkins. Such a move had been anticipated by the Confederates. John Thompson and a member of the Border Rangers were on vidette on the Bills Creek Road when they caught sight of blue uniforms:

> *"...the Yanks (were) moving by skirmish line through a cornfield some 300 yards away. (We) sat on (our) horses until the line came within a hundred yards....the Yanks opened fire on (us) both succeeded in getting away without getting hurt. Thompson lost his hat and false teeth. This was at 9 o'clock in the morning...."*[8]

Prompted by this brush with White's skirmishers, Thompson and his friend fell back to Camp Tompkins to warn Patton, and to the mouth of Coal to inform Jenkins. While the two messengers were so occupied White continued his advance to Scary, throwing scouts out on both sides of the road, encountering no resistance until they arrived at the mouth of Little Scary Creek. At this point Captain Barbee's advance pickets, hidden in a log house, fired upon White's command. Since White had only been ordered to reconoiter the enemy position, and not to bring on or enter into a general engagement, he retreated back to the main camp to confer with General Cox on further strategy.

At that meeting of Federal officers, Col. John Lowe of the 12th Ohio requested permission from Cox to "clear Scary of the rebels" to which Cox readily consented, ordering Lowe to take with him the 12th Ohio, Capt. Charles S. Cotter's Independent Battery Ohio Volunteer Artillery, and Capt. John S. George's Independent Company Ohio Volunteer Cavalry. Just before departure Cox's adjutant, Charles Whittlesey, a West Point graduate and veteran of the Black Hawk War who was made chief engineer for the Ohio troops when the war broke out, suggested to Cox that Col. Jesse S. Norton of the 21st Ohio should accompany Lowe as he had previous knowledge of the area. Cox, who had originally planned to go himself but decided against it, agreed and Norton was sent with two companies of the 21st: Company K, of Gallipolis, under Capt. Samuel A. Strong and Company D of Capt. Thomas G. Allen. All told, Lowe had a total force of approximately 1500 men. Reportedly, he was told to dislodge the enemy if it appeared feasible or to pull back and await reinforcements if not.

The Virginians had not been idle in the interim. Thanks to Thompson and his friend, Patton had already awakened the soldiers at Camp Tompkins. Three companies were already at Scary: Barbee's, Sweeney's Wheeling

FIELD OF SCAREY'S RUN, WEST VIRGINIA.

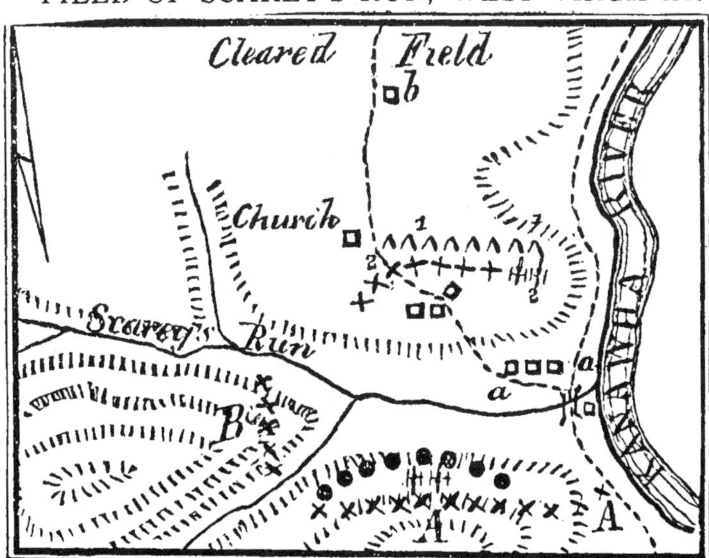

Scale 200 yards to the inch.

A A.—Rebel line of infantry, two guns and rifle pits.
1 1.—Col. Lowe's first position with the guns.
2 2.—Col. Lowe's second position with the guns.
a a.—Houses, mill and bridge captured by Col. Norton.
b.—Barn where the Rebel pickets were met.
B.—Major Hines' position.

SCARY CREEK BATTLEFIELD MAP—As drawn by Charles Whittlesey, adjutant to Gen. Cox. From Charles Whittlesey's "War Memoranda"

JOHN MORGAN FARM
As it looked during the war. — Courtesy: West Virginia State Archives

POSTWAR VIEW OF THE JOHN MORGAN FARM
Federal soldiers camped on the land in foreground. Note stables, cribs, and carriage houses to the right, with poultry and meat houses to the left, and the original slave quarters to the extreme left. A second story has been added to the main house. — Courtesy: Rembrandt Morgan

BREVET BRIGADIER GENERAL [then Lieutenant Colonel} CARR B. WHITE
12th Ohio Volunteer Infantry. He met Confederate skirmishers at the mouth of Little Scary. — Courtesy: U.S. Army Military History Institute (MOLLUS Collection)

CHARLES WHITTLESEY
Adjutant to General Cox. — Courtesy: U.S. Army Military History Institute (MOLLUS Collection)

COLONEL JOHN W. LOWE
12th Ohio Volunteer Infantry. The scapegoat at Scary Creek. — Courtesy: Ohio Historical Society

boys, and the Kanawha Riflemen under 2nd Lt. Nicholas Fitzhugh, a total of "around 200 muskets." Patton, the Kanawha Artillery, and the cavalry companies of Jenkins and Lewis, "armed with shotguns and a few carbines," were on the River Road by 10:00 A.M. hoping to arrive before the battle broke. Jenkins' men were slightly detained by some Southern ladies who stopped them in order to present them with a flag. Jenkins accepted, gave a short speech, and the flag became the only Confederate flag on the battlefield of Scary, where it was "literally shot to pieces." Back at Camp Tompkins were about 189 men comprising the commands of Capts. Bailey, Tyree, and Thomas Broun (Broun himself was not present as he had become a proficient recruiter and was up Coal River drumming up new enlistees at this time), and at the bridge over Coal River was a 150-man contingent of the Wise Legion cavalry under Col. Frank Anderson. In addition, the companies of Capt. James Corns were stationed along the Guyandotte Road at nearby Coal Knob (Mountain), so that the total Virginia force consisted of slightly less than 900 men with "only one-half...near enough to prove of much service."[9]

While the Federals were eating breakfast and planning their strategy in the Morgan farm kitchen prior to their advance, a loyal citizen of the area arrived and informed them to use the Bill's Creek Road to go to Scary, as it was a little used country road which departed the River Road slightly west of the Morgan farm, curving around and into the Teays Valley Road near the mouth of Scary. Apparently Lowe decided to send the main column by way of the Bill's Creek Road while sending a smaller detachment by the River Road, posting scouts on the flanks of the marching columns:

> *"....The road (Bill's Creek) being steep, as well as dusty, while a hot sun came down 'the near way,' a number of halts were necessary, which rendered the march a slow one. Long before the first shots were exchanged, great fatigue was manifested by the men, and it was evident that some of them would never be able to engage in that day's fight...."*[10]

While the main column proceeded on Bill's Creek Road the Federals on the River Road apparently stopped by the river-front home of Mary Ann Simms, about two miles below Scary, and took all her hay to feed their horses.[11]

The two companies of the 21st under Col. Norton had been the first to advance, probably sometime between 10:00 and 11:00 o'clock. Accompanying Norton were Capt. David Gibbs of the 21st and his chief commissary, Lt. Andrew J. Roosa (Rosa) of the 12th; Gibbs' adjutant; and Charles Whittlesey, adjutant to General Cox. At approximately 11:00 o'clock Col. Lowe caught up with them and informed the officers that Cox had told him that reserves would soon follow.

At 1:30 P.M. the Federal column forced the Confederate pickets at Little Scary Creek out of the log house and back to their lines. At about this same time Robert Garnett Simms, son of Mary Ann Simms, and Anthony Fukery, one of his grandfather's slaves, were playing marbles in front of the Scary church, apparently unaware of the events transpiring about them, and somehow having missed the evacuation of July 16. Suddenly they spotted blue-clad soldiers approaching by way of Bill's Creek Road and immediately ran to Scary Creek, either waded or swam across, and watched further proceedings from a distant hill.[12] The advance detachment of the Federal cavalry, which had fallen behind on the Bill's Creek Road, was called up and drove the Confederate pickets out of Scary church. One Ohio officer rode back to the main column and boasted, "We have flushed the infernal scoundrels."[13] Just as this transpired Patton arrived from Camp Tompkins and began deploying his units: "Capt. Sweeney's company was thrown across the creek below the houses."[14] Once occupying the houses Sweeney and his men removed chinking from the ten or twelve "log huts" comprising Scary (town) and improvised "loop-holes" through which to shoot. "Barbee's company was deployed partly across the creek; and on the extreme left the Kanawha Riflemen under Lt. Fitzhugh" were "deployed as skirmishers, in advance of the troops, in front of Hale's Battery extending up the ravine along a brush fence."[15]

At approximately 2 P.M. the Fedral soldiers began to arrive at Scary in ever increasing numbers. One area resident later recalled:

> *"I was in the road near our house when two Confederates went riding by. They were laughing and nudging each other. I didn't know what the matter was till one of them said, 'There they come.' I looked up and saw the hillside black with Yankees. I went in the house to tell mother and the others about it. I thought we would go around the hill and watch the soldiers as they came down. But as I started out the back way I met them coming in."*[16]

Kanawha Rifleman Levi Welch, brother of Lt. James C. Welch, was posted on the far left where he reported, "....I saw a glittering line of steel extend through the thin woods and cover our front."[17] At the same time, Lt. James C. Welch, his waiting over, observed the Ohio cavalry action at Scary church and opened his battery upon them in conjunction with the Confederate infantry killing one and causing the remainder to retreat in wild disorder to an area slightly to the rear of the Robert Marshall Simms house. One Ohio soldier recalled the incident:

> *"Suddenly there broke a flash and curling column of white smoke, succeeded immediately by the hissing sound of grapeshot overhead. The battle had been opened by the rebels. Discharges followed each other in rapid succession, with but slightly damaging effect, owing to inaccuracy of aim. One man was shot through the body and died almost immediately; another was knocked down by a shot which struck his cartridge box, he recovered from the force of the shock before the battle terminated, and performed good service."*[18]

The 12th Ohio was ordered to try to knock out Welch's battery and Private Elijah Beeman took part in that unsuccessful effort:

> *"When within 100 yds. they opened with grape. The battery was screened by a grove of timber we didn't see until we were almost upon it. But we knew where it was. The enemy opened upon us with grape but most of the Balls passed over our heads. One spent Ball struck Roderick Schlossmiller in the Breast. A grape shot of 4 oz. weight. But it didn't hurt him any. The Boys waddled like a parcel of geese when you throw stones amongst them."*[19]

Within minutes, though, Captain C.S. Cotter's Artillery arrived, viewed the situation, "tore down the fence," unlimbered their iron six-pounders and ran one of them up to a bench back of Teays Valley Road near the Simms house, under a clump of trees. The other cannon was placed near the church. Captain Cotter positioned himself to the right of the guns just as two enemy "balls whistled over his head, cutting the topmost branches of the trees."[20] The Virginia artillery continued to overshoot the Ohio battery and struck a woodpile back of the Simms house, scattering wood and splinters in all directions, causing the Virginians to believe that the Federals had thrown up breastworks. Cotter's artillerists finally began to return the fire but also overshot their target until Captain Cotter yelled, "a little lower, boys," and they began to ascertain the proper range of about 500 yards.[21] Levi Welch found himself within Cotter's range:

> *"I saw, I think, the first puff of powder smoke and a bullet hit the stump on which I sat. A large beech tree was opportunely near me, and I immediately sought the protection of its trunk. As the puffs of smoke increased the beech tree seemed to wonderfully decrease in size. But for personal reasons I stuck to it."*[22]

Before Cotter's men could cause any strategic damage, the company 'pet,' young Private John Haven of Scholersville (Putnam County, Ohio), had his right hip removed by an enemy six pound solid shot while he was passing a ball to his gun. Captain Cotter saw this an ran to his aid, attempting to pick him up and carry him to safety, when Haven said, "Never mind me, captain, but don't let that flag go down."[23] Whether or not this incident instilled Cotter's artillerymen with a sense of revenge is unknown, but suddenly, the artillery duel took on full effect:

> *"The loud-mouth cannon, bursting shells, crashing small arms, and 'shouting captains' made a royal tumult which tested the nerves of the raw recruits from the field and from the shop; but they stood their ground like veterans and gave shot for shot."*[24]

The Ohio battery was devastating and their third shot made a victim of Lt. James C. Welch, whose head was nearly ripped off by a richocheting ball which made a direct hit on his field piece, striking the axle and splintering it into pieces. Another soldier, a private, was mortally wounded in the incident. The enemy 'shot' continued to roll through the Virginian ranks causing quite a stir. Lt. William Quarrier, in charge of the other Virginia field piece, reportedly was forced to run for safety, but Patton later claimed he had ordered the gun shut down in order to be used at a later time. As a result, the Ohio artillery, in the span of some fifteen minutes to a half hour (beginning at 2:00 P.M. and ending at either 2:15 or 2:30) had put the Virginia artillery to silence.

And while the artillery duel had been in progress, action continued elsewhere on the battlefield. The 12th Ohio had one soldier who was adverse to drill and had a habit of falling down which he blamed on his toes. When the Confederate artillery opened upon his company they fell to the ground upon instinct, all except the one clumsy oaf who proclaimed, "There, that's what comes of all your drilling; every man's killed deader'n a hammer, and I'm the only one left to tell the tale," which obviously amused his comrades even in the thick of battle.[25]

Another soldier of the 12th, a Lt. Roberts, who was an adjutant, had earlier proclaimed his bravery, although his fellow soldiers highly doubted it. And during the first exchange of gunfire, he sure enough reversed his horse and ran away in haste, with an equally cowardly company dog at his side, "and the two were never seen afterward."[26]

Capt. Ferdinand Gunkle of the 12th Ohio, a Dutchman who could never seem to issue his orders correctly, panicked when he was unable to get his men into some sort of battle formation, finally yelled, "Attention, Company I; shoulder-e-r-r guns; forwards walk, do sumpting, quick."[27]

By the time the artillery duel ended the two Confederate cavalry companies had arrived and Patton posted Lewis' company in "the woods to the left to prevent annoyance by a flanking party, while Capt. Jenkins' men were held in reserve."[28] Bailey's Fayetteville Rifles, whom had hidden their blankets and jackets in a barnyard while en route to the battlefield, had arrived at the same time as Tyree's men and both companies were posted to the front and to the left. William F. Bahlmann of the Fayette Rifles later remembered:

> *"Our company had crossed Scary Creek to the West, but when the enemy advanced they fell back to the hill on the East side of the creek. I stayed on the brink of the creek behind a very comfortable tree. A plank was lying edgewise behind the tree. A bullet struck the plank just below my right foot and I lifted my foot pretty high. At another tree stood Bill Baber of Co. A. After a while an elderly man appeared between Baber and me. He had a double-barrelled shotgun. He would fire one barrell, hurrah for Jeff. Davis, curse Lincoln and then fire the other. Everytime he fired he would go through the same program of hurrahing and cursing. He seemed to be angry. After the fight was over I asked Baber what the old fellow was mad about. He replied, 'I don't know.' "*[29]

Shortly after the arrival of Bailey and Tyree the company of John Swann arrived but took little active part in the engagement.

The bulk of the Ohio troops had reached the battlefield and formed their line "on the left of the road towards the river, near the northern bank of Scarey's run, partly protected by a rise of ground, by a fence, a field of corn and some houses on a level with the enemy's guns." Pvt. J.H. Collins of Company H of the 12th Ohio reported:

> *"No sooner had we emerged from the woods which lined both sides of the road (Teays Valley) than the pop, pop, pop, warned us that we were in the vicinity of the enemy. Companies H and K of the 12th were deployed to the right and passed down the hill in rear of an old church. Companies A and B of the 21st and D of the 12th deployed to the left, passing in the rear of the Simms house, over a steep bluff to the river road and were soon engaged. The balance of the 12th Regt. marched down the (Teays Valley) road with arms at shoulder, through a withering fire from the Confederates."*[30]

Private Elijah Beeman of the 12th found himself in the midst of some of the heaviest fighting of the day as a result of this maneuver, but he held his ground and did not falter:

> *"We advanced to within 800 yards of the Enemy's ranks and fired upon them with our Rifles. They would pop up their heads, fire and fall back. I and John Kelley crept up within 900 yards of the enemy in a ravine. We fire(d) turned over upon our backs and loaded. The Battle was fought in Indian style."*[31]

Sweeney's Wheeling company still held the houses but, with the Virginia artillery temporarily out of action, the Ohioans began to concentrate on driving them out. A lieutenant led a section of Captain George's cavalry in an attempt to clear the houses but were met with a deadly volley which killed one cavalryman. Captain Cotter's artillerists immediately moved their guns from their right flank to their left and turned them on the houses in an effort to support an attack on the houses by men under Col. Jesse Norton and Lt. Col. White. These two men, reportedly angered at Cox for not putting them in charge of the entire affair, moved their men down the hill through a wheatfield where they were met by enemy fire, to the riverbank, with hopes of charging the houses from that position. Simultaneously, Cotter opened with deadly accuracy, rarely missing a house, the "manner in which the logs, guns, and the limbs of men were scattered about, as his percussion shell would strike, must have been anything but encouraging to the rebels."[32] Sweeney held on as long as possible but Norton reached the houses as the Ohio artillery was taking its toll, driving Sweeney's men out and across the Scary bridge position. As they fell back, a "coatless boy of about 16 years, carrying a gun, fell behind," only to be shot dead by a bullet in the back from Norton's soldiers.[33]

But as Norton took possession of the houses, Cotter's ammunition ran perilously low. Like all the other Ohio units involved, Cox had issued them only fourty rounds of ammunition (or eighty depending on source) and one day's ration, therefore three messengers were sent to Cox to obtain more, although one was killed by enemy fire as he departed. Norton's men made a feeble attempt to cross the bridge 'position' but were unable to gain any ground without strong artillery support.

It was now 3:00 o'clock and the majority of the Ohio boys began to assault the bridge 'position.' The Virginians held their fire until the enemy was almost to the bridge, opening upon them with horrendous effect, putting the attackers to flight. After some consultation amongst the Federals, it was decided that since ammunition was low, a bayonet charge would be made on the bridge 'position' in conjunction with a strike on the enemy left flank. Placed in charge of this flanking movement was Col. Lowe and a detachment of the 12th, who were to move to the right of the Ohio line, attempt to find a fordable section of Scary, then position themselves on a bluff where they could command the enemy rifle pits.

Lt. Col. Carr B. White, leading the frontal assault troops, composed of the two companies of the 21st, assisted by Norton's men in the houses, moved his men down the hill, across the wheatfield and to the bridge position where a number of them forded the knee-deep stream. The Virginians met and engaged them in intense hand to hand combat. Captain William B. Smith, of Company B, "snapped his revolver several times at a rebel and, then throwing it away in disgust, leapt forward, knocked him down with his fist, and brought him away prisoner."[34] A few Ohio boys crossed the stream and started to attack the enemy entrenchments, composed mainly of Bailey, Swann, and Sweeney's men, and it appeared that the Federals were near a victory.

About three-fourths of the Confederates not actually engaged began to panic and flee the battlefield. Taking note of this was Patton, who rode his horse onto the battlefield and attempted to rally them, but his horse became unruly for a short distance and the men mistook his movement as a signal to retreat. He still managed to rally a portion of them, but fifteen minutes later was severely wounded in the left shoulder and knocked from his horse. Once Patton was removed to a safe place behind lines, Capt. Jenkins took over and began rallying the men. And suddenly the tide of battle turned in favor of the Virginians.

Responding to the sounds of battle the Sandy Rangers of Capt. Corns arrived from Coal Mountain, riding mules and horses and singing "Bullets and Steel" as they raced down the hill toward the bridge. In addition, Col. Anderson and his portion of the Wise Legion cavalry had arrived, placing themselves on the far left of the Virginians' line where they observed their comrades at the bridge breaking. Men on the Confederate left flank mistook these new arrivals for the enemy and fired into them, wounding several:

"About this time a lot of men pushed in our left with blue trimmings on their uniforms. One of them fired at me, and I yelled to the next file on the right, that we were being

outflanked by the Yankees. The man on my right, taking the same view of the situation as I did, with a sudden aim, he shot one of the supposed yankees through and through. I do not remember how the mistake was rectified, but it was before the poor boy died.''[35]

To make matters even worse for Norton and White, accompanying the Sandy Rangers was B.S. Thompson's Kanawha Militia and the artillery piece of Lt. Thomas E. Jackson, the ''Peacemaker'' which had been cast at Mr. Job Thayer's foundry at Malden.

But the real tragedy for the Ohio boys was that Col. Lowe was having severe problems with his flanking movement. It appears that Maj. Jonathan D. Hines of the 12th Ohio had requested three or four companies in order so that he could make the maneuver. Col. Lowe ordered two of his captains, stationed to the right, to go with Hines but one of them was hiding behind a corn crib with part of his men and refused to go. If that wasn't bad enough, the men who did proceed with Hines, having arrived at a position above where the old Kirtley Store was later built, ran into trouble locating a place to ford the stream. Some believe they managed to get tangled up in the heavy foilage and underbrush and were fired upon by Col. Frank Anderson's men who were located in a higher elevated position. Records indicate that at least one company did successfully cross the stream:

''Captain Carey, with his company, succeeded in getting within thirty yards of the rebels main work. Captain C. requested to be re-enforced by one company, when he would charge the position, but owing to some mistake the needed assistance did not arrive, and so the intention failed.''[36]

Whether or not Capt. Edward M. Carey and Company H or anyone else crossed the creek to a strategic position was pointless, as they were too late to be of any effect to the main assault. Already Col. Norton realized his position was in jeopardy at the bridge and began to move up the creek under the south bluff in front of the Ohio line, at which point he was severely wounded in the hip (or thigh). 1st Lt. Ashley Brown of the 12th Ohio remained with Norton to care for his wound and both he and Norton were captured. Capt. Thomas G. Allen of the 21st fell mortally wounded at the bridge. Capt. James Sloan(e) of the 12th, a Gallipolis resident, was wounded in the pit of the stomach while stationed at the last held Federal position on the extreme right.[37] Cox's adjutant, Charles Whittlesey, had his horse shot out from under him.[38]

Yet with the beating they were taking there was still hope that the Yankees could win if reinforcements arrived in time. The soldiers were asked to hold their positions while Whittlesey went to the riverbank to see if any boats were being sent from Camp Poco. And while so occupied the men on top of Simms Hill, including Col. Lowe, caught sight of a steamer coming from the direction of Camp Two Mile. Their immediate reaction was that Gen. Wise had sent Confederate reinforcements although Col. Lowe doubted it and ignored the boat while the battle continued.[39]

The Federals had already converted the log Scary church, by now torn by shot and shell, into an impromptu hospital where the wounded, brought from the battlefield in the only available wagon, were treated by Dr. Trotter of the Kentucky regiments and Major Hines.[40] In much more danger than most of the wounded, though, were soldiers from both armies who were unable to stand the extreme heat and knowingly risked exposure to enemy fire by going to the creek to get a drink.

Company A of the 12th Ohio, led by Capt. James D. Wallace, Elijah Beeman's commanding officer, had an English cook known as "Spider" who prided himself on his foraging abilities but prior to Scary had not had much luck. Taking note of a flock of geese caught between enemy fire:

> *"Spider's penchant got the better of his reason, and he darted after the flock, chasing them hither and thither, at one time getting almost inside the enemy's works, until he secured as many as could conveniently be carried, when he started off. How he escaped is a matter of perplexity, for at one time no less than one hundred bushwackers directed their fire at him."*[41]

Thomas L. Mason and William Mason were fighting in the Confederate ranks at Scary. Their father, an overseer for the Lewis Bowling plantation, made his home directly across the Kanawha River from Scary, where the remaining Mason children "huddled behind heavy furniture" at the height of the battle. Both Mason brothers survived the battle although both were killed later in the war.[42]

The Confederates, yet shy of victory, needed a stimulus at this stage of the battle, and besides the reinforcements that had arrived, that stimulus came in the form of Capt. Albert G. Jenkins:

> *"Captain Albert G. Jenkins, afterwards Brigadier General, came up the line of skirmishers, with his hat off and the blood streaming down his hair and neck, and called for someone to go and get his horse, tied to a stake behind Hale's Battery. He did not, like King Richard, promise a kingdom for his horse, but was thinking of the kingdom to come, and a chance to dodge it. So I left the beech tree, and ran through the brush, over the hill and untied the horse. I rode up to the battery and saw a dismounted cannon being propped up for service by a lot of determined men. I asked of them, 'Where is my brother?' 'Who is your brother?' 'Lieutenant Welch of this Battery.' 'There he lies. He has done his duty.' I looked where the soldiers pointed, and saw my brother upon the ground lying where he fell, with his head almost severed by a flying piece of iron from the cannon that he was aiming when it was struck and dismounted by a cannon ball. As he lay with both arms extended in the form of a cross, he reminded me of Christ crucified. One died for all mankind, the other for his native state, with the same willingness.*
>
> *I rode the horse to where I left Captain Jenkins, and when I tried to dismount, I could not get my foot loose from the stirrup, and he could not mount. I was very much afraid that the tangle would be undone by the bullets, but solved the riddle by pulling out my camp knife and cutting the stirrup leather in two. I then repaired rapidly to my friend, the beech tree, and Captain Jenkins went his way in the fight, while I got the stirrup off my foot."*[43]

The combination of Jenkins rallying his men, the "Peacemaker" firing "trace chains, mashed horse shoes, and other kinds of scrap iron" at the enemy, and the fresh reinforcements from Coal Knob had nearly driven the Yankees away from the bridge and the Confederate left by 5 P.M. In addition, Charles Whittlesey had returned to the top of Simms Hill to report that no boats had arrived from Camp Poco. It's possible that Cotter's Ohio Artillery had six or eight rounds of ammunition left at this stage of the battle and unsuccessfully attempted to counter Thomas Jackson's artillery piece. But the Federals had had enough, as well as falsely assuming that the men of Capt. Corns were reinforcements from Camp Two Mile, and immediately took flight to the Morgan farm where the kitchen was converted into a hospital. Along the River Road the "disorganized...tired, thirsty, and exhausted" Ohio men met the remainder of the 21st Ohio, under Lt. Col. James M. Neibling, about two miles from camp, whom Cox had belatedly sent to their aid. It was decided that without more ammunition they would

MORGAN PLANTATION KITCHEN MUSEUM
It was used as a hospital after the Scary Creek battle and is now located at St. Albans Park. — Courtesy: Gary Bays

not attempt to renew the Scary affair.

Capt. Jenkins assumed the Federals had pulled back in order to plan another, much stronger, attack and ordered his men to retreat from the field. Ironically, this mistake left the battlefield deserted by both armies. Col. Frank Anderson, with his two companies on the extreme left flank, took note of this and brought the retreating column back to their defenses, resulting in a Confederate victory at Scary Creek.

On a scouting expedition not far from Scary was the Rocky Point Grays (Company F, 22nd Virginia) with member James H. Mays:

> *"We could plainly hear the rattle and roar of guns and see above the treetops the smoke of battle, and I dare say that the sight of that smoke and the sound of those guns caused more fear and trembling than any of the succeeding battles of the four years of the war."*[44]

Although a message arrived to hurry the Grays to the scene of battle by the time they arrived the Federals had retreated and the battle had concluded.

Led by Lt. Nicholas Fitzhugh the Kanawha Riflemen, the Fayetteville Rifles, the mounted Border Rangers, and skirmishers, were ordered to cross the creek, rally on the Green, and guard the Teays Valley Road near the Simms house. Their final order of business was to burn the buildings so that the Federals could not return and occupy them.

As dusk fell upon the Scary battlefield, Cox and his army suffered what was probably the most embarrassing and humiliating incident of the entire Kanawha campaign.[45] As the Virginians reveled in victory on the battlefield (reportedly they were a bit intoxicated) they set fire to a cooper shop, an outbuilding located near the river, and the Robert Marshall Simms home, although family members returned in time to extinguish that particular fire (verified by a door key which burned an imprint on the floor which could be seen long after the war). Quite unknown to the victors, the Federals had made an arrangement earlier in the day whereby if a victory were obtained, a fire, such as the one now created by the enemy, would be lit upon the battlefield.

The confused situation had originated as early as 2:30 P.M., during the course of the battle, when a messenger arrived at Cox's camp with a request for more ammunition for the troops engaged. Just as Cox ordered forth reinforcements a second messenger arrived with premature news of a Federal victory.

COLONEL [then Lieutenant Colonel] JAMES M. NIEBLING
21st Ohio Volunteer Infantry. Led belated Federal reinforcements to Scary. —
From S.S. Canfield's "History of the 21st Ohio"; Courtesy: Library of Congress

MAJOR [then Captain] CHARLES S. COTTER
Independent Battery Ohio Volunteer Artillery. He led Federal artillery at Scary Creek. — Courtesy: U.S. Army Military History Institute (MOLLUS Collection)

As a result, Col. Charles A. DeVilliers of the 11th Ohio, and four officers of the 2nd Kentucky: Col. William E. Woodruff; Lt. Col. George W. Neff; and Captains George Austin of Co. B. and John R. Hurd of Co. F. rode three miles above Camp Poco to get a better view of the action but found the view obstructed. Observing the smoke from the burning structures, the officers, without any official authorization, decided to cross the river and congratulate their colleagues in victory.

Two versions exist of what transpired next. One is that they rode to the riverbank and found a male Negro whom they persuaded to ferry them across in a "flat." The Negro gladly obliged since the Federals had been winning the battle when he had been on the other side of the river earlier in the day. The other version says that the officers "went to a house on the bank of the river at the foot of Johnsons Shoals and prevailed a man named Dudding to ferry them across the river." Although Dudding warned them of the potential danger they paid him no heed.[46]

DeVilliers, undoubtedly motivated by his ego, and the men of the 2nd Kentucky with overconfidence brought on by their relatively easy victory at Barboursville, raced across the river, past Federal pickets, rode up the River Road and onto the battlefield, where they approached one of the burning buildings and confronted the surrounding soldiers. Unable to discern the figures of the enemy in the darkness, DeVilliers and his cohorts began yelling hearty congratulations as they rode up to Capt. Albert G. Jenkins screaming "That's right, boys, give the damned rebels hell. Shoot every mother's son of 'em."[47] as well as something such as, "Well, you have given the rebels a good sound thrashing today."[48] The response, quite to the surprise of the Federal officers, was for the "damned Yankees" to "dismount and surrender" or they would have the "hell" blown out of them.[49]

COLONEL WILLIAM E. WOODRUFF
2nd Kentucky Volunteer Infantry. Captured at Scary. — Courtesy: Library of Congress

The five Federal officers soon found themselves on their way to Libby prison where, at a later date, Neff and Woodruff found themselves held as hostages for the privateers taken aboard the ship "Savannah." DeVilliers escaped from the prison late in the fall and rejoined his command at Gauley Bridge. Upon their capture, Jenkins gave Neff the gentlemanly treatment promised him by Mrs. Jenkins prior to the battle of Barboursville.

Cox was understandably infuriated with the actions of these officers but the 2nd Kentucky was particularly "disconsolate at the loss of their gallant leader, whom they loved as a father."[50] But if the morale of the 2nd Kentucky was at a low ebb, the loss of DeVilliers was a blessing to the 11th Ohio. At this stage of the war the Federal army could do without bungling idiots and DeVilliers was one of the worst. Even more disheartening to the Federals was that this bonus catch made the rebels twice as thrilled with their oddly won victory at Scary and undoubtedly raised their morale. These officers would later claim that they had acted with permission, that they thought the smoke signaled victory, that loud shouts of jubilation lured them across the river, that they had spotted a Union flag being hoisted on the battlefield, that the Negro on the ferry had lied to them, and that their view being obstructed they had sought a closer observation. It was all to no avail. It was a matter of record that all five had acted without official permission in total disregard of military regulation.

Later that night General Wise finally decided to strike Cox's force at Camp Poco, which could have possibly been a resounding piece of military strategy had it been applied much earlier in the day while nearly half of Cox's men were occuped at Scary Creek. Seemingly taking a cue from General McClellan, Wise let his opportune moment slip by. It is very feasible that a well coordinated attack on Camp Poco in conjunction with the Scary battle could have destroyed Cox's army and sent them running back to the Ohio River, giving Wise a double victory and a much stronger foothold on the Kanawha. More important, the time gained by such a Federal setback would have allowed Wise to more strongly reinforce Charleston and Gauley Bridge so as to defend against any attack from his rear, possibly eliminating the later necessity of evacuating his men from the valley. But as it were, Cox's men were only slightly bloodied at Scary, and he continued to retain his position at Poca.

But Wise did indeed decide to make such an attack, even if it was applied hours too late to be of any service. Slightly after 10 P.M. he issued orders to Col. John McCausland and Col. Chirstopher Q. Tompkins to lead the movement. They were to:

> *"Advance at once cautiously & slowly 600 Infantry, including three companies ordered to reinforce Coal, and which reinforcement is countermanded & 150 cavalry & a corps or artillery. One Company of Cavalry and two of Infantry to move down the Brush Fork Road; and the remaining Infantry about 500, and the other two companies of Cavalry, and corps of artillery, to move down the River Road...."*[51]

All together there were about 800 men involved in the movement, including the Richmond Light Infantry Blues, and some more were to be added at Coal Post if there were any there that could be spared. Wise ordered the entire contingent to "put the cold steel of their bayonets into their (the Yankee's) teeth."[52] A steamer was also sent along "to be ready at the most eligible point to cross the river in every emergency requiring it."[53]

By the time of the proposed attack Cox had reorganized from his defeat at Scary and was well prepared for Wise's surprise. When McCausland came within view of Camp Poco he reportedly found Cox's men, three regiments strong, well entrenched and in possession of some heavy artillery, including some 12 pound howitzers. McCausland, much brighter than Wise in military matters, realized an attack was out of the question and began the journey back to Camp Two Mile. On the other hand, Cox's adjutant Charles Whittlesey later claimed that, "Pocataligo was not entrenched, nor did McCausland's command come within sight of our camp."[54] Regardless of who was telling the truth, earthworks are yet barely visible at the mouth of Poca River, although they could have been erected after July 17. But the primary point to remember is that by not initiating this move during the battle at Scary, General Wise lost his chance, a slim one perhaps but still a chance, to control the Kanawha Valley for the Confederacy. This was Wise's greatest failure in the Kanawha campaign.

The night of the 17th passed wihout any incident of particular note. At Scary nothing beyond scattered sniper fire transpired. At about midnight Fayette Riflemen William F. Bahlmann and Sam ("Flint") Wingrove, posted as pickets on the Teays Valley road, were aroused by the sound of approaching cavalry, but after requesting proper identification the mounted men were found to be their comrades.[55]

JAMES H. MAYS

About 1860

JAMES H. MAYS

Rocky Point Greys Co. F, 22nd Virginia. He helped bury the Scary dead. — Courtesy: Lee Mays

WHITELAW REID
Noted Ohio newspaper correspondent who covered the Kanawha campaign. — Courtesy: Library of Congress

CHAPTER SEVEN

Aftermath and Retrograde Movement

Early on the morning of July 18th some of Jenkins' Border Rangers went to the riverbank to wash their faces for breakfast and found a frightened Federal hidden in a hollow tree. "He was the worst scared man I ever saw," claimed James D. Sedinger.[1] James H. Mays of the Rocky Point Grays from Monroe County (Company F, 22nd Virginia) remarked that the cook from his company found a Federal seated inside a hollow log writing and captured him. Another Scary participant said, "We even captured two Ohio men in an old hollow sycamore, but they were not scared anymore than we were."[2] Whether or not these references were being made to one incident or more than one is not known.

At about 8:00 A.M. the Fayette Rifles, and the majority of the Confederate units at Scary, returned to Camp Tompkins, having been at Scary for a total of 19 hours with but little to eat or drink. William Clark Reynolds, of the Kanawha Riflemen, wrote: "Returned from picket after passing a sleepless night and had a scanty coffee-less breakfast, being the first morsel of food we've had an opportunity of eating in 26 hours."[3]

A short time later the Confederates began performing the gruesome chore of burying the battlefield victims, including the Federals, as their comrades had left them behind during their retreat. James H. Mays later recalled:

> *"....we went over the battle ground gathering up the dead for burial. Fourteen dead Yankees were found, which we dragged together. We dug a pit about 6 by 20 feet and spread some straw in the bottom. We then laid the bodies side by side on the straw, put more straw over them, and covered them with the dirt that had been dug out. It was a rather rough piece of business, but was the best we could do under the circumstances.... In assembling the bodies, I carried one of the men's caps. The name I noticed on the cap was Captain Allen. I left it with the body...."*[4]

Of course this was Captain Thomas Allen of Company D, 21st Ohio, and upon further inspection of his body a letter was found that revealed he was engaged to a young lady in Dayton, Ohio. Captain A.R. Barbee sent Allen's belongings to her and a letter praising her fiancee's gallant fall in battle.

The exact spot where Captain Allen and his thirteen comrades were buried is not known but is believed to have been 100 yards from Scary Creek, 30 yards from the road, somewhere between the river and the junction of the River (Winfield) and Teays Valley road. Through the years some people have come to believe the bodies are still there but, reportedly, they were removed after the war and transferred to a national cemetery. Another account indicates that in 1868 some military men excavated the site but found no remains.

Levi Welch, brother of Lt. James C. Welch, obtained permission from Lt. Fitzhugh to go to Upper Falls of Coal River to report his brother's death to his mother who was staying there. Although she had probably heard the sounds of battle, little could she have realized that one of her sons was one of its few Confederate victims.

Although there appears to be no definite report on the casualties at the battle there have become some generally accepted figures which are most often quoted. The Confederate loss being one killed, two mortally wounded, and four slightly wounded. In contrast, the Union forces had a much higher toll of fourteen killed in action, thirty wounded, and twenty-one missing. This is not unusual, though, as the Federals were engaged offensively, exposing their ranks quite often, while the Confederates remained defensive. (For author's researched conclusion of casualties, see Appendix.)

Many other casualty figures have been given and most vary to some degree. 'Political generals,' men quickly promoted to military rank due to political influence or background as both Cox and Wise were, often were prone to exaggerate their official reports so as to make a favorable reflection on themselves. So, undoubtedly, the statistics given by these men are open to question. Wise, in the *Official Records,* says his Confederate forces killed thirty Federal soldiers and captured six officers and ten or twenty privates. He gave his own losses as one killed, two wounded (one mortally), and no mention of the number missing. Cox, on the other hand, in his *Military Reminiscences,* written after the war, listed his casualties as ten killed and thirty-five wounded, but gave no report on what he thought Confederate casualties to be.

Newspaper accounts, composed at the time, also were blown largely out of proportion, although such outstanding newspaper correspondents as Whitelaw Reid accompanied the Federal forces. The *Cincinnati Commercial* set Union losses at twelve killed and thirty or forty wounded, and supposedly quoting a neutral source (Dr. Thompson), gave Rebel losses as sixty-five killed and 150 wounded. To add to this confusion, the *Cincinnati Gazette* gave a completely different version, stating the Federal losses totaled fifty-seven, including nine killed, thirty-eight wounded, and nine missing. Although admitting to being unaware of actual Confederate figures, the paper did state that the Rebel losses were "at least equal" to the Federals.

One newspaper account, written many years after the war but supposedly quoting Wise from the *Official Records,* said Wise reported thirty Federals killed and twenty-three captured, and his own casualty list consisted of one dead, three wounded, and again no mention of missing in action. Although the same source was used by both accounts the figures do vary slightly.

The common foot soldier, the actual participant, had his versions to tell as well. Being the one most prone to bragging, his figures usually exceeded the official and accepted accounts. One Confederate, writing to his sister, boasted of his troops killing 260 Union soldiers at Scary and wounding an unknown amount.

Border Ranger J.D. Sedinger said his comrades killed eighteen of the enemy. Private Elijah Beeman of the 12th Ohio, wrote his parents and said his forces lost seven killed and twenty wounded and that the enemy admitted to a preposterous 65 killed and 200 wounded. At a later date, Private J.H. Collins, also of the 12th Ohio, remembered that the 21st had one known killed and one known wounded and the 12th had seven killed and eleven wounded to some degree. Even Lt. Col. Patton gave a different account saying, "The Confederate loss was 3 killed and 9 wounded of whom two died of their wounds—The Yankees left 12 or 15 of their dead in the field, but by their own confession their loss was not less than 200 killed and wounded."[5]

As if the massive confusion surrounding battlefield data isn't sufficient enough already, writers and historians have continued to uncover or create new figures. *The History of Putnam County* by William Wintz and Ivan Hunter says total losses for the Scary action was twenty-one dead and thirty wounded. Forrest Hull, a questionable source, according to his colleagues, wrote in the *Charleston Daily Mail* that the Union loss was thirty dead and one wounded. Shirley Donnelly, a more credible source, writing for the same newspaper listed fourteen Union soldiers killed, thirty wounded, and four missing. William Wintz, in a specially prepared piece on Scary written in 1972, says the Union had fourteen killed, thirty wounded, and twenty-one missing, while the Rebels lost three killed and three wounded. In *War of the Union* by Allen Nevins there is mention of nine dead Federals, thirty-eight wounded and three missing, as well as the five captured officers. Finally, the *War Memoranda* of Charles Whittlesey has the Federals with nine dead and twelve wounded, the Confederates with three dead and nine wounded.

None of this contradictory information is unusual as it practically became a custom both during and after the Civil War for every person, combatant or non-combatant, to create his own picture of what transpired. And later writers can't be too heavily faulted for quoting what they had been led to believe were accurate reports. Certainly future historians will unveil new accounts and most will probably go unquestioned, as all the veterans of Scary, the only ones who could possibly give an accurate version, have long since passed away.

Whatever discrepancies existed in casualty reports, there was certainly no doubt as to the response of various officials involved. McClellan was infuriated, condemning Cox and requesting better officers. Cox himself later admitted that he took the affair too lightly and did not commit enough troops, but felt that McClellan was unjustifiably harsh in his criticism. General Wise being the victor, called it a "glorious victory"[6] while Lt. Col. Patton felt that his troops "whipped at least 4 times their numbers of armed and disciplined Yankees & put them to a shameful & disgraceful flight."[7]

Many reasons were offered by the Federals to explain their loss besides Cox's blunder, including unfamiliarity with the terrain, the greenness of the soldiers and, in particular, their ineffective arms, which the 21st Ohio even included in a poem:

"We were men. We were patriots, four years and more.
We clung to our colors, we fought at the fore.
From that daring Kanawha, fixed bayonet onslaught.
Where our smoothbore muskets we found worse than nought."[8]

But in reality their arms were no worse than those of the men they fought. The real victim and scapegoat of Scary was Col. John W. Lowe of the 12th Ohio who received the bulk of the blame for the Federal loss due to his failure to flank the Confederate left. He became tagged as a cowardly old man, a burden he had to carry until he proved himself when he fell in action at the battle of Carnifex Ferry, (West) Virginia, on September 10, 1861. Actually, McClellan had been correct in blaming Cox; his mistake was that he used his own victories as a comparison to Cox's loss. Such a comparison held no weight as McClellan had more men, with better arms, and who were better trained. But Cox probably could have grabbed a victory at Scary. He knew of the enemy position from Col. Jesse Norton's July 14 scouting attempt and, since Cox was a new and unknown military commander, his presence on the battlefield might possibly have given his men a better sense of confidence; but to belatedly admit to not commiting enough men was an invalid excuse. Fortunately, Cox, like Lowe, later proved himself a capable officer although McClellan's wrath almost cost him his rank after Scary.

The remainder of July 18th was relatively calm in both camps. Cox had outposts about three miles above camp at the White House near Rock Branch which were lightly attacked, as well as a picket in a tobacco barn about a mile above the outposts, but this resulted in nothing more than slight skirmishing, probably brought on by Wise's scouts.

On the morning of the 19th Jenkins' Border Rangers left Camp Tompkins, somehow managed to bypass Cox without notice, and returned to Greenbottom. Here, while his "company dismounted and hid themselves in a pawpaw thicket," Jenkins posed as a potential passenger and lured the boat *Fanny McBrownie* to shore. When the boat's captain, a Mr. Blagg realized the dupe he hid behind the smokestack and ordered his pilot, Mr. Holloway to back the boat out. Holloway refused and told the captain to do it himself. As a result, the Border Rangers boarded the boat and confiscated military stores, consisting of nothing more than a case of swords and four revolvers. The soldiers then rode to the Greenbottom farm but when about 100 yards from the farm Mrs. Jenkins met them and Captain Jenkins "proposed three cheers for his little wife."[9] Later, the Jenkins family was placed in carriages and began the return to Camp Tompkins.

The return was not a pleasant one. General Wise had sent a detachment under a flag of truce to Poca to obtain the baggage of the captured Federals. He had received news of McClellan's victories in the north and, realizing his position was in jeopardy, began what he called his "retrograde movement," a retreat from the valley the Yankees preferred to call the "Great Skedaddle."[10] This did not go well with the men and many officers were proclaiming that western Virginia had sold out. Preparations began on July 19th by removing the forces at Camp Tompkins by the steamers *Julia Maffitt* and the *Kanawha Valley*. Wise's orders to Col. Tompkins for the 19th explained the movement in detail.

Charleston, Ka. July 19th 1861

Sir,

You will proceed promptly to retire all forces from Scary Creek, and remove them from the camp at Coal. Take the strongest position you can select under guidance of Colonel Adler at the mouth or bridge of Coal River on the right bank and at Coal Mountain, placing your battery of artillery in the strongest position on the right bank of the river, so as to defend the pass of the Bridge. You will also post strong guards of Infantry and Rifles at the points where the road crosses Tacketts Creek & Coal river, Fall creek and Coal river, and when it crosses Coal River between Island Creek and Fuqua Creek, or at the mouth of Crooked Creek, and also at Alum Creek and a guard at Elk Shoal to protect the ferry above. And at Bunker Hill, on Upton Creek, you will make a strong hold against emergency of retreat, regarding the mouth of Coal, the crossing at Fall creek, and the crossing Alum Creek, as the most dangerous approaches, to be most strongly guarded. You will make a strong outpost also at the point where the road forks to Fall creek and the mouth of Crooked Creek, between Trace Fork of Mud River, and Trace fork ridge.

Upon all these points you will distribute for the present 1000 men. You will take to the artillery post the gun which was disabled at Coal, have the carriage repaired and the gun unspiked. The Steamer will be sent immediately to aid there. You will exercise a sound discretion in departing from this plan of defense, but report any material departure before execution. The sick must be immediately removed to the Hospital at Charleston, and all ardent...in reach of the camp must be destroyed. Send the prisoner Dr. Thompson, whom I wish to deal with strictly to me at this place.

By Comd. of Brig. Genl. H.A. Wise
Signed E.J. Harvie
Capt. A.A. Adjt. Genl.[11]

They arrived at Chandler's Landing on the 20th. On the 23rd they left the steamers and marched to Hunter's Stretch, or Stretcher's Neck as one soldier called it, where they erected impressive intrenchments "running from the river to the mountains. We placed empty salt-barrels in a zigzag line, filled these with earth and then threw earth among and on top of the barrels until they looked and were solid."[12] Colonel Adler, using Private William Bahlmann as a translator, supervised the project.

Cox himself had decided to stay put. He wanted to continue his advance on land, free of dependence upon the boats, in order to be able to initiate flanking movements, but to do so he had to await the arrival of more wagons. He knew that any further advance by boat, attempting to run Johnson's Shoals, would put him in an exposed position to enemy fire. In addition, he had to wait on the arrival of Company K of the 11th Ohio, the mechanics and engineers who were to construct a bridge over the Poca River. But they didn't arrive until nightfall of July 18 and for some unknown reason didn't dock until the next day. These delays, as well as rains that had plagued Cox's men since the affair at Scary caused much agitation amongst them.

Robert E. Lee wrote General Wise on July 21st informing him that Confederate President Jefferson Davis was "....much gratified at your success, and particularly at the handsome repulse given to the enemy at Scarey Creek and his subsequent ejection to the Pocotaligo...,"[13] yet went on to remind him of the Confederate losses at Rich Mountain, Laurel Mountain, and Corricks Ford, including the death of General Garnett, making it clear that a retreat from the Kanawha Valley was essential, a thing of which Wise was already well aware.

On that same day, Pryce Lewis arrived by steamer at Red House where he found Cox on a boat which was tied to a wharf which served as headquarters. Although he had a sealed letter from McClellan introducing him and gave a vivid account of his adventures, Cox was a bit suspicious and called in Maj. Charles Whittlesey to get his opinion. Lewis repeated his story, including vital military information:

> *"I gave the number of troops in Wise's command as 5,500, including those under Patton and Browning, told the number of rations issued at Charleston, and the number of pieces of artillery there. I gave my opinion that, in going to Charleston, he would have two fights, one at the junction of the Coal Mouth and Kanawha, the other at Elk River suspension bridge. When I got through the General appeared astonished."*[14]

Lewis then toured Cox's camp in order to compare it to that of General Wise, concluding that Cox had fewer troops but his men were better equipped and had better artillery. Later that day Lewis learned for the first time of the battle at Scary.

According to Lewis the remains (probably the personal effects and not the body) of Capt. Thomas Allen, killed at Scary, were brought into camp and sent to his family. The next day Lewis was planning his return to Cincinnati when he caught word that a combination of land and water troops was going to make a reconnaisance of Scary. He decided to cancel his departure and join the troops in their excursion, going with the boats as the land troops had already departed. Just as the boat was leaving General Cox appeared and, still showing signs of suspicion, asked Lewis if he was coming back. Feeling a bit insulted, Lewis replied, "Where in the hell do you think I'm going?", to which Cox shouted a satisfied "All right."[15]

As the boats approached Scary they noticed smoke in the distance, which they correctly assumed was the bridge over Coal River, put to the torch by retreating rebels. The boat docked near Scary and some of the soldiers advanced toward Coalsmouth, soon afterward sending back a prisoner, a Confederate cavalryman who had not been able to get across the bridge before it was burned. As they continued to Scary a number of other prisoners were taken, but when they finally neared Camp Tompkins one of the advancing Federal soldiers came to Lewis' group and requested the aid of a surgeon as the Federals had captured a badly wounded Confederate officer. When Lewis learned that the wounded man was in Valcoulon Place he surmised it may very well be Patton, and probably feeling some guilt for having duped him, refused an offer to go in the house.

Indeed, Lewis was correct. Patton was apparently left behind in the Confederate retreat, his wounds too severe for him to be moved. But the Confederates had the wounded Colonel Jesse S. Norton as a prisoner, and before departing they had made an agreement with the Yankees to exchange Norton for Patton, an agreement that infuriated Cox when he learned of it, although he later upheld it and paroled Patton. The Federal surgeons attempted to amputate Patton's arm, but he somehow got hold of a pistol and prevented them from performing the operation. Finally one young doctor "rigged up a sling and a bucket with a hole in it, which dripped water onto the wound and apparently "saved the arm."[16] Although Patton recovered from his wound and later rejoined his command, he was no longer a participant in the Kanawha campaign of 1861. He would be out of the picture for quite some time.

When Pryce Lewis returned to Cox's headquarters he found the General once again in doubt, having recently received information from Col. James V. Guthrie that two loyal Union men had come into his camp stating that Wise had 60,000 men, to which an astonished Lewis reassured Cox that these were only wild rumors which were quite prevalent in the country at that time. He said, "I am no soldier, but with the men you have here and in the vicinity, I would promise to be in Charleston in twenty-four hours. The way is now clear."[17]

After more deliberation Cox was finally satisfied with the information and issued General Orders No. 7 at Poca through his Acting Assistant Adjutant General, J.N. McElroy:

> *"The troops will move from Poca at 5 a.m. on the morning of the 24th instant. The 11th Ohio Volunteers will move tonight to the White House, throw out their pickets, and then await further orders."*[18]

Although Cox invited Lewis to accompany the movement he rejected the offer and returned to Cincinnati the next day, the 24th, having fully served his purpose in the Kanawha Valley.

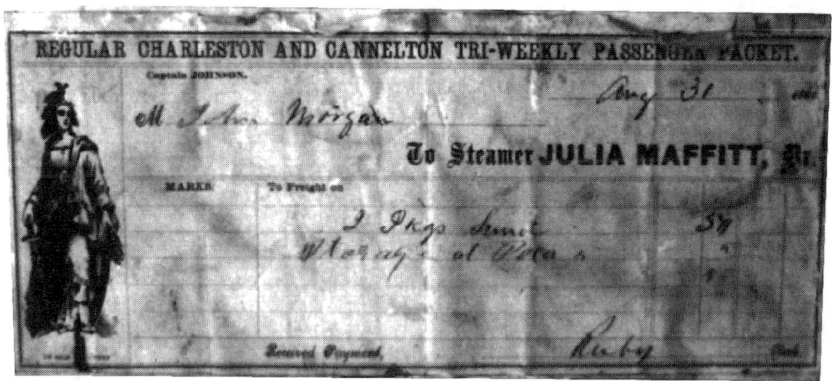

REGULAR CHARLESTON AND CANNELTON TRI-WEEKLY PASSE[illegible] PACKET.

Captain JOHNSON.

Aug 31

To Steamer JULIA MAFFITT, Dr.

MARKS

To Freight on

Received Payment,

EARLY RECEIPT

An 1860 cargo receipt from the "Julia Maffitt." Located in the Morgan Museum at the West Virginia State Farm Museum Complex at Point Pleasant.

— Courtesy: West Virginia State Archives

Sinking of the Julia Maffitt

As previously noted, Wise had already begun his retrograde movement by the 24th and Cox had all the wagons and supplies he deemed necessary to renew his advance on Charleston. The Federal troops, with two days rations, were ready to move from Camp Poco by 5 A.M. although they didn't depart until eight. The 11th Ohio held the advance, keeping three miles ahead of the main column. Following the 11th were the wagons, then Cotter's artillery, and bringing up the rear, the 21st Ohio, commanded by Lt. Col.

THE WHITE HOUSE
At Rock Branch today (rear view). — Courtesy: Gary Bays

THE WHITE HOUSE
At Rock Branch today (front view). — Courtesy: Gary Bays

James M. Niebling who had replaced Colonel Norton. Also, four companies of the 12th Ohio, with Lt. Col. Carr B. White, remained with the main column. Covering the entire main column was the 1st and 2nd Kentucky led by Col. David A. Enyart and Acting Col. Thomas D. Sedgewick respectively, with Sedgewick filling in for the captured Colonel Woodruff. The river fleet was commanded by Commodore Beltzhoover, the flagship *Economy* used as the lead ship with a cannon posted on her bow. Upon the boats were six companies of the 12th Ohio under Maj. Jonathan D. Hines and three companies serving with Col. John Lowe remained at the rear of the fleet.[19]

Cox's men were certainly not the only ones in motion on the 24th. During the early morning hours, after having sunk all coal barges in Coal River belonging to the Rosecrans owned company, Col. Christopher Q. Tompkins and some seven hundred soldiers, the bulk of the 22nd Virginia, proceeded to evacuate Camp Tompkins and Hunters Stretch. The commissary stores and infantry were placed on the *Julia Maffitt,* a somewhat small but spacious steamboat with one, and possibly two, flatboats in tow. The boat was designed for passenger travel with plenty of eating and sleeping accomodations as well as pleasant staterooms. Although definitely not a warship, her crew was composed entirely of staunch Southern sympathizers, including the captain, Lawrence (or Lawson) M. ("Nat") Wells; the pilot, Phil Doddridge (the original roll of the Kanawha Riflemen listed a Phil Doddridge and this is probably one and the same); and the mate, Bob Wilson. In addition, there was an engineer and a "full crew of deck hands, stewards, stokers, and other help."[20] The rear guard, composed of the mounted men such as Jenkins' Border Rangers, probably approximated the route of the boat via the James River and Kanawha Turnpike. Some veterans of the incident later recalled that there were no soldiers on board but undoubtedly this was not the case.

The first of the two enemy fleets to run into any trouble was the Federal boat *Economy* which came into contact with entrenched Confederates on the right side of the river about seven miles from Poca. Major Hines desired to engage the enemy and sent word to Colonel Lowe, on a boat one mile back, of his intentions but when Lowe arrived he decided against it and after checking with Cox was ordered to move on.

The main column under Cox, after crossing the Poca River, passing the White House at Rock Branch, took a little known back country road which enabled them to arrive in the rear of Wise's advance picket camp at Tyler Mountain. The pickets, not expecting the enemy to approach from such a direction, were caught totally off guard, were driven in, and departed in such haste that they left their still cooking meals over the campfires. Simmonds' Battery was involved in this action but to what extent is unknown. Further inspection by the Federals found a couple of bridges in flames, indicating that Wise had abandoned camp only a short time before. At this point it was decided to return to the Kanawha and check on the progress of the boats. But instead of finding their own river expedition they found the *Julia Maffitt.* Somewhere above the mouth of Davis Creek, Colonel Tompkins' army had apparently decided to dock on the south shore and take on some wheat that had been cut in a nearby field and placed in a sheaf. Some fellow Confederates had previously been stationed there but for some unknown reason had withdrawn. When Cox's men caught sight of the boat from the opposite shore they were unable to determine if it was one of their own due to poor visibility brought on by twilight. Some accounts indicate that the Federals called out from shore for an identification, while at nearly the same time, Sgt. Gary Carr, aboard the boat, requested the same from the Federals. At this point there is much dispute as to what followed.

Some accounts suggest that the obvious responses followed and a short conflict ensued. Another version indicates that the Federals attempted a bluff by pretending to be Confederates. Astride a white horse and dressed in civilian clothing Col. Christopher Q. Tompkins rode through a cornfield to the riverbank and assessed the situation. Possibly taking note of a Union flag being hoisted at the former Rebel entrenchments across the river, he detected a trap and wheeled his horse about. At approximately the same time the *Julia Maffitt,* with the soldiers on shore, apparently decided to attempt to run past the Union artillery of Captain Cotter then trained upon her. Being dark and at a rather long distance from the boat, the artillerists had difficulty in finding their target, finally resorting to the glare from the boat's boiler furnace as a target. George B. Hewitt, acting gunner, fired twice, his second round piercing the hull and hitting the boiler setting the boat on fire.

The Confederates gave a different account of the fire. According to them, as the *Julia Maffitt* began to run past the Federal artillery a shell pierced the hull but didn't cause any severe damage. Finding the artillery barrage too much to deal with, Doddridge reversed the boat and headed in the opposite direction at full speed. At just about the time when the crew felt secure, the lookout stationed on the upper deck, caught sight of more blue uniforms advancing from the vicinity of present day Dunbar. Within minutes the crew found themselves caught midstream between two artillery barrages. Having already absolutely rejected surrendering as an alternative, the crew had no other choice but to ram the boat into the south bank of the river. As they did the officers and crew, and probably some horses, quickly jumped ashore and fled through the nearby fields.

Suddenly, Phil Doddridge glanced back at the boat and realized that its wealth of supplies was about to fall into enemy hands as the Federals were already beginning to cross the river in small boats. Not wishing for such an event to transpire, Doddridge ran back to the boat, scoured the cabins gathering mattresses which he covered with oil from the engine room and set ablaze. As he hurried to depart the boat for a second time a few Federals had already come within reach of the boat. With not a second to spare, he jumped ashore, crept a short distance away and covered himself in a bed of dry leaves, keeping a small breathing space.

A Federal search party attempted to locate him and came so close he could hear their conversation, and one soldier practically fell over him. But he was not caught, nor were any of the rest of the crew of Colonel Tompkins' men. One Wheeling newspaper indicated that there was one Confederate killed but there were actually no known casualties. And the cargo of the *Julia Maffitt,* estimated to be worth at least $100,000 went up in flames.[21]

The troops on the southern shore, including the Border Rangers, "ran the gauntlet of infantry and artillery fire" from the opposite shore and proceeded eastward. A short time later the retreating Confederates were told enemy cavalry were to their front. Immediately some 800 men jumped over a fence and ran to the nearest mountain. Further inspection revealed it as a false alarm as the supposed enemy cavalry was only Mrs. Albert G. Jenkins arriving in a carriage. Still under fire, the Confederates moved on and reached Charleston after dark, where the Charleston companies hastily bid farewell to their families. From Charleston they marched to Brownstown (Marmet), arriving at about midnight and spending the night. The Border Rangers went into camp at the mouth of Lens Creek and became the rear guard from that point on.[22]

As for Cox, the loss of daylight and an insufficient number of boats to cross the Kanawha after the *Julia Maffitt* was set ablaze caused him to feel any further pursuit by crossing the river would be fruitless. As nightfall arrived, Cox decided to camp on the mountainside in the prevously occupied Confederate camp where his men feasted on the abandoned Confederate supper.

While the *Julia Maffitt* incident had been in progress, General Wise had been occupied, probably in Charleston, with interrogating a Kentucky businessman who had an "establishment for distilling coal tar from cannel

PHIL DODDRIDGE

Purported hero of the steamer "Julia Maffitt." — Courtesy: Charleston Newspapers

GAULEY BRIDGE
An artist's conception of the original covered bridge at Gauley Bridge that Wise burned in his retreat. Shown here as it looked in 1860. Man on the horse paying toll is Colonel Christopher Q. Tompkins.. — Courtesy: Fayette County Historical Society

coal on Elk River." Wise reportedly said, "I can stand a Yankee abolitionist with his hands under his coat-tails; but, by God, I can't stand a Kentucky abolitionist, and you ought to be hung. But I will for the present send you to Richmond." Fortunately for the young man, Wise turned his attention to the artillery firing on the *Julia Maffitt* and had his carriage brought forth in order to make a quick exit from Charleston. These distractions gave the Kentucky man the opportunity to escape to Federal lines.[23]

The Confederate retreat from Charleston was quick and effective, having caused considerable damage to the Elk River wire suspension bridge and "about everything that would make a light must have been ignited" in Charleston.[24] The rebels boarded a steamer which they rode about a half a mile above Charleston where some fellow Confederates fired upon them in the belief that they were Yankees. As the troops on the boat also believed that the men on shore were Federals, a short exchange of gunfire ensued until the situation was corrected before any harm was done.

The next day, July 25, the rebels arrived at Clifton at 2 P.M. and went into camp for the remainder of the day. On the 26th they departed at 1 A.M. and later arrived at Gauley Bridge where they quartered in the Fall's House. The majority of the Confederate army remained at Gauley for a few days during which time it rained almost constantly, creating a vast wasteland of mud. In order to remain dry many of the soldiers slept inside of the covered wooden bridge over Gauley River. This escape from the elements ended one rainy night when Wise arrived and ordered the torch put to the bridge, an act which the soldiers reluctantly performed until "the bridge burned in two and fell with a crash into the swollen stream."[25] At daybreak began the retreat to Bunger's Mill near Lewisburg, well out of the zone of danger from Federal troops. Wise would later claim that his retreat from the Kanawha Valley was orderly and without incident except for the desertion of many of the volunteer troops, but Beuhring H. Jones of the Dixie Rifles gave a more vivid account:

> *"Such demoralization as then ensued have been seldom witnessed. One entire company, perhaps two, deliberately filed off and went home. Another scattered like frightened sheep; but the captain marched boldly on alone until he encountered a barrel of whiskey; there he halted, got 'tight,' broke his sword and wore his bars no more, and was never heard of again. Huge sides of bacon were pitched into the mud and trampled underfoot. The heads of whiskey and molasses barrels were knocked in, and every man helped himself. The Gauley Bridge that had cost $30,000 was burned although the river was fordible for infantry and cavalry about one hundred yards above. It was said, though I never credited the report, that the famous Hawks Nest was examined with an eye for its destruction, but was declared non-combustible, and was thus saved for the admiration of future tourists. Every man went it on his own hook. For the first twelve hours, despite the efforts of the General, orders were disregarded and system was lacking."*[26]

General Wise, standing at the gate to Gauley Mount, greeted each company as it arrived from Gauley Bridge and halted them in order to verbally grant a furlough to every man who wished to go home, causing Beuhring Jones to complain: "Nine tenths of my company wanted to go home, and the result was, I entered Lewisburg with ten men out of a company of eighty eight."[27]

On August 1st Wise arrived at Bunger's Mill where he finally felt at ease, although his soldiers were not too pleased with the entire affair. One day the fiesty General overheard a private speak of "Wise's retreat from Gauley" to which Wise thundered, "Retreat!!"—"never dare call it a 'retreat' again, sir. It was only a 'retrograde' movement, sir." To which the poor fellow

GAULEY MOUNT
Home of Col. C.Q. Tompkins before the war. — Courtesy: Fayette County Historical Society

replied, "I don't know nothin' about your retrogrades, General, but I do know we did some damn tall walkin.' "[28]

At Bunger's Mill Wise wrote to Robert E. Lee on August 1 to apprise him of his present situation and a valid, if somewhat prejudiced, defense of his movements in the Kanawha, stating that after the battle at Scary Creek the enemy fell back and increased to five thousand in numbers, while Wise had only 1000 at Gauley; another thousand at Coal; and 2000 at Elk and the immediate vicinity. So outnumbered, and with additional Federal troops closing in from other directions, Wise felt he had no alternative but to abandon the Kanawha Valley. He also felt his Legion had performed admirably in the retreat, having only one man desert, while the State Volunteers lost three to five hundred by desertion. But the final paragraph of his letter expressed his sentiments best:

"The Kanawha Valley is wholly disaffected and traitorous. It was gone from down to Point Pleasant before I got there. Boone and Cabell are nearly as bad, and the state of things in Braxton, Nicholas, and part of Greenbrier is awful. The militia are nothing for warlike uses here. They are worthless who are true, and there is no telling who is true. You cannot persuade these people that Virginia can or will ever reconquer the northwest, and they are submitting, subdued, and debased. I have fallen back not a minute too soon..."[29]

He closed with the usual request for more and better weapons, a plea that by this time he should have known would not receive the proper attention. Actually, this well known (and often printed) letter was only one of three he wrote on the same day, the others being to Samuel Cooper and to Gen. W.W. Loring. Although the information in each was basically the same as that relayed to Lee, Wise did mention to Cooper that his men "have marched and countermarched incessantly, and fought well at Scary, and have scouted the enemy to their teeth, and are now without shoes..."[30] To Loring Wise reported his strength at Bunger's Mill as 3500 effectives, while the enemy at Gauley purportedly had 5000, with eight pieces of artillery.[31]

General Wise actually didn't need to alibi or condemn anyone, and his best defense was probably given by Col. Christopher Q. Tompkins when he wrote a brief history of the war:

"Much has been said of the policy of this retreat and the manner of its execution. There can be no doubt as to the policy. The Army of the Kanawha with all its aggregations barely numbered three thousand & never were forces in the field at such distances from their depot of supplies in worse condition for a retrograde movement, in fact, the Regiments and Battalions were barely organized & totally unskilled in the elementary principles of military life. Companies were grouped together in some approximation to homogenous arrangements but the exercises of the service were such that detachments of corps were constantly drawn into active duty before the officers & men had learned the first lessons of tactics."[32]

Cox's army also resumed activity on the morning of the 25th when the mayor of Charleston and a few prominent citizens arrived at Cox's camp at Two-Mile in order to surrender the town. Cox, well aware of the fear of Union soldiers instilled in the population by General Wise, ordered his men to march orderly and without disturbance through the streets of Charleston. That march was delayed a bit, though, when they found that Wise's retreating army had partially destroyed the wire suspension bridge over Elk River, an act which reportedly didn't have the blessings of O. Jennings Wise who cursed his father for the act of destruction. Regardless, Wise's army had managed to burn about forty feet of the flooring but, however, did not damage the wires. General Cox called up the mechanics and engineers of the 11th Ohio, the same men who had built the bridge over the Poca River earlier, and they hurriedly gathered nearby barges in order to construct a crossing for the army.

That night a detachment of men under Maj. Jonathan D. Hines boarded the steamer *Economy* and went six miles above Charleston to Malden to search for the foundry that had cast the rebel cannon but returned to camp empty-handed although a cannon that had been disabled in the battle at Scary was found in a wagon shop fully repaired and ready for use. It was quickly placed with the Federal artillery. In general, the Federal entrance into Charleston was calm and without incident with the residents, for the most part, receptive to them.[33]

On the 26th Cox was ready to resume his advance to Gauley Bridge, not yet having received the dispatches from Gen. William Starke Rosecrans who had replaced McClellan when he had been called to Washington to command all Federal forces in the east. At 10 A.M. the steamer *Eunice* arrived with Col. James V. Guthrie and the remainder of the 1st Kentucky, and by noon the army was on the march, camping that night eleven miles above Charleston, "in a lovely nook between spurs of the hills."[34] News apparently traveled slowly. From Parkersburg Arthur I. Boreman wrote Francis H. Pierpont expressing his concern at Wise's presence in the valley, unaware that Cox already had him on the run.[35] Although General Wise had threatened to throw numerous obstacles in the face of the invading Federal army the most he managed was a few felled trees, some brisk skirmishing with Cox's advance unit, and the destruction of bridges. At the time, as well as through the years, Wise has been harshly criticized for not taking advantage of the rugged terrain to ambush Cox, but to do so would only increase the possibility of having his army cut off in the rear by Rosecrans. It was imperative he get out of the Kanawha Valley quickly and into the high mountain ranges of Gauley and Sewell. Wise did not have to be an experienced military man to see that he was about to get caught in a deadly trap. In retrospect, this was probably the most intelligent move he made while in command in the valley. And as for Cox, his biggest problem between Charleston and Gauley Bridge was his own army rather than Wise. During the course of the march he had to deal with some insubordinate officers and some haughty newspaper correspondents, one being William Swinton who later became a noted historical writer. But these people were dealt with accordingly by Cox and on the 29th the Federal army marched into Gauley Bridge unopposed. The march could go no further though as the rebels had destroyed the bridge over Gauley River and as the river was very swift and high it would take an extended amount of time for the 11th Ohio to constuct a new bridge. However, all was not a loss. A small part of the bridge had escaped the fire and on it the Federals found "a large number of old regulation muskets, made in 1802, which the state of Virginia had preserved for emergencies like this. The bayonets were about two feet in length. There were also accoutrements and supplies...."[36]

For all practical purposes the war in the Kanawha Valley proper in 1861 ended with the occupation of Gauley Bridge by Gen. Cox. While the Federal forces would be threatened a number of times at Gauley, most

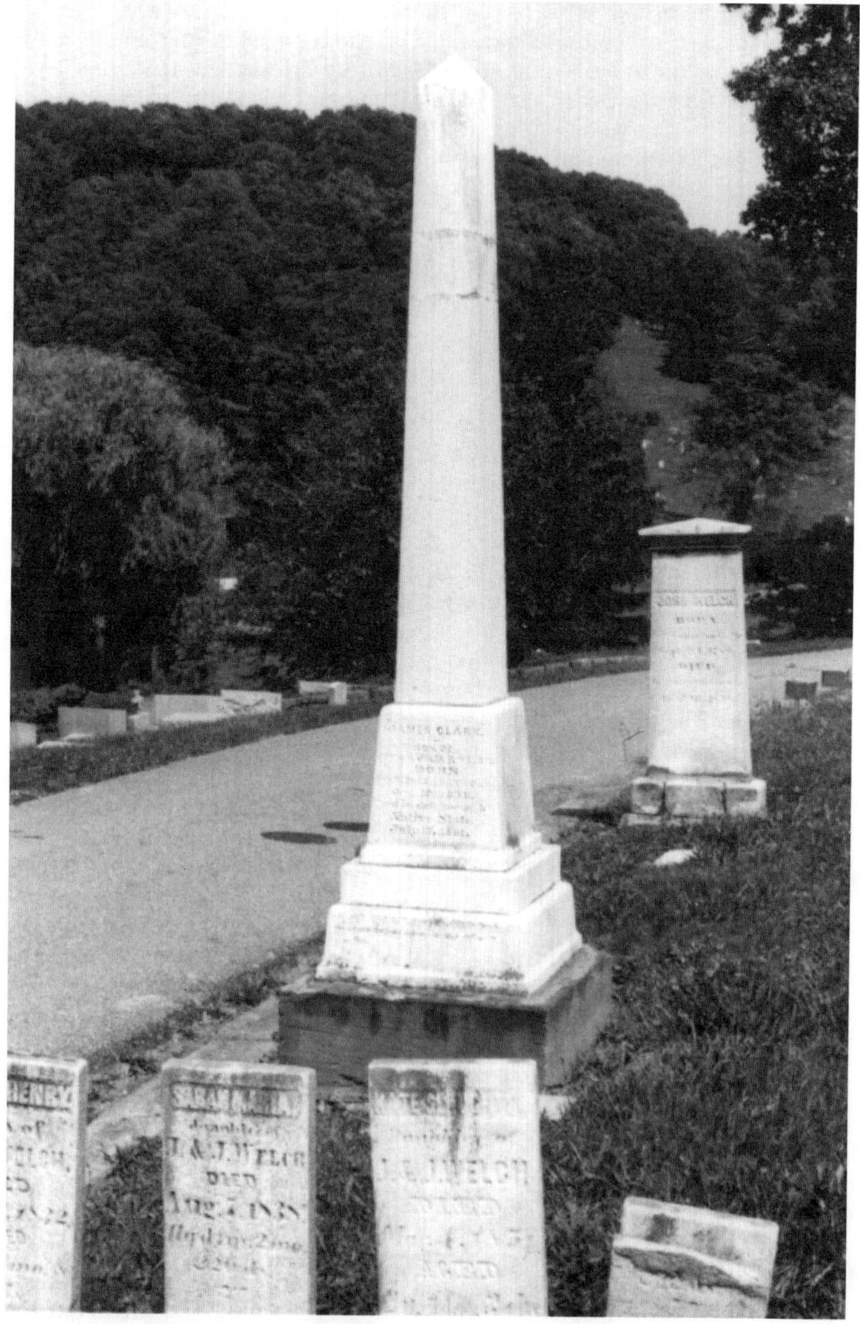

GRAVE OF LIEUTENANT JAMES C. WELCH

Inscription reads "Died in defense of his native state, July 17, 1861," Spring Hill Cemetery, Charleston. — Courtesy: Gary Bays

notably by Gen. John Floyd on Cotton Hill, there would be no fighting of note along the banks of the Kanawha River for the remainder of the year. Yet the war was far from over, and hostile activity would return to the valley in 1862, involving many of the soldiers who had served on either side in the Kanawha campaign and then going on to participate in the many larger and more historic engagements of the war.

For now, though, one had already fallen—young Lt. James C. Welch. His dreams and future shattered, his life ended—for a losing cause. Yet upon closer examination maybe his was a better fate than for many who survived the conflict. When he died there were no certain victors in the war; it was much too early to predict such a thing. But by 1865 the end of the Confederacy was obvious. Perhaps Welch actually died a winner while many of his comrades survived as losers.

And Welch was far from being the only Scary participant who failed to survive the war. His commanding officer, George S. Patton, who gradually rose in rank as predicted, was wounded a second time at Giles Court House (Pearisburg, Virginia), and finally mortally wounded while astride his horse at the third battle of Winchester, Virginia, September 19, 1864. A tragic end to a gallant officer who was under consideration for promotion to Brigadier General at the time of his death.

Albert Gallatin Jenkins rose to the rank of Brigadier General of the 8th Virginia Cavalry, was wounded at Gettysburg, and mortally wounded at the battle of Cloyd's Mountain, Virginia on May 9, 1864. Buried near the battlefield, he was later removed to Greenbottom and finally laid to rest at Spring Hill Cemetery, Huntington, West Virginia.

Capt. Obidiah Jennings Wise of the Richmond Light Infantry Blues fell mortally wounded while bravely leading his men in the battle of Roanoke Island fought on February 7 and 8, 1862. Capt. Robert Augustus ('Gus') Bailey of the Fayetteville Rifles was mortally wounded at the battle of Droop Mountain, West Virginia, November 6, 1863 and is buried near the old Stone Church at Lewisburg. Kanawha Rifleman 3rd Lt. Alanson Arnold, killed at the battle of Cold Harbor, and Lt. Gay Carr of the same outfit lost at the battle of Dry Creek (White Sulphur Springs). These were just a few of the (West) Virginians never to return.

And as the death of Pvt. Elijah Beeman at the battle of South Mountain, Maryland in 1862 proved, neither army would return with a full roster. As earlier noted, his commanding officer at Scary, Col. John Lowe, the scapegoat of the whole Scary affair, redeemed himself as he fell in action while leading a charge at the battle of Carnifex Ferry only a couple of months after the Scary incident.

Yet there was a bright side. Many of the soldiers involved in the Kanawha campaign distinguished themselves both during and after the war. Gen. Henry A. Wise became prominent in the defenses of Petersburg and was noted for his bravery. Although Col. Christopher Q. Tompkins became disgusted with Confederate military affairs and resigned early in the war, John McCausland became a brilliant Confederate General, infamous for his burning of Chambersburg, Pa. After the war he eventually returned to the Kanawha Valley and became one of its most prosperous farmers, living to a ripe old age.

On the Federal side, Gen. Jacob D. Cox rose above McClellan's remarks and became one of the North's most highly respected military leaders, prominent in the Atlanta campaign, becoming governor of Ohio in the years after the war. Although Col. Jesse S. Norton resigned from the army in 1862, and Col. Charles DeVilliers was "booted out" of the army, such men as Lt. Col. George Neff and Lt. Col. Carr B. White became Brevet Brigadier Generals.

Despite whatever fortunes or misfortunes befell these survivors of America's greatest crisis, little would any of them ever forget their early war experiences in what Maj. Jed. Hotchkiss, Confederate map maker, would later refer to as "The First Kanawha Valley Campaign, April to July, 1861."[37]

THE OLD SOLDIER

The old Confederate soldier, John McCausland, as a prosperous farmer in the postwar period, is shown here with his daughter Charlotte. — Courtesy: Mike Price of South Hills Antiques

THE BATTLE OF SCARY CREEK

ADDITIONS AND REVISIONS TO THE ORIGINAL TEXT

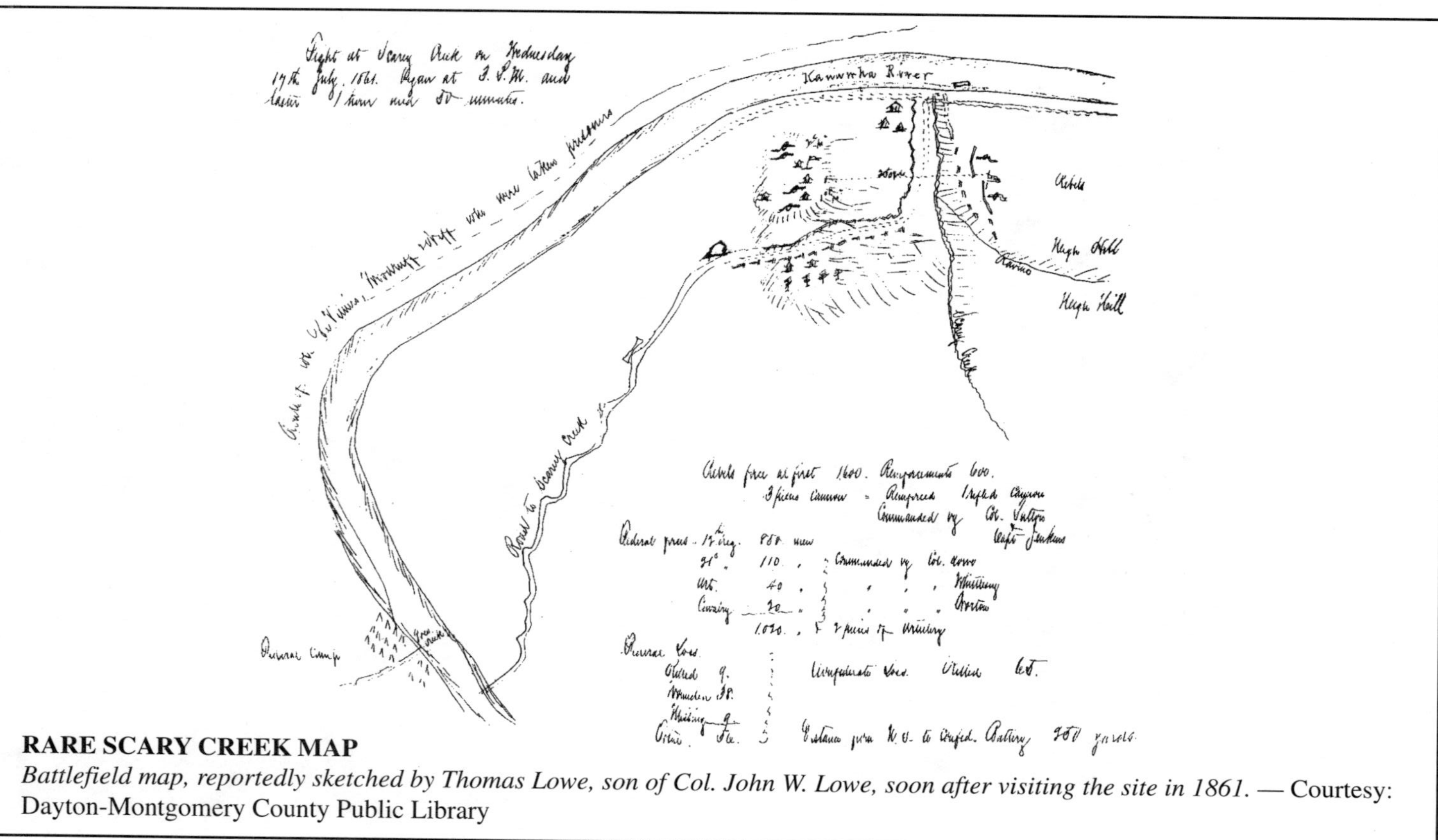

RARE SCARY CREEK MAP

Battlefield map, reportedly sketched by Thomas Lowe, son of Col. John W. Lowe, soon after visiting the site in 1861. — Courtesy: Dayton-Montgomery County Public Library

FOREWORD TO REVISED EDITION

When *The Battle of Scary Creek* was first published in 1982 there were very few contemporary works in print relative to the Civil War in West Virginia. In fact, a pictorial history by Stan Cohen, and two works by Jack Zinn on Rich and Cheat mountains, were about all that existed beyond older works by such noted historians as Boyd Stutler, George Moore, Roy Bird Cook, and a few others. Aware of this huge gap in historical research, it became my largest and sincerest hope that my Scary Creek book would inspire others to pursue different areas of the West Virginia campaigns and to correct and add to previous information and works, including my own. My wish certainly came true as many other fine studies have since evolved by such outstanding authors as Tim McKinney, Joe Geiger, Jr., Michael Pauley, Dave Phillips, William D. Wintz, Fritz Haselberger, Jack Dickinson and a host of others. Their contributions to the West Virginia campaigns are invaluable.

Due to this interest in the Scary Creek book, it quickly sold out and has been out of print for over fifteen years. As a result it has become heavily sought after as a collector's item and I continue to receive numerous requests for copies even today, although I have written four other highly successful books on the Civil War in West Virginia since its original publication. Because of this strong demand I finally felt the time was right to reprint the book for the first time, but I only agreed to this on two conditions, the first being that the original text would be kept as intact as possible, and secondly, that a new section would be added with new material uncovered on the battle since the original publication. Those additional sources do not change anything in the original text, and are presented in a new section in their original form so the reader can interpret them and add them in. Some of the material, particularly newspaper accounts, are highly biased and inaccurate and must be taken with the traditional grain of salt, but the basic information is there for consumption. Grammar and spelling in some of the original documents is incorrect but has been retained in its original form, illegible portions have been noted. Also included are additions to the original casualty lists as well as assorted other materials.

Not only has the Scary Creek book become so influential to other authors and readers but it has spurred interest in the actual battle site. On the opposite page of the original title page I included a photo of the then existing state historical highway marker of the site, which included incorrect information. This situation, which bothered me, drew the attention of a number of area Civil War buffs and historians including Nobel Wyatt of the Kanawha Valley Civil War Roundtable, Robert Skinner, Steve Wyatt, and Joe Ferrell, who graciously took on the project of correcting this error, and on July 17, 1988, a new sign was unveiled with many area notables in attendance. Additionally, on July 17, 1995, the Charleston, West Virginia Post Office and the Kanawha Valley Civil War Roundtable celebrated the 134th anniversary of the battle, which included a special one day postal cancellation and an exclusive cachet envelope. During 1996 the new state historical marker, ravaged by salt placed on the Scary Creek bridge and road during winter, was refinished by Roy Honaker and family.

Unfortunately, what little was left of the original battle site has not fared so well, and has continued to suffer from commercial development. Simms Hill has been cleared and turned into a housing development, St. John's of the Valley Episcopal Church was destroyed, and a number of new houses and business structures have been built on the grounds.

I am so honored and pleased that *The Battle of Scary Creek*, despite some minor typos and flaws in the original text, has become such an influential work and I hope readers will enjoy this new revised and expanded collector's edition.

[*Special thanks to Tim McKinney, Fayetteville, WV, and the Fayette County Historical Society for use of the Dickinson and Huse Family Papers; William D. Wintz, St. Albans, WV for use of the Molly Hansford material; Nancy R. Horlacher, Special Collections Librarian, Dayton-Montgomery County Public Library for use of material in the Colonel John W. Lowe papers; Richard Marker of South Charleston, WV for use of his computer; Joan Marker of South Charleston, WV for technical and computer assistance; and all the others who contributed new material.*]

Terry Lowry
1998

OPERATIONS PRIOR TO THE BATTLE OF SCARY CREEK

Letter of Harlow Huse, Kanawha Rangers (originally Co. K [1st], 22nd Virginia Infantry, then Co. I, 8th Virginia Cavalry), written on June 6th, 1861 from the rebel camp at Coals Mouth Va. (W. Va.) —Camp Tompkins

I thought i would drop you a few lines this morning we are all here 3 company all got down safe we will be stationed two miles below elk in a few days we are quartered in a steam mill now i think there is but little danger from the troops on the Border of Ohio Being with drawn further Back all here seem to Be alive to there duty i am acting as quartermaster for our company i am very well give your selves no uneasyness about me i will let you no when there is any thing wrong if ther is any thing wrong with you all i would like to hear it This is not much of a place for writing we had prayer last night some preachers are with us when i get a Better opportunity i will write again

Yours H Huse

Letter written by Harlow Huse from Camp Tompkins, Coals Mouth Va. (W.Va.) June 25th, 1861

Mr. James Montgomery and Wife i Rcd your letters and present By george the other day i am enjoying good health we are getting along verry well now we have variouse reports from down the River Just the otherday there was 16 steam Boats loaded with soldiers landed at the point to march up this River But as it happened there was need up at Graffton for them so the last one went up the Boats have gone down it is supposed for more troops there will be no fight with us unless Wise comes on as expected and goes down to the point to Blockade the River if that is done we will have hot fighting sure i understand Ben Linquois is at Charlestown with 115 men there is over 500 hundred men in this camp at this time i dont know how many above this our company drills twice and go out on dress parade every day we can march with any of them there are some men at the head of affairs that have been trying to improve on this company in diferent ways But our men have got the pluck to assert their rights and fight for them in any way that could be called for we have some oficers in our company that will not do certain Jack Miller that used to be about Raleigh is here as a lieutenant in a company from Waine County He got drunk the other night and was shooting his gun about the camp He was promtly put in the guard house last night John Smith was in the Boys have to walk verry straight if the boys at home are drafted send them word to stay at home they are not compelled to come this is no place for a weekly person it is no uncommon thing to see men drop off there feet as that man did at your House in Ranks i have been present at all the drills have not been sick a minute

H Huse

Letter from Harlow Huse's niece where she forwarded his letter to her parents on July 2, 1861

Dear Pa & Ma

I thought I would send you Harlow's letter We got it today. I was up to see Thomas last Sunday I took him a pie some seet cakes and a plug of tobacco. He came down to Billy Riggs to meet us.

He seemed in good spirits he does not like joining Wises Legond he and Burt Huddlesston are down on C. Bailey for ever I think Pa you and Uncle Harlow ought to try and get him out of Wises Legond he voted against it but the majority ruled Tom is not very stout and he could not stand to be draged about as Wises men are.

We are all well I do not know when I will be up
you must all come down soon love to the children and all the family

Your Daughter
BTR Montgomery

Letter of L.B. Montgomery, Kanawha Rangers (originally Co. K [1st], 22nd Virginia Infantry, then Co. I, 8th Virginia Cavalry), written on July 14th, 1861—Camp Two Mile

Dear Father

I thought that I would write you a few lines this morning by Stephen Rigg we arrived here Monday about 5 Oclock and are all well except a few that have the measles we are all verry well satisfied here we have plenty to eat we were aroused at 11 Oclock last night to prepare for a Fight and we are expecting to be called every minute it is reported here that there are five thousand northern Troops between here and the Ohio River the men here are anxious to meet the invaders it is useless to write to me unless you see some one that belongs to our company our company has increased to 90 men I saw Harlow last Tuesday here he had ben over to Ripley there is between 3 & 6 Thousand Soldiers on Kanawha tell them all howdy for me good bye

L.B. Montgomery

Letter written by Harlow Huse from Camp Tompkins, Coals Mouth Va. (W.Va.) July 17th, 1861

Dear Parents Having a few idle moments and thinking you would like to hear from me i will drop you a few lines i am still in good health Sunday morning 3 companys of us went down to Scary Creek below this place 3 miles we fixed round alittle expecting an attack of course from the enemy that was above Winfield we got two cannon ready and about 2 o'clock they made there appearence and halted just as they stopped our cannons fired 3 shots at them they wheeled and run beautifully only one man killed several more wounded none of our men hurt at all They did not come on us anymore they have 3 steamboats at the mouth of Poky The Valley Rangers a cavalry company from Rockingham county down at Poky killed 18 of them yesterday and only lost two horses the militia have been whipping them below in some places Capt. Jenkins with his cavalry and the militia whiped them at Barboursville very decently leaving 65 new graves over there 2000 of them have been on the Old Valley Road Some yesterday they crossed over to the river this morning they took fifteen thousand pounds of bacon from old bolin do not be uneasy about Tom because he is in Wises Legion he will only have to serve twelve months as the balance of us volunteers if not sooner discharged he is in a healthy place and will be well cared for in everyway a great many of the boys wishes they were in Wises Legion i would for myself as soon be there as any other place several of our company are in the hospital at Charleston Bob Mosely amoung the balance tell Jim to grind all he can save all he can take care of his hogs and not allow the news to interfere with any of youre business you will not get the truth often tell Warren to work his wile mow an cradle save all the cow feed he can if you need him some John Rodes would help you harvest and put a credit on his note i have make Sam Huddleston pay you what he owes me and hire some work with that trade some of my hogs to work tell uncle i have never written to him but it was not because i had forgotten him or any of his family but remember me to them all and every one of the family

Your son, Harlow Huse

Letter of Hudson Meriweather Dickinson, Kanawha Rangers (originally Co. K [1st], 22nd Virginia Infantry, then Co. I, 8th Virginia Cavalry), written on June 1861 from the rebel camp at Coals Mouth Va. (W. Va.) —Camp Tompkins

My Dear Father

I am safely housed in camp at Coals Mouth Va. Cpt. Lewis company received further orders at Charleston. Our first commands were to march to Buffalo When we reached Charleston in the evening of our first days march we were over taken by Col. Tompkins and commanded to rendez-vous at coal, where we are at this time. We have a delightful place to camp—we are quartered in a very large brick building of Wm.Tompkins—our duty is plain & substantial. Something as to the conduct of my company will relieve you no doubt, rest assured there is no drinking here. Since my arrival at this point I have seen no one intoxicated.

I have often heard it said that a soldiers life is a constant scene of [*illegible*]iation. If all other camps are alike ours it is a mistake. I promised mother to write to her touching this point. The evening we arrived at coal was one well calculated to cheer a soldier. The Kanawha sharpshooters reached here and spent the night with us. They were in camp at Buffalo together with the Kanawha Riflemen (under Cpt. Patton). The Boone Rangers were also here. Today the Cabell & Mason Rangers arrived under command (Capt. Jenkins—late Congressman.) The Sharpshooters the Boone Rangers the Border Rangers together with all other companies in Kanawha Valley are in camp at two mile except the Ka Rangers at Coal <u>No</u> troops quartered at Buffalo anymore

It is too close to the enemy—if we were all quartered at Buffalo it would not give us no time to concentrate our forces from above; if we were attacked. The policy of our encamping above is to be where we can concentrate on short notice to be ready to meet the enemy should they attempt to cross the Ohio at the point.
I was out on a scouting expedition yesterday—Some 6 in Company—we went as far as Winfield. The Federal troops came to the point as we heard, but were advised by some Union men near there to stay on the other side—Hence they marched up the Ohio on the Ohio side to Marietta, farther than that I have not heard—There are some 800 Federal troops in Parkersburg (So report Says)

All foot companies together with 2 Cavalry companies (One from Cabell & Mason—the other at Hurricane Bridge) are quartered two miles below Charleston. The mouth of Coal & above to Charleston is the present encampment—. No telling how long we may remain here—My health is very good—save a bad cold—which is much better—Dont feel at all uneasy about my health, Comfort & etc. to live & die in defense of my country. My rights & my interest is the height of my ambition. Do not think me at all dictatoral—but my advice to you my dear father—is to remain at home until some further developments are disclosed. Do not leave home yet unless there is a great immergency & that will be made fully known to you—

Ever your devoted Son
HM Dickinson

[*Written along the letter's edge is*:] Where ever we go our company is said to be the best in the service. P.S. Direct your letters to Coals Mouth care of Cpt. Lewis & all other letters that may come to me. —Hand my letter to sister Ella & Anne, I have written it on the floor so it will not be very well done.

Letter written by H.M. Dickinson from Camp Tompkins, Coals Mouth Va. (W.Va.)
June 5th, 1861

My dear Sister,

I wrote to father a few days ago but since the mails are so irregular, I thought perhaps he might not get it. So I will write you a short letter agreeable to promise—Coals Mouth is quite a military looking place—there are a number of companies here at this time, & others arriving daily We are expecting several companies tomorrow. We have a beautiful place to camp—our fare is rough but substantial—bread bacon and coffee is our principle diet sometimes—The farmers around here send in something better—but very seldom—My health is very good at this time. We have fine music every day—Cpt. Pattons company has a band. Our officers are very strict. We have to come up to the scribe Military rule is very rigid, & unless adhered to the institution is rendered worthless.

Mr. Graves the circuit rider preached in the camp for the soldiers last Sunday. All is quiet about Point Pleasent now. I think the Federal troops will hold off for awhile. This note I have written in a great hurry I would write more but for want of time. Please write to me soon my best love to all—

Youre devoted brother
HM Dickinson Jr.

P.S.
Direct youre letters to Coals Mouth Va.

WHEELING INTELLIGENCER
July 19, 1861

THE KANAWHA EXPEDITION

The Passage up the Kanawha—Concentration of Gen. Cox's Brigade—Skirmish with Cavalry—Three Companies of the Twenty-first Ohio Surrounded—Relief Dispatched—The Relief Fired on from an Ambuscade—One Killed and Several Wounded—Hot Times Ahead.

Red House, Virginia

31 Miles up the Kanawha, July 16

The morning of the 14th opened with a heavy fog over the river. Colonel Guthrie, with the land forces, comprised of Companies A, Capt. [*Joseph J.*] Wheeler; F, Capt. [*Jesse J.*] Stappleton [*Stapleton*]; C, Capt. Coninet; D, Capt. [*David Y.*] Johns; and I, Capt. [*Thomas*] Cox [*Jr.*], took up his line of march for Ripley at five o'clock, with the baggage wagons all in line. The "boys" stepped off with a quick and elastic step, highly pleased with changing the monotony of camp life for more active service, and with the hope of soon meeting a foe worthy of their steel.

Those on board of the boat under command of Lieutenant Colonel [*David A.*] Enyart and Major [*Bart G.*] Leiper are companies H, Captain [*Frank*] Cahill; E, Captain [*Seth J.*] Simmons; K, Captain [*John*] Becker; G, Captain [*James W.*] Mitchell, and B, Captain [*Alva R.*] Madlock [*Haddock*]. It was not until seven o'clock that the fog cleared away sufficient for the boat to proceed up the river. Having now had some opportunity to witness the movements of the First Kentucky Regiment, I must acknowledge my surprise in finding them so perfect in their drill and other exercises. The companies all move with the precision of veterans, and in the regimental drill they make a most magnificent appearance. In their evolutions they move with rapidity, and in perfect order. They are a splendid body of men, and only ask to be shown the foe, to prove their worthiness of being pronounced soldiers in the cause for which they have so gloriously shouldered their muskets and taken up their line of march to support. The Rev. J.F. Wright, Chaplain of the First Kentucky, joined the regiment this morning. He had been detained at Guyandotte with the Second.

Brother Wright is full of martial ardor, and feels anxious to have the "ball" opened. We passed the town of Buffalo at half past nine o'clock. Buffalo is a neat little town on the left bank of the river as you ascend. In times of peace it contains about five hundred inhabitants, but in this place of late, has been a rebel rendezvous, it had been partly deserted, all the Union men having been driven from here; but they are now returning, as the Federal troops advance. As soon as we passed this place, Capt. Cahill formed his company on each side of the hurricane deck of the boat, ready to answer any little incivilities which the rebels might see proper to extend to us, by bullets or otherwise, from the shore. They, however, considered discretion the better part of valor, and made themselves invisible in those parts. We arrived at Red House, nine miles above Buffalo, at meridian, and reported to Gen. Cox. At this point the "Wise-acres," some time since, sunk flatboats, loaded with rocks in the river, to obstruct the channel, but their efforts were not as successful as they had wished, the boats all having succeeded in passing these obstructions without difficulty. At this point is situated the town of Winfield, the county seat of Putnam; it contains about 130 inhabitants.

One mile above Red House we found encamped the following troops: Twelfth and Twenty-first Ohio, and four companies of the Eleventh Ohio. They are encamped in the bottom, surrounded with hills. The Eleventh Ohio has two pieces of rifled cannon planted on the heights, completely commanding the position. Scouts have been sent out in all directions, and picket guards are extended upon the heights around.

There is quite a stir among the troops just at present; some employed in moving camp kettles, some in gathering fire-wood, and others in building fires, preparatory to preparing their rations for the morrow—Sheep meat bears a very conspicuous part in the contributions for the festive hoard. The "boys" hugely enjoy the relish of this Secession mutton, which was intended for the greasing of other chaps.

Gen. Cox received a dispatch this evening stating that Gen. McClellan had engaged the rebels at a point called Rich Mountain and gained a glorious victory, and capturing many prisoners. You, of course, are correctly informed of his movements.

Whether true or not, this news has its effect upon our boys here. They are all in a perfect fever of excitement, and anxiously looking for a brush with the rebels in this section. We have received information here of the rebels having burned the bridge at Pocatalico, seven miles above here, and it is supposed they intend to make a stand at that point or the mouth of Coal river, eight miles above the former place. The rebels are reported as being entrenched at the mouth of Coal River, defended by batteries of artillery, and the bridge well protected. Should they not be able to hold the bridge, they will let it down, as it is a draw-bridge. Our men are afraid, however, that they will not keep their position long enough to give them a glimpse of their countenances. The column will all move from this point tomorrow morning at daylight.

The river fleet which is comprised of four steamboats—the Economy, Mary Cook, Marmora, and Silver Lake—will proceed on up the river with a portion of the troops, and the baggage and stores. This morning a company of rebel horsemen was seen across the river, just below Red House. A company of the Twelfth Ohio crossed in pursuit, when the rebels wheeled and ran. The Twelfth fired upon them, killing one of their number and his horse.

7 o'clock P.M.—A scout had this moment arrived in camp, and reports the rebels on a knoll in position at Scarey Creek, 800 strong, with two pieces artillery, seven miles above here, and that Colonel Norton, with three companies of the Twenty-first Ohio is also on a knoll, three miles this side of them.

7+ o'clock—Another scout has just arrived, stating that the rebels are marching on Colonel Norton, with the intention of surrounding him. One discharge of artillery, the signal to strike the tents, has just sounded. Tents have been struck, armor buckled on, and the lines formed in marching order.

The 21st Ohio has landed on the right river bank and taken the line of march toward the enemy. The 2nd Kentucky has also crossed the river and are on their line of march. I should have gone on the march with them, but I do not expect any fighting until morning when the boats will be there, and your correspondent will be among them taking notes. The boys started in great glee at the prospect before them. Capt. Cahill got up out of a sick bed to march at the head of his column. I was sorry to see him leave in his weak condition. All the boys on the sick list shouldered their muskets and formed in the column, determined to see the fun and be in at the "killing," not one man would stay behind.

11 o'clock at Night, Sunday, 14th—The column had not been moving more than twenty minutes before we heard rapid firing of musketry. Wishing to ascertain the cause, I started up to where the firing was heard. Proceeding a short distance, we found the dead and wounded in the road. They were all taken on board the steamer, Economy, and the wounded were properly cared for by Dr. White, of the 1st Kentucky. Your correspondent made himself useful in assisting the doctor in his attention to the wounded. The cause of the firing, as near as I can ascertain at present, was from the column being fired upon by some stragglers in a wheat field on the road. The following is a list of the killed and wounded.

I must close this. In my next I will give you all the particulars. All the troops from this point—3,000 strong—are moving this morning to the seat of the troubles.—You may expect stirring events in the next.

Yours,
C.W.B.

THE BATTLE OF BARBOURSVILLE (MUD RIVER)

[In the original text the battle of Barboursville was incorrectly placed on July 14th 1861 due to a misprint in the original dispatch concerning the battle, when in fact, it actually took place on July 13th 1861]

OFFICIAL REPORT OF THE BATTLE OF BARBOURSVILLE (MUD RIVER)

[From the Jacob D. Cox Papers, Oberlin College, Oberlin, Ohio]

Head Quarters, Camp Woodruff
July 14, 1861

Col. W.S. Woodruff

Sir, In compliance with your orders I left Camp Crittenden on the morning of the 13th inst. with the following companies. Co.'s A, B, D, F, and K, three hundred and sixteen (316) men and proceeded in accordance with your orders to take possession of Barboursville. I found the enemy in force said to be six hundred and ten (610) men, stationed upon a ridge 100 feet in height about 100 yards wide, all sides being almost inapproachable by a bluff bank, covered by and with trees, bushes and stones protecting the road for about 3/4 of a mile. At the base of the ridge a bridge crossing the Mud river the floor of which had been removed. I was obliged to cross on the "string pieces."

We were exposed to a galling fire for the space of about half a mile. I saw there was no means by which I could obtain possession of the place except by storming at the point of the bayonet. I therefore ordered the charge to be made. Company K being on the right. But in consequence of the refusal or neglect of the officers in command of Co. K to make the charge I ordered Co. A to take the right and charge which they did in a most gallant manner. I desire to make particular mention of Lieut. Wm. R. McChesney of Co. H who acted in the most brave and gallant manner, also of Capt. A.J.M. Brown [*Alfred J.M. Brown*] of Co. A, Capt. Warner Spencer [*Co. D*], Capt. [*John R.*] Hurd [*Co. F*] and Capt. Geo. Austin of Co. B. After scaling the heights the batallion rallied and formed in line on the summit, where we flaunted our flag the day being won by us. I also desire to make mention of the gallant conduct of Serg't Major [*Oscar*] Mitchell, Serg't [*Charles A.?*] Smith of Co. A and Serg't Kuhn of Co. K.

Hereon I attach the list of killed and wounded. [*no list found*]

Yours respectfully

Geo. W. Neff Lt. Col. 2d Ky. Regt.

[*For more details on the Barboursville battle refer to* Civil War in Cabell County,

West Virginia 1861-1865 *by Joe Geiger, Jr., (Charleston, West Virginia: Pictorial Histories Publishing Co., 1991)*]

THE IRONTON REGISTER
July 18, 1861

MILITARY OPERATIONS IN THE GUYANDOTTE REGION

It is well known that Guyandotte, Va., has been the meanest "Secession Hole" on the Ohio river, that the Secessionists there, under the lead of A.G. Jenkins, late member of Congress from that district, have for a long time been carrying things with a high hand, committing diverse outrages on Union men in that vicinity, and driving from their houses many old and respectable citizens of that portion of Virginia for no other crime than that they did not wish to destroy their Government. Appeal has often been made by Virginians themselves to the U.S. and Ohio military authorities for the protection of Union men in that quarter, but to no purpose.

CAPTURE OF THE STEAMER FANNY MCBURNIE

On Thursday morning of last week, Jenkins with a guerrilla squad of forty men concealed in the bushes on the river bank, at Green Bottom, took the steamer Fannie McBurnie. Jenkins himself appeared alone and hailed the boat, which went in, there being no other thought but it was a man wishing to take passage. As the boat neared the shore, Jenkins whistled, and his men rushed down the bank, and took forcible possession, Jenkins swearing terribly at the Captain and Pilot for their slow movements, threatening them with instant death, his men having their guns drawn on them. Jenkins took from the boat a case of revolvers and other of swords, consigned to private parties, and had the passengers drawn up in line, and with an oath threatened them with summary treatment if they deceived them in the least as to their private arms, but he found only two valuable pistols, which he took, one from C.A. Haley, of Ironton, Mr. Hawley and Geo. Willard, of the Iron Bank, being passengers and old acquaintances of Jenkins who looked very badly, bloated, haggard, desperate, and in the examination never recognized Willard and Hawley, but after he was through remarked that he was "sorry to meet any of his old friends, but couldn't help it," told Mr. Hawley to call on H.S. Neal, his (former) agent in Ironton, and he would pay him for the pistol—a revolver worth $16; also he remarked that "*he was a ruined man*;" true enough! The boat was then permitted to pass.

THE 2D KENTUCKY TAKES GUYANDOTTE

The 1st and 2d Kentucky Regiments passed Ironton on boats for the Kanawha on Wednesday evening of last week; but advises of the alarming condition of things in the Guyandotte region caused a change, and the 2d Kentucky, Col. W.E. Woodruff, lay by for the night, and on Thursday morning, 11th, landed below Guyandotte, marched up at "double quick" and took quick possession of the town, the Secessionists remaining there generally making very hasty flight—Some straggling shots were fired, but no one killed. Col. Woodruff went into camp a mile back of town.

FIRST AT BARBOURSVILLE

On Friday afternoon. Mst. Noble, whom Col. Woodruff had taken from Burlington, as a scout, rode in the direction of Barboursville, the county seat of Cabell county, eight miles back of Guyandotte. The flying Secessionists from Guyandotte had reported horrid tales about Col. Woodruff's men, and a force of over six hundred had gathered at Barboursville, to resist the "invaders," under the notorious Jenkins, who was there with his cavalry company. Noble, before he was aware of it, was within their picket lines, was fired upon several times, just below Barboursville, escaped up a high point, lost his horse, concealed himself until after dark, when he returned to camp. Past midnight four companies, under Lieut. Col. Neff, left for Barboursville, to attack the rebels who had been discovered by Noble. They were the Woodward Guards, the company of Capt. J.R. Hurd, raised in this Iron Region, the German company, and company B. The enemy were in a singularly advantageous position, on a high and long point, a backbone ridge, with very steep banks, accessible at only one place with a wagon and that something like a third of a mile from the point, which is right at the bridge over Mud river. The four companies numbered 316 men, and reliable authority places the rebels at 615, including Jenkins' cavalry. When near the bridge our men were fired upon, one instantly killed, being shot in the neck, another mortally wounded. The men rushed into the bridge, which was covered; some twenty feet of the planks had been removed, but they pushed on over the stringers, and amid loud yells and the wildest whoops immediately charged up the high point, when the rebels, who were mostly armed with old fashioned rifles and shot guns, with few if any bayonets, took to their heels, and scattered in all directions, over the bottom the other side, and Jenkins' cavalry rushed in utter confusion through town, but formed about a mile distant and like cowards waved their Secession flag at the victors on the hill.

Our loss was one killed, thirteen wounded, two mortally, one of whom said to be Harper, a young man from Franklin Furnace, was shot under the left eye, and died the next morning. According to the best authority we could get at Barboursville, the next morning, the rebel loss was *eight* killed, and many wounded.

It is singular, from the nature of the ground, that one half of the Federal troops were not slaughtered; but the truth is, the men of the rebel force had no heart at all in their unjust cause, and the rapid and vigorous charge of the gleaming bayonets and the enthusiastic shouts of our men at once struck terror into them. Many of them threw away their coats and rifles, which were taken, together with a splendid sword belonging to an officer we heard called "Col. Mansfield," who was reported wounded.

IRONTON VOLUNTEERS TURN OUT

On Saturday forenoon the steamer Victor No. 2 went up to Guyandotte carrying some thirty of our citizens. Just before night the boat returned with the word that there had been a battle at Barboursville, with the first exaggerated report, giving a large number killed; that the Kentucky 2d was all at Barboursville, except one company at the camp with all the baggage, stores, etc. that there was extreme danger of an attack upon the town and camp that night and all the Ironton military was needed. In a very short time, the Zouaves, Capt. Savage; Guards, Capt. Johnston,

Grays, Capt. McFadden; Blues, Capt. Cronacher a company of Independents under Col. High; and a squad of Artillery, Capt. Frailey were on the boat, which left at about dark. A few came on at other points.

Disembarked and formed at Guyandotte 12, midnight and immediately the word was, that we were wanted to march to Barboursville that night with Capt. Ball's company of the Kentucky 2d, and the baggage of that regiment. The Blues remained in Guyandotte as guard and a few of the Independents. The rest of our battalion, 180 men, took up the line of march. Arriving at the camp, Capt. Ball called in his pickets, struck tents, and had the wagons with the baggage and stores soon in the line. We were told that one of his pickets had just been shot and wounded; that there were five shots; that we were in the enemy's country," with great danger that the train would be attacked; and, of course, many felt some would be killed, and doubtless to say thought, "it may be me." Arrived, however, all safely at Barboursville, at 5 o'clock in the morning, our boys generally standing the march finely; found Col. Woodruff encamped on the hill occupied by the rebels, the morning before, our Ironton squad with the brass 6-pounder, which went up last week, entrenched and guarding the entrance to the camp. We (that is, this writer) viewed the battlefield in astonishment, that the rebels should have fled from such a strong position; saw the blood-stains on the ground; visited the hospital, found two dead in it, laid out, 12 wounded men, one in a dying condition, shot through the body; many buildings in town vacant and open, occupants having fled; got a good breakfast from soldiers in camp—when, at 9 o'clock, Sunday, our volunteer column took up the line of march for home—arriving at 4 o'clock, P.M., having been to the "seat of war," had a steamboat ride of 45 miles, and a march of 16 miles, one meal, a few slept a little on floor of the boat, and twenty hours only out from Ironton. Of course, we can all now tell our *exploits* in the actual service of our country, to our children and our children's children!

We must say our column of troops behaved themselves in most exemplary manner, Judge Johnson being our Commander-in-Chief. And let us remark, that, under all the circumstances, we think the severe censures cast by many upon the German Blues for not going to Barboursville, uncalled for. We were sorry that they did not go, but there was no obligation whatever on their part to do so, and that they are nay more "cowards" than the rest of us, who did go, we do not believe.

MORE ABOUT THE BARBOURSVILLE AFFAIR

A Kentuckian writes us that a portion of the men at Barboursville, who assembled to resist the Ky. 2d, were really Union men maddened by "the *lies* of the Secessionists that the Federal troops at Guyandotte, were stripping women and children and whipping them in presence of their defenseless husbands and fathers, and committing other atrocities upon them." He states that one of the duped Union men, after the first fire, looked around and saw about 200 Secessionists running like cowards and Jenkins nowhere to be seen, when he, too, wheeled and made the first three-quarters of a mile in "a little less than no time," determined to give Jenkins the contents of his revolver, but he couldn't catch Jenkins. Many of the Secessionists laid down their arms, not to take them up again unless in defense of the "stars and stripes," swearing vengeance on Jenkins.

THE LATEST INFORMATION

We have from that quarter is that Col. Woodruff, Ky. 2d, had moved from Barboursville, to join Gen. Cox, who has the 11th, 12th and 21st Ohio. 1st and 2d Ky, three field pieces, and Capt. George's Cavalry, under his command and would undoubtedly route the rebels under Ex-Gov. Wise, from Charleston.

WHEELING INTELLIGENCER
July 18, 1861

The Fight at Barboursville, Cabell County Between the 2d Kentucky Regiment and the Command of Jenkins.
(From the Cincinnati Commercial of last night.)
Camp Woodruff, near Cabell C.H., Va.
July 14th, 1861

You have probably been advised of the great activity of the 2d Kentucky Regiment since its putting foot upon the soil of Virginia, an activity which has been attended with such fortunate results that waiting to starve them out begins to look like—fallacy—as it certainly is in Western Virginia. My last hurried letter left us in occupancy of the troublous town of Guyandotte. We remained there but a few hours, a number of companies moving out to Camp Crittenden, as it was christened, the same afternoon the town was captured.—Camp Crittenden was situated on the Charleston road, about two miles from Guyandotte, and was pitched on the wheat field of Col. Everett, now in the Secession army. His mansion adjoined the field, and his family was one of the few of that persuasion that did not flee when we landed.

Our position there was not a strong one, and much apprehension was felt the first night concerning an attack from the rebels encamped some six miles distant, at Cabell C.H. (or Barboursville, as the town is called.) Our men were aroused by the long roll half a dozen times before daylight, and formed in line of battle on the parade ground, and the pickets alarmed by stragglers through the adjoining wooded hills, fired their guns and withdrew to camp. No enemy appeared, however, and the next day our position was made comparatively secure, by the arrival of the balance of the regiment, which evacuated Guyandotte, leaving a small detachment to hold the place.

Once encamped, scouts and skirmishing parties were constantly sent out. Of all the small detachments of infantry that left camp to reconnoitre, not *one* returned, although we were also joined the same day by corresponding parties of cavalry mounted on secession nags left standing in stables, uncurried and unfed, or tumbling through neglected fields. The most scrupulous respect has, however, been evinced for the property of the Unionists, whilst they in turn cheerfully volunteer, both their chattels and their services, in our advance. Colonel Woodruff was, in the meanwhile, turning attention to the rebel camp at Barboursville; gleaning such information as he could from scouts and loyal residents. He found they were receiving reinforcements so rapidly, that a most vigorous action on his part would be necessary. He could learn nothing positive concerning their number, or the military strength of their position; but he planned an immediate attack. Accordingly, at mid night, on the night of the 12th, companies A, B, D, F, and K were aroused from their slumbers, and placed under the command of Lieut. Col. Neff, and, with one day's rations in their haversacks, they proceeded on their march—after a short but stirring address from Col. Woodruff. The column was conducted by a strong Union man, a resident of Barboursville, who had been driven thence some weeks since.

It was proposed to make the attack at early daylight, but the deep silence observed along the route, together with the halts to send forward scouting parties, deferred their coming into sight of the enemy until the sun was two hours high. When they *did* catch a first glance, if there had been any fear in their compositions, it would have overpowered them at once. The rebels were drawn up in line of battle on the brow of a high hill, apparently inaccessible on all sides, and commanding a view for two miles around of a magnificent level plain, with all its roads in full sight, until they dwindled into the distant forests.

Near the base of the hill wound the Guyandotte river, and within pistol shot of their position was the only bridge which spanned it from the side on which we were advancing. Our brave boys took but one glance and passed on.

As they neared the bridge, they discovered a large body of cavalry on the road which wound around the base of the hill on which the enemy was ranged, retreating and dividing in order to intercept our flight—a natural inference, but a matter of opinion nevertheless. The rebels very considerately reserved their fire until the head of our column had set foot upon the bridge, and then they fired a terrific volley, killing one man instantly, and wounding a number of others.

To escape this terrible shelving fire, our men were double quick into the covered bridge where the bullets pelted, pattered and whistled like a leaden hail storm. They rushed onward, however, until they halted with such a sudden shock, that it sent the whole column into disorder. The planks of the bridge had been removed on the opposite side, and the mule on which the guide was mounted had fallen through, and he barely escaped sharing its destruction, by clinging to the timbers.

The rebels, encouraged by our delay at the fearful impediment, broke into wild shouts and cheers. Fired by their assurances of Victory our boys could be restrained no longer; they answered with terrific yells, some ran to the pathholes of the bridge, and discharged their muskets at their foe, and Co. A; led by Capt. Brown, made a dash in single file across the bare stringers and rafters on the bridge, followed by Company D (Woodward Guards) and the remaining companies. As they emerged from the bridge, the rebels flanked and charged front from the mouth of the bridge, to the road which encircled the base of the hill, and sent another bitter volley at our men, which luckily was aimed too high, and did but little damage.—Our men by this time had all cleared the bridge, in total disorder, but blazing away with excitement, yelling and leaping like madmen. They turned suddenly up the side of the hill at a charge bayonets, and literally dragging themselves up by bushes and jutting turf. They cleared in a few moments, rushed at the enemy, who had, as they commenced the ascent, fired again with effect. It was their last volley. As the glistening bayonets reached the top of the hill, and met their wavering gaze, and those yells continued, which meant victory if there had been a thousand opposed. The enemy swayed for a moment, a leap was made from their flank and rear, and then the whole body scattered like sparks from a pin-wheel, down the rear of the hill, streaming in every direction in the fields below, at full speed, with white faces in a conflagration. Our men were too breathless for pursuit, but they cheered as only men who have conquered can cheer, and planted immediately the stars and stripes on the summit of the hill.

There was some firing at the retreating foe, and their commander, Col. Mansfield was hit and fell from his horse, but was immediately seized and carried off by his companions, as is supposed others were.—They left but one on the field, an old gray haired man, whom we are informed, was pressed into the service, as many of his companions had been. He was taken care of by our troops, but he died in the afternoon.

The victorious battalion, when the rebels had disappeared marched through the town with the banners flying and band playing airs which the inhabitants never hoped to hear again. The Woodward boys planted their flag on the flagpole of the Court House and seemed to regard as a coincidence, that precisely two months after it was presented it was streaming from a spire in one of the hot-beds of secession.

CINCINNATI, JULY 17

On Friday night a detachment of three companies of Colonel Woodruff's Second Kentucky regiment attacked six hundred rebels between Mud river and Barboursville on the Kanawha river, completely routing them. Ten or twelve rebels were killed and a number wounded. The Kentuckians had only one killed.

Gen. Cox's brigade was rapidly moving up the Kanawha.

INCIDENT AT RED HOUSE

[Refer to page 164 of the original text]

THE IRONTON REGISTER
July 25, 1861

In the unfortunate affair on Kanawha, Sunday night, 14th last, in which parties of the Kentucky 1st and Ohio 21st fired into each other, by mistake, two men were killed, one fatally wounded, and three slightly wounded. The man fatally wounded, who was shot through the body, and whose wound was dressed here at Ironton, Monday night, was Alex Mordecai, of Cincinnati; he died on the boat near

New Richmond. The killed were John Hogan [*Dugan*], of Cincinnati; and John J.W. Roberts [*Robins*], of *Union Landing*, in this county. He was a young man of less than 18, was raised by Thomas W. Means; he went to Camp Clay, and volunteered in company G, 1st Kentucky Regiment.

The man killed, of the Kentucky 2d, at the Barboursville Fight, 13th inst., was John Jordens; and Barney McAvey [*McEroy*] of Louisville, was the young man shot just below the left eye, who died on the next morning. Elihu Harper, whose name we mentioned last week of Franklin Furnace, was only slightly wounded.

PERRYSBURG JOURNAL
July 28, 1861

Another Great Bethel Affair.

Gen. Cox, on his march up the Kanawha, last week, encamped one night in the vicinity of the Red House, about 38 miles up that stream; and during the night occurred another Great Bethel affair, only on a smaller scale. It seems that a portion of the 1st Kentucky Regiment, with the General commanding, was called out shortly after dark (for what purpose is not stated) and while in line a gun was accidentally discharged, which led to the belief that they were surprised by the enemy. The wings of the line, which seem to have been crescent-shaped, immediately fired upon each other. Two men were instantly killed, both having been shot through the head, and several others wounded.—Among the wounded were two Wood county boys—William Stewart of New Westfield, and Morrison Lewis of Milton Center.

FEMALE SPY

GALLIPOLIS JOURNAL
August 1, 1861

A female was last week discovered in the First Kentucky Regiment dressed in male attire. She enlisted at Camp Clay under the name of John Thompson, and was about as efficient a "soger boy" as could be found in the Regiment. She is at present confined in our jail by order of Col. Guthrie, but for what reason we have not learned. We are told her appearance is rather masculine, and "trowserloons" become her remarkably well. She is not the only woman in this community that wears *britches*. Her age is about 20 years. If she wishes to serve her country in the capacity of a soldier, we say turn her loose— "or any other man."

GALLIPOLIS JOURNAL
August 8, 1861

The Female Spy—The female discovered in the ranks of the First Kentucky Regiment, who was arrested as a spy and confined in jail here, was taken in charge by the officers of the 21st Ohio Regiment, who left Gallipolis for Camp Chase on Sunday last with their command. She enlisted under the name of John Thompson, and if the Western Virginia correspondent of the Cincinnati Commercial is correct, she is certainly a dangerous character. He says:

A female spy has been discovered in the First Kentucky Regiment. She is from Ga., and enlisted at Cincinnati. She was detected by writing information in regard to the movements of our troops to the enemy. She is a member of the Knights of the Golden Circle, says she knew the punishment of a spy is death, and is ready for her fate. She is to be sent to Columbus

LETTER OF WILLIAM N. CURRY, 60TH VIRGINIA INFANTRY, WRITTEN THE NIGHT PRIOR TO THE BATTLE OF SCARY CREEK

Charleston Kanhaway Co. Va.
July 16th 1861

Dear Father and Mother

Your of 9th & 11th inst. came to hand last Sunday you must excuse me for not writing you sooner as I had to march from camp in an hour after receiving it. You may rest assured that it gave me much pleasure to record the receipt of your letter. Was glad to hear that you were all well. The friends also. We have gone down the river about 2+ miles below 2 mile bridge where we have a fortification thrown up. We have lain in our trenches 2 nights. Last night was a very disagreeable night for it rained a right heavy shower late in the camp. I was out as guard last night stood from 2 o'clock till daylight. I haven't had [*illegible*] but 4 four reliefs since I started. I don't regard standing guard an agreeable thing. We only have to stand 2 hours in a night probably only that once in a week or more.

I haven't been sick one hour since I left home. I feel stouter than when I left home. I believe that every one of the company have been sick except me. I have had the diarehea once or twice a little but not to absent me. I want you to send me the name of the medison you got while you was at [*illegible*] and send it to me. The enemy are at the mouth of Cole. We expect to fight them today. We are all ready for fight. Would like to try the yankees pluck once. One of the wild cats company met with a sad accident yesterday evening, while fixing up a shelter he cut his knee cap

nearly off. It will make him a cripple all his life. Was so sorry it happened I heard that the militia of greenbrier & monroe was ordered down here. If it is so I am sorry to hear of it. I think that we have force enough in the valley to stand against any force that will be sent against us. We have very exciting tours at present.
Some of our men complain very much of the hard times but I take it very easy knowing every thing will work out for the best—in the future my trust is in a kind provience he alone can bring me safely through this world of trouble. I wrote Anderson last Sunday morning a soldiers life is very far from being a normal one. I hear on the [*illegible*] ringing on every side of me it fairly made me shudder at first to hear the oaths that were vollied forth. You haven't no idea what a soldier has to go through I thought our company was wild enough but they are much more moralized than the other companies are. I expect to see the enemy today, a dispatch came just now that the enemy were within four miles of us. I feel just as calm as if I were going right down to my breakfast. I haven't been the least scared as yet. It seems to me that I am to be killed by the yankees

My prayer is that it will not be so. (that I will be killed by the Yankees). You must make yourselves easy about me. If I am [*illegible*] to see you again in this world. I hope to meet you in another where [*illegible*] and disappointment will be no more. Give grandfather [*next line illegible*]
-friends except the same for yourselves. Tell grandfather that he receives my warmest thanks for the money he sent me. Also tell him that I will write him a letter in a few days if I get back to the camp I am spared a man hasn't but one time to die. He will not die until that time comes up—it can when it will. Nothing more at present but will remain you most affectionate son.

Wm. N. Curry

James Curry
Rush A. Curry

P.S.—you asked me how long I expect to stay at our camp. I can't form the least idea of the time as we are subjected (?) to be called out at any moment.

You must excuse my hand writing as I have written this on my bible on my knee.

[*Original in the collection of Terry Lowry*]

ADDITIONAL PERSONAL ACCOUNTS OF THE BATTLE OF SCARY CREEK

PERRYSBURG JOURNAL
July 28, 1861

The Engagement at Scary Hill — Colonel Norton Wounded and taken Prisoner

The report which reached here on Saturday to the effect that Col. Norton had been wounded and taken prisoner in an engagement with the rebels at Scary Hill, about forty miles up the Kanawha, produced a profound sensation in this community. The particulars, as near as we can gather, are as follows: On Wednesday morning, the 17th inst., Gen. Cox had information of a supposed rebel battery near the mouth of Scary River, about three miles above Gen. Cox's encampment, and detailed Col. Lowe's 12th regiment, and two companies of the 21st regiment, under Col. Norton, the artillery and cavalry to reconnoiter the enemy's supposed position on the opposite side of the river. Afternoon heavy firing was heard from the direction which Col. Lowe's detachment had gone, and Colonels Woodruff, De Villiers and Neff, two captains and several lieutenants went up the northern side of the river to take a view of what was going on from a commanding position, and failing to return, or their whereabouts known up to twelve o'clock, Thursday, it is believed that they have been captured by the rebels and made prisoners of war. The firing was kept up briskly for fully an hour, when Colonel Lowe's ammunition gave out, and he dispatched a messenger to the camp for re-inforcements and for more powder, ball and cartridges; but before the assistance could reach him he was compelled to make a hasty retreat, leaving six to eight killed on the field, and carrying forty-seven wounded off. Our men, after firing forty rounds, crossed the creek and silenced the masked battery, but their ammunition giving out they were compelled to retire. One gun of the masked battery was afterwards remounted and opened fire on our men. The Union troops acquitted themselves nobly, and but for the unfortunate exhaustion of their ammunition, their victory would unquestionably have been complete.

Five privates were retreating with Col. Norton who was badly wounded, when the rebels closed upon them so nearly, that at Col. Norton's request they dropped him on the field, and caught up with their companies. Our troops succeeded in capturing five rebel prisoners, who stated that the rebel forces were under the command of O.J. Wise, and numbered 1800 men; but that during the engagement a regiment of Georgians arrived on a steamer from Charleston. The enemy had five pieces of cannon, while our troops had two 12 pound rifled guns. As our troops were retreating they met 8 companies of the 21st and the ammunition sent for but they were too late. The enemy was intrenched, and is represented to be well fortified. Col. Norton's regiment was composed of companies from the North-western part of the State—one from Huron county, two from Wood, two from Putnam, two from Hancock, and one each from Seneca, Ottawa and Defiance counties. Two companies only of the regiment were in the engagement, Capt. Allen's and Capt. Strong's.

Gen. Cox's Brigade consisted of the 2d Kentucky regiment, Col. Woodruff; five companies of the 1st Kentucky regiment, under Lieut. Col. Enyart; the 12th Ohio regiment, Col. Lowe; 11th Ohio regiment Col. De Villiers, and the 21st Ohio regiment, Col. Norton; Capt. Carter's company of the artillery, and a cavalry company from Ironton, which were encamped at Poca Tablequa, on the Kanawha river, about fifteen miles below Charleston, and Col. Guthrie, with five companies of the 1st Kentucky regiment, was at Ripley, Va.

Gen. Cox had not attacked the enemy up to noon on Thursday, 24 hours after the engagement. The wounded soldiers were placed on board the steamer *Economy*, which has been converted into a hospital, and every possible attention given to the wounded. The *Mary Cook*, Capt. Hugh Campbell, left the camp Thursday p.m., bringing Lieutenant Pomeroy who was wounded in the engagement, but he died while the steamer was below Gallipolis. His remains were forwarded to his friends.

A number of secessionists who had been taken prisoners by Col. Norton, and were detained at Point Pleasant, circulated a petition addressed to Colonel Tompkins, in charge of the enemy's forces at Scary Hill, begging him to release Col. Norton, who had shown them great kindness in their confinement, and also asking that the Ohio troops might be allowed to remove their dead under a flag of truce. No reply had been received when the boat left. It was ascertained, after the boat left the landing, that Col. Woodruff had returned. Gen. Cox was preparing to attack the rebels with his entire force on Thursday afternoon, and the probability is that the battle was fought on Friday.

P.S. Since the above was in type we learn that Col. Norton has been released, and is now at Gallipolis. He was wounded in the thigh, but not severely. He was well treated by the rebels, as were also others that fell into their hands. The dead were buried. No intimation of another battle.

THE FIGHT ON THE KANAWHA.

The steamer Dunleith, Capt. A.D. Wilson, arrived from Parkersburg yesterday bringing the latest intelligence from the Kanawha River. The reports being somewhat contradictory, we give the statements of both loyal and rebel authorities.

Capt. Hugh Campbell, of the Government transport steamer Mary Cook, who came passenger in the Dunleith, reports that a severe action took place on Thursday afternoon, between the rebels and the Federal troops under Col. Lowe, of the 12th Ohio regiment and seven companies of Col. Norton's regiment. Capt. Campbell did not learn any satisfactory details, but states that our troops exhausted all their ammunition, and retired, after severe loss, with their two field pieces. The Federal fleet was lying below Pocatella creek, and the action took place at "Scarey," some distance in the interior. It appears that our troops were sent out with orders to make a reconnaissance, but not to attack the enemy, who were in a strongly entrenched position, numbering 1500 strong—unless it appeared the position could be easily carried.

Capt. Campbell reported that Col. Norton was severely wounded while gallantly encouraging his men to charge, and he was left on the field and captured by the enemy.

The extent of our loss is not known, but we infer that it was quite serious. The enemy also suffered severely. Col. Lowe sent back during the action for ammunition, and Gen. Cox sent it forward with reinforcements, but our troops were met returning from the field. Lieut. Pomeroy, of Ottowa, O., was mortally wounded, and he was sent to this city on the steamer Dunleith, but he expired at Gallipolis.

One private in the cavalry company which forms part of Gen. Cox's brigade, was killed. Col. Woodruff and Lieut. Col. Neff, of the 2d Kentucky Regiment and Major De Villiers, of the 8th [*11th*] Ohio, were at the engagement as spectators, and when Captain Campbell left Pocatella creek twenty hours after the conflict, they had not returned. The inference is strong that they were taken prisoners, and we are afraid our troops met with a severe reverse. Capt. Campbell reports that they fought gallantly and did not retire until their ammunition was completely exhausted.

A REBEL'S STATEMENT.

Capt. W.O. Roseberry, who it will be remembered was arrested at Pt. Pleasant, Va., and taken to Columbus, Ohio, but subsequently released, being charged with sympathy with the rebels, was also among the passengers by the steamer Dunleith. The following is his version of the conflict:

On the 17th, Gen. Cox ordered the 12th Ohio, Col. Lowe, two companies of the 21st Ohio together with the Cleveland Artillery and Capt. Rogers' Cavalry company from Ironton, Ohio, to cross the Kanawha river at the mouth of Pokey Creek, twenty miles below Charleston, and reconnoiter the rebel camp two miles above, on the south side or right hand bank of the Kanawha, three miles below the mouth of Coal river, and to cannonade and draw them out in order to estimate their force, and, if easily captured to take their batteries, the enemy being fortified. When within three hundred yards of the battery, they were fired into by rebels under command of Col. Tompkins, from three to five pieces of artillery, when a general engagement ensued, lasting about two hours, when the rebels were reinforced, and the Federal troops compelled to retreat. Col. Norton, of the 21st Ohio, was wounded shot in the hip and taken prisoner; Capt. Allen killed-ball in the forehead, just between the eyes; Lieut. Pomeroy was shot through the hip. He died on the Dunleith, when the boat was near Gallipolis. The remains will be forwarded to his home in Ottowa, Putnam county, Ohio, today. Lieutenant Pomeroy and Captain Allen were in Company B [*should be Co. D*], 21st Ohio, Colonel Norton. During the engagement, Col. De Villiers, 11th Ohio Col. Woodruff, Lieut. Col. Neff, and several Captains, of the 2d Kentucky, mounted, rode up opposite the scene of action, and had not returned to their camp up to 12 M., on the 18th inst. The rebels were reported to be 1400 strong, previous to being reinforced. A flag of truce had been sent out by the federals asking the privilege of visiting the rebel camp to gather the dead and wounded. Petitions were also sent from Pt. Pleasant signed by Capt. Roseberry, and other prisoners, recently in charge of Capt. Norton, asking the privilege to bring the Colonel back, who was reputed wounded.

LIEUT. POMEROY.

Lieut. Pomeroy, of Co. B [*should be Co. D*], 21 Ohio Regiment who was mortally wounded in the battle, and brought on board of the steamer Dunleith, received every attention from the officers of the boat. He died as the boat was nearing Gallipolis.

STATEMENT OF AN EYE WITNESS.

A gentleman who was in the engagement and whose character and rank are sufficient guaranties of the correctness of his statement, gives the following version of the affair on Wednesday afternoon:

The 12th Ohio and parts of two companies of the 21st, started to capture a battery at the mouth of Scarey creek, about thirteen miles from Charleston. The battery was supposed to be supported by about 700 men. When we reached the hill where the battery was planted, the rebels opened fire upon us from two pieces of artillery. We had also two pieces, and tearing down the fences, the guns were placed in position and our forces wheeled into line on the brow of the hill in such a manner as to bring our fire to bear upon the enemy, while we had partial protection from theirs by a fence on the top of the hill.

We were seriously annoyed by a flanking fire on the river, and also from a large log house on the bank of the creek. Detachments of two companies of the 21st and two companies of the 12th, charged upon the house and routed the rebels at the point of bayonet. They retreated across the creek covered by the fire of their own men-fording it, as they had previously burnt the bridges.

In the meantime our artillery had silenced their battery, entirely destroying the carriage of one piece, and our boys twice silenced the fire of their infantry. At this juncture they received reinforcements, (their force was nearer 1,500 than 700 at the outset) and our boys had completely exhausted their ammunition. They therefore commenced a retreat, in good order, so soon as they had got beyond the range of the rebel's single re-mounted piece, reserving their last single shot in the cannon for any emergency, should the enemy attempt a pursuit.

In this manner the retreat was kept up till we fell in with the balance of the 21st Ohio, under [*Lt.*] Col. Nibley [*Neibling*]; the boys had then exhausted every round in their cartridge boxes, that the attempt was given over.

Our informant puts the loss on our side at 4 killed, 2 mortally wounded, 3 missing and 17 or 18 more or less seriously wounded. Of those instantly killed were Capt. Allen, Co. D, and Geo. Blue, Co. K, 21st. Lieut. Pomeroy has since died of his wounds. One man had his hip torn away by a cannon ball, and must die. Capt. Sloan of the 12th was wounded, but not dangerously. These were all the names he could recall. Col. Norton was supposed to be a prisoner. He had been wounded and taken to a house a fourth of a mile from the hospital, but the guard placed over him had been called off to take charge of some prisoners taken during the engagement, and he was seen or some one supposed to have been him, in the hands of the rebels.

The painful news that Col. Woodruff and Lieut. Col. Neff of the Second Kentucky, and Col. De Villiers, of the 11th Ohio had been captured while reconnoitering, needs confirmation. They had left Gen. Cox's Camp to ascertain what was going on, at the time of the fight, and had not returned when our informant left, though, just as the boat was pushing out, he heard the boys in Camp give three cheers, and saw some one that he took to be Col. W., riding into Camp. It is not infrequent that officers on reconnoitering expeditions remain out for a considerable time longer than they anticipate when setting out and the friends of these gentlemen should not be uneasy about them, at least, till further intelligence arrives.

WHEELING INTELLIGENCER
July 20, 1861

Another Battle on the Kanawha

Cincinnati, July 19—The Kanawha correspondent of the *Gazette* says, on the morning of the 18th Gen. Cox ordered the Twelfth Ohio, two companies of the Twenty-first Ohio, two guns of the Cleveland Artillery, and Ironton Cavalry, to reconnoitre for the supposed masked battery, near the mouth of Pope [*Poca*] Creek. On reaching the creek, four miles from Gen. Cox's headquarters, they discovered the enemy, fifteen hundred strong, strongly entrenched on Scarey Hill, with a masked battery of two guns. On reaching the creek our men were fired upon from the masked battery and from a log house. Our men after firing forty rounds, crossed the creek and silenced the battery, but ammunition giving out they were compelled to retire.

The gun of the masked battery was afterwards re-mounted and opened fire. Capt. Allen and Lieut. Pomeroy, of the 21st Ohio, and 2 others killed, 17 wounded and 3 missing. Col. Norton, of the 21 Ohio, was badly wounded and taken prisoner. The rebels were commanded by Col. Tompkins, Col. Woodruff and Lieut. Col. Neff, of the 1st Kentucky, and Col. Devilliers, of the 11th Ohio, left Gen. Cox's camp on the 17th and nothing has been heard from them. At last accounts it was supposed they had either been killed or taken prisoners.

THE IRONTON REGISTER
July 25, 1861

OPERATIONS ON THE KANAWHA

The Brigade of Gen. Cox, it would appear had concentrated on the Kanawha, at the mouth of Pocatalico, by the middle of last week, forming "Camp Poco." And on Wednesday, 17th July, 1861, was fought the

BATTLE OF SCAREY

Gen. Cox having learned that the rebels were preparing to make a stand at the mouth of Scarey Creek, five miles (by land) above "Poco," and fifteen miles below Charleston, sent a force forward to reconnoiter, consisting of the 12th Ohio, Col. Lowe; two companies of the 21st, under Col. Norton; Canton Artillery, two rifled guns, under Capt. Colton [*Cotter*]; and a squad of the Lawrence County Cavalry, under 2d Orderly J. [*Joseph*] L. Barber, of Ironton, in all about 1,200 men. It is stated that the instructions were to dislodge the enemy, if it could be done easily; if not, to take position, and hold it until the main body could advance.

The detachment moved slowly and cautiously, and at about 3 o'clock, P.M., came upon the rebels, entrenched on high ground with a deep valley at the base of the hill, having two rifled 6-pounders in their battery and squads of riflemen in log houses outside of the entrenchments—their force reported at 1,500 and soon strongly reinforced. The strength of the rebels was not known at first, and to draw it out, the column was ordered to advance, our squad of Cavalry *leading the advance,* under orderly J.L. Barber, with 20 men, including himself, to wit: [*Corp.*] Dr. D.C. Ellis, of Adams county, [*Pvt.*] Thos. Hamilton, [*Sgt.*] Fletcher Golden, [*Pvt.*] Arthur T. Dempsey, [*Pvt. W.*] Geo. Crawshaw, [*Pvt.*] S. [*Silas*] H. Curry, [*Pvt.*] Jas. Steece, [*Pvt.*] John Irwin, [*Pvt.*] Wm. Smith, [*Pvt.*] Richard Lambert, [*Pvt.*] Milton Davisson, [*Pvt.*] Jackson Culp, [*Pvt.*] G. [*George*] W. Shattuck, [*Pvt.*] M. [*Martin*] Vanvers [*Van Every*], [*Pvt.*] Geo. Primm, [*Corp.*] J. [*John*] T. [*F.*] McCartney, [*Pvt.*] Good [*John L.*] Godman, [*Pvt.*] Jos. Ricker [*Richer*], and — McFadden. As the Cavalry rounded a point, the rebels opened a fire of grape shot upon them; they returned the fire until six rounds from the cannon had been fired upon them, when they were ordered to retire. An old house somewhat protected them, and the cannon were aimed too high, so that the shot passed mostly over their heads. In the first discharge, Richard Lambert, son of Esq. Wm. Lambert, just below Ironton, was instantly killed—one of the grape shot tearing through his body, near the heart, another penetrating his brain.

Capt. Colton's [*Cotter*] Artillery followed, took position on a hill, and silenced the enemy's battery in about fifteen minutes, losing one of his men killed. The Infantry advanced, and the fight continued, it is said, over two hours, when, at last, the ammunition of our boys gave out, the rebels had been reinforced, and the Federal troops were compelled to retire, having lost 9 killed, 37 wounded, two mortally, and some 8 or 10 missing. Capt. Allen was killed, and Lieut. Pomeroy mortally wounded, (since dead) both of the 21st Ohio; also Col. Norton was severely wounded in the thigh and taken prisoner. The loss of the rebels is said to have been, on very good authority, 67 killed, a larger number wounded, and 4 prisoners; another account puts the rebel loss at 65 killed, 150 wounded. Our troops fell back to "Camp Poco." Our officers and men had been too confident, and were repulsed.

THE ENEMY MAKE A LARGE HAUL OF OFFICERS

We have already mentioned the wounding and capture of Col. Norton, by the rebels.—Well, Col. DeVilliers, of the Ohio 11th, Col. Woodruff, Lieut. Col. Neff, and Capt. J.R. Hurd, of the Kentucky 2d, together with a Capt. Austin—five officers—went out *by themselves*, in a reckless manner, to see the "fun" up at Scarey, and fell into the hands of the rebels—*"prisoners of war!"* Good enough for *them!* That is a pretty good haul of the enemy, three out of five of our Colonels.

THE LATEST

We heard from Gen. Cox, he was still at "Poco," Saturday, 21st. The rebels were stated to be falling back on Charleston.

Xenia *Torch-Light*
William B. Fairchild, Editor
Xenia, O.
Saturday, July 27, 1861

Letter from Kanawha
Camp Coaco, Kanawha Valley,
July 21, 1861

Editor of Torch-Light: We have had a battle; a hard-fought, desperate battle, and this time somebody has been hurt, and this beautiful valley has been stained by the blood of some of Ohio's noblest sons. Our own loved county of Old Greene had her representatives there; and she never will have cause to blush for them. Their deeds are on record, and they are not ashamed.

The Shawnee Rangers were in the hottest part of the fight, and are terribly cut up. The details of the battle may reach you before this will have been received, but I will give some of the facts. As we advanced up the Kanawha, the marauding parties of the rebels were driven before us without offering battle, they fell back on their fortified camps at a little creek called *Scarey*, two miles [*?*] south west of Charleston. Their number and position could not be definitely ascertained, but they were known to have some pieces of artillery. At the importunity of some of the officers of the 12th Regiment, Gen. Cox ordered that regiment, with two pieces of Brass Rifled Cannon under Capt. Carter [*Cotter*]; a squad of Cavalry, and one Company of the 21st O.V. under Capt. Allen. The whole was commanded by Col. Lowe of the 12th, with the assistance of Col. Norton of the 21st, and numbering 1,020 men, to make an attack on the enemy wherever he might be found.

The order was received with delight by officers and men, and by 9 o'clock on Wednesday morning, the 17th our baggage and knapsacks had all been stowed on board the steamer Marmora [Matamore] and we were ready to march. We crossed to the west bank of the Kanawha on steamboats, and took up the line of march. Company A, Capt. [*James D.*] Wallace, and company D, Capt. [*William B. "Buck"*] Smith, formed the advance guard; company H, Capt. [*Edward M.*] Carey, the rear guard and the Artillery and Cavalry, in the centre. The battalion proceeded cautiously, and when about a mile from camp skirmishers were deployed to the right and left of the road, which wound around between steep, high, rocky hills, covered with timber and a thick underbrush; save here and there, where a small patch had been cleared, and on which log houses had been erected; but all closed and tenantless of their once heroic dwellers, save where the affrighted crying woman and everlasting tow-headed children had crowded together for mutual protection, or as they said *to be killed together!* When we talked kindly to them and assured them that we came as friends, and not as enemies of women and children, and that no harm would come to them, their pale, terrified countenances were changed and their fear quieted, and they would tell us of a husband, a father or brother that was in the Southern Army, and implore us to save them; but on this point we could not, under the circumstances, give them much assurance, and the boys would kindly hint that those whom they wished us to spare had better not 'gone a soldiering.'

After marching five miles in this manner we emerged from the woods, and the valley of the Kanawha lay again before us; and suddenly we saw two or three men running and heard the report of their muskets discharged in the air. They were the enemy's pickets. A halt was ordered by Major Hines, who led the advance, and the artillery ordered forward, and forward they came at a thundering speed and moved along the road, while the infantry deployed rapidly and without halting for a moment, moved forward for over a half mile, when we discovered the position of the enemy. Their left wing was posted on a high hill or promontory covered with thick timber and underbrush, whose point reached to within one hundred yards of the river. On this point their artillery was posted, numbering four [*two*] pieces, one of which was a rifled ten-pounder. Their left rested on the river. Here was several log cabins, piles of lumber and cooper stuff, in and behind which the rebels were posted. When we approached within five hundred yards of the enemy, he opened upon us a terrific fire of round shot, grape and musketry, doing but little damage however, as the balls passed entirely over our heads. Our artillery advanced rapidly and took up a position at a distance of about 600 yards from the enemy's lines; unlimbered got the range and sent round shot and shells right in and through the rebels at their guns, mowing down whole platoons at every discharge. For more than an hour the artillery kept up their thunder, when the enemy's batteries ceased to respond, while ours thundered on, doing terrible work in the ranks of the foe. Meanwhile, the riflemen and musketeers of the enemy, posted in the log cabins down by the river, kept up a galling fire on our left and centre. Col. Lowe ordered Lieut. Col. White to dislodge them, and turn their right flank and drive them back upon their centre, while Major Hines was directed to assault their left. Company D occupied the left of our line, and were stationed on a bluff with two sides, one fronting the enemy, the other fronting the river. Along the river, at the foot of the bluff, on a road which led up to the enemy, Col. White came riding along coolly and apparently unconcerned, the balls whistling around him, and ordered Capt. Smith to take his company and dislodge the enemy from his position in the log cabins, and down over the rocky bluff we went, tumbling over rocks, followed by company I, Capt. [*Ferdinand*] Gunkle, and company D, Capt. Allen of the 21st, and Col. Norton of the same regiment; and away we rushed. Company D, headed by Capt. Buck Smith, led the advance. The enemy opened upon us a murderous fire just in range. But nothing daunted, our men rushed on, and with a shout entered the houses and drove the enemy before us at the point of the bayonet, taking four prisoners. It was in this charge that we sustained our heaviest loss. The enemy were routed and in full retreat, when they received a re-enforcement of five hundred men, fresh and well armed, when they returned. When our men found that they were out of ammunition, there were cries of rage and despair. It was found that a deeply imbedded creek, with steep banks on both sides lay in front of the enemy's line, crossed by a bridge near the river, across which their right were advanced, and when driven across they blew up the bridge. Some of our men crossed on the stringers, but were driven back by superior numbers, when they took post in and behind the log cabins. The re-enforcement of the enemies brought with them one piece of cannon, which they brought to bear upon us. Human power could do no more. Completely exhausted, having eaten nothing since morning, and then only a few doughnuts and fat bacon, and-it being now 6 o'clock-out of ammunition, wet with sweat and covered with dust, we retired slowly from the field, bearing our wounded and two prisoners-two having escaped. We were unable to carry off our dead, which amounted to four. Capt. Allen and his 1st Lieutenant of company D, 21st Reg't; a private in company I, 12th Regiment, and here we left poor Perry Taylor of our own company D, of the 12th. He had discharged his musket and was just retiring behind the house, when a ball struck him in the breast in the region of the heart, when he fell and expired without a groan. Capt. Allen was shot in the forehead and fell dead. Col. Norton was wounded in the hip, and falling, he took off his hat and cheered on the men.

When we regained the hill on which the artillery was posted, we found that they too had spent all their ammunition, and the artillerymen crying and swearing with rage and mortification.

The right and center of our force had by some means failed to execute the order of Col. Lowe, and we were ordered to rally to the artillery, and retired slowly and sullenly from the field. Loss in killed and wounded amounting to 25-seven of whom were killed, and one mortally wounded, who died yesterday. One half the entire loss fell on Company D, but one, however, was killed, and all the wounded will recover. Most of the wounded were sent to Gallipolis yesterday. Abe King, who was wounded in the temple by a musket ball, refused to be sent down, and today he is walking about the quarters, his fine brown eyes shinning with their usual luster, and looking none the worse for wear and tear.

The cannonading was plainly heard at camp, where were stationed part of the 21st and 11th Ohio, and the 1st and 2d Kentucky. These Regiments instantly flew to arms, with wild shouts, and implored Gen. Cox to let them come to our assistance. He refused. At last a courier reached him from Col. Lowe asking for aid, when six companies of the 21st was dispatched for our relief—but too late. Had this aid been one hour sooner all would have been well—the enemy would have been routed from his position—but the heads of the advancing and retiring columns met half way between the camp and the battle field.

The Lieut. Col. of the 21st, and his men, as well, were furious at the loss of their beloved Colonel, and, with tears in their eyes, insisted to storming the enemies camp, and it was only on promising them that they would be led on, on the morrow, that they could be induced to come back. But when the morrow came Gen. Cox thought best to wait re-enforcements—and here we are yet.

We have learned by deserters who came into our camp that the force of the rebels was 2,000 men, and that their loss amounted to 65 killed. But two companies of our Regiment were armed with Enfield Rifles which did terrible execution. The other companies had the old muskets.

Your, &c.,
Sigma, Jr.

GALLIPOLIS JOURNAL
Oct. 9, 1861

Secession sympathizers say the rebel loss at Scary was only four killed and thirty wounded. We learn from a reliable source that the rebel loss was not far from seventy-five killed and one hundred and fifty wounded, among them Capt. Patton, who had his right arm shattered, the same ball passing through the muscles of the right breast, creating a terrible wound, from which he is not likely to recover. On calling the roll after the battle four hundred of the rebels were among the missing. Albert G. Jenkins had his scalp lock grazed with a musket ball, but escaped uninjured. A rebel soldier who was in the battle states that at least one hundred shots were made at the brave Capt. Allen before he was struck. Capt. [*Andrew Russell*] Barbee [*Co. A, 22nd Virginia Infantry*] claims the honor (?) of having shot this brave soldier, but he lies. The fatal shot was made by a rebel standing near the foot of the hill, who was himself killed a moment afterwards.

TWO ACCOUNTS CONCERNING EDWARD SETTLE GODFREY, 21ST O.V.I. AND THE BATTLE OF SCARY

[*Edward Settle Godfrey, whose letter written the night prior to the battle of Scary Creek appeared on page 104 of the original text, entered West Point in 1863 and graduated in 1867 with a commission as 2nd Lt. assigned to the 7th Cavalry and later became a 1st Lt., Capt., and Major. He served 33 years with the 7th Cavalry and was in 40 important Indian fights, becoming one of the country's noted Indian fighters. In 1876, at Little Big Horn, he was credited with helping to save seven companies of the regiment. The following year he was in the fight with the Nez Perces Indians at Bear Paw Mountain where he was wounded and won the Con-*

gressional Medal of Honor. Between 1879-1883 Godfrey served as cavalry instructor at West Point and in 1901 was first a Lt. Col. in the 12th Cavalry and then Col. of the 9th Cavalry in the Philippines. In 1904 he was in command of Ft. Riley, Kansas and in 1907 was a Brig. Gen. and retired. During World War I, at the age of 73 he offered his services in any capacity — for this information thanks to Roy Kiely, Morehead City, North Carolina]

Godfrey's son recounting what his father told him about Scarey Creek

"... I have a recollection of Scary Creek being spelled "Skerry Creek" —perhaps "Scary" had unfortunate connotations for the survivors since they were scared and did run. I asked father one time whether he ran. He said "not till the rest of them."

I think, Thomas Allen was the captain of the company (was it "D"?) 21st Ohio Vol. Inf. organized in Ottawa and enlisted for 3 months service in April ? 1861. Being less than 18 years old, he (father) had to have his father's consent which was given on the promise that he would not re-enlist. As I remember the story this "battle" was only a small skirmish, the company was surprised and I suppose broke and ran when the company commander was killed. I seem to remember quite a few headstones in Pomeroy Cemetery that were marked "killed at Battle of Skerry Creek" or died of wounds received there.

THE PUTNAM COUNTY (Ohio) GAZETTE
March 16, 1933

His [Edward Settle Godfrey's] first military experience, however, was in the so-called three months service in the Civil War, in Company D, Twenty-first Ohio Volunteer Infantry, that lasted from April 26 to August 12, 1861. That Company was mustered in at Camp Taylor, Cleveland, Ohio, May 21, 1861 and was mustered out at Columbus, Ohio, August 12 following. It was recruited in and near Ottawa by Lawyer Thomas Godfrey Allen, who became Captain, and the volunteers mainly were enrolled by him at the railway station and on the street. The drilling was done on the village common, just east of the Blanchard River and just north of the Ottawa-Kalida road, and the drill instructor was Jacob Wolf, a then recently discharged regular army sergeant from Delphos, Ohio, who was visiting in Ottawa, was persuaded to enroll for the Company, and was made a Corporal. During the last few days before entraining for Cleveland, camp was made at the large barn of Dr. Calvin T. Pomeroy just south of the village and just north of Williamstown Road. Before being mustered in our young volunteer experienced two rejections before acceptance could he had. He there stood in the physical examination line three times, going immediately from the head to the foot twice. Finally and although his age was below the minimum, persistence and resourcefulness won over the examining surgeon—Dr. Miller. And in vindication it may be noted that during that Company's sole engagement, at Scarey Creek, West Virginia, July 17, 1861 Private Godfrey while under fire carried water to the wounded.

And he assisted in carrying from the field Second Lieutenant Guy Pomeroy. For a time that wounded officer was carried in a blanket, so that eventually the carriers' fingers were much pained. Arriving at a tobacco shed and finding therein a ladder, immediately there was discussion as to the right and the wrong of taking and utilizing it for litter purposes to ease the injured one and his comrades. As a result the ladder was not left.

In that Company was a family connection of twelve cousins and one uncle. Seven of them were officers. And they sustained the only casualties in the only engagement the Company had, Second Lieutenant Guy Pomeroy being fatally wounded and Captain Thomas G. Allen being killed. The former expired on an Ohio River steamboat while being taken to Gallipolis, Ohio by Sergeant J.L.H. Long. Captain Allen had said- "If I am killed I want to be shot right here," placing a finger at the center of his forehead. And that was where the bullet struck. First Lieutenant Charles William Allen, a student of medicine under Dr. Charles Moore Godfrey and brother of the Captain, re-enlisted and died at home of wounds received at the battle of Chickamauga in September 1863. Those brothers lie under a double monument erected in Pomeroy Cemetery, Ottawa, Ohio, and Second Lieutenant Guy Pomeroy also lies therein and nearby. Captain Allen had bequeathed his sword to Ottawa Lodge No. 325 F.A.M. Ottawa, Ohio. Many, many years afterward the writer of this delivered to the widow of Lawyer Guy Pomeroy letters that had been written by him to Thomas G. Allen. She instantly recognized the handwriting and expressed sweet gratitude. He was one of the committee that acted for resident voters to petition the County commissioners for incorporation of Ottawa Village, the other members being Lucius Hubbard and Dr. Charles Moore Godfrey. And their petition was allowed February 13, 1861.

John Adams, Company C, 21st Ohio Volunteer Infantry, captured the camp flag of the enemy at Scary Creek, "...which was the first Confederate flag brought to Ohio."[*according to records Private John Adams, Co. D, 21st O.V.I. (3 years service) enlisted August 26, 1861, which if true, would indicate he was not present at Scary Creek*]—*Biographical and Historical Sketches*—Parlee C. Gross & Others, General Publishing, McComb, Ohio

---

THE IRONTON REGISTER
August 1, 1861

Milton J. Ferguson, Esq., the leading Secessionist of Wayne Co., Va., on last Friday night appeared at or near Ceredo, with six men, it is said for the purpose of arresting Col. Zeigler, the leading Union man—his own story is being that he went to make peace with Zeigler. He was arrested and handed over to Deputy U.S. Marshal E.F. Gillen, of this place, who left with him last Monday, for Columbus, or perhaps Wheeling.

Ferguson admits having been at Barboursville and Scarey Fights. He gives as an instance of the good firing of the Canton (O.) Artillery at Scarey, that a gun was aimed at one of the rebel batteries, some half a mile distant; the first shot was a little too low, the second a trifle too high; but the third struck the gun of the battery about in the center, taking off the top of Lieut. Welch's head, killing him instantly, also killing the gunner. It was then turned upon another battery, and the second shot destroyed another gun, and exploded its magazine—five shots destroying two of the rebel cannon.

The Kanawha correspondent of the Cincinnati Gazette says that before leaving Camp Poca, July 24th:

"A young man named James M. Gray, from Ashland, Ky., a member of Company F, Second Kentucky Regiment was accidentally shot by a comrade while on guard and died a few hours afterward."

John K. Thompson of Company A (Putnam County Border Rifles), 22nd Virginia Infantry, "... first experience in actual war came when a Union force attacked a Confederate force at Scary on lands adjoining the Thompson estate, opposite Putnam County, where he spent most of his life. The advice of the young V.M.I. cadet was sought and he pointed out the most advantageous position to place the cannon."—John K. Thompson obituary, *Charleston Daily Mail*, Jan. 25, 1925

2nd Sgt. C.L. Rowan, Co. A, 60th Virginia Infantry, stated: "My first battle was at Scary's Creek; lasted about two hours. Whipped the Yankees and had only temporary breast works. Had only 1,000 or 1,200 men, the Yankees had three men to our one. Fought under Col. Patton, commander."—United Daughters of the Confederacy Report, Craig County, Virginia

---

Pvt. Thomas D. Webb, Company A, 22nd Virginia Infantry, suffered a "hernia rupture caused by extricating himself from water and mud at Scary Creek during the battle." He was discharged for a scrotal hernia caused at Scary Creek on Feb. 26, 1862—from Confederate Service Records, 22nd Virginia Infantry, National Archives, Washington, D.C.

From the Colonel John W. Lowe Papers, Dayton-Montgomery County Public Library, Dayton, Ohio

[*Col. John W. Lowe's unofficial report of the battle of Scary Creek written the day after to his wife. Some of the letter is illegible as it is written in pencil and somewhat faded. indecipherable portions are indicated by blanks or question marks.*]

Scary Creek—

Kanawha, Va.

July 18, 1861

My Dear Wife

My regiment had a very severe fight yesterday. I was under fire for an hour and a half but was not hurt—thank God for that—Willie was not in the fight but remained on board the boat 5 or 6 miles distant listening to the firing that decided our fate. I was disappointed to my loss cannot be ascertained as yet. Timberlake the 2—was killed.

killed — missing and — wounded

I cannot give you the particulars—we fought them very well & the 12th has covered itself with glory. You will see by the papers more than I can write—but one thing you can rely on—the 12th did nothing that would tarnish their fame. My horse Charly behaved nobly in the fight. Col. Norton of the 21st is wounded & missing—Ashley Brown was with him & is probably a prisoner Capt. Buck Smith behaved nobly, he fought Co. D like a hero.

We whipped the enemy fairly until they were reinforced and all our cartridges were expended—we fired our last artillery cartridge at the instant we retired—by great exertion we brought off 30 of our wounded—among them was Capt [*illegible*] of Hillsbrough, Taylor of Middletown, Lt. Wilson of the same [*illegible*] Abe King & his brother were both taken prisoner but got away. Abe was wounded in the head—but not dangerous.

I can write no more at present—remember me again to all my dear friends & relatives—tell them I am safe.

Your [*illegible*] affectionate husband

J. W. Lowe

[*Two additional letters written by Col. John W. Lowe following the battle of Scary Creek indicating his depressed state of mind following charges of cowardice in the battle.*]

Charleston, W.Va.
Aug. 11, 1861

To Kate from Father,

The treatment I have rec'd from my countrymen for whom I have sacrificed all that made life desirable to me makes me wish most earnestly to leave the army and retire to the seclusion of private life, but duty and an injured name forbid it and urge me onward to the destiny that awaits me whether it be good or bad. I am in the hands of my God, let him do with me as seemeth him good.

Camp Scarey
23 July [1861]

To Mother,

I feel as though my life's journey was nearly ended. The chances of War render it highly probable that this is so, but don't despond. God has given us many, very many happy hours together and now if it be His will that we meet no more on this earth you must thank him as I do for what he has already granted us & submit with resignation to his Holy Will.

THE CAPTURE OF THE COLONELS

GALLIPOLIS JOURNAL
August 8, 1861

The Captives—We learn from the *Wheeling Intelligencer* that Major Leiper, of the 1st Kentucky Regiment has been informed of the removal of Colonels Woodruff, De Villiers, and Neff, together with Captains Hurd and Austin, from the town of Charleston to the city of Richmond. Col. Woodruff was represented to have been effected to tears from the humiliation of his position. Col. De Villiers pronounced their capture is contrary to all honorable military rules. They all claim that they were treacherously ensnared into the enemy's camp by the enemy displaying the American flag. They have been kindly treated by their captors, and complain only of the mode of their capture.

THE IRONTON REGISTER
September 5, 1861

LETTER FROM CAPT. J.R. HURD

Richmond, Virginia, August 4, 1861

Cousin E.: I hope you do not yet think I have intentionally neglected to fulfill the promise made to you all, previous to our departure for the seat of war in Western Virginia. Owing to various circumstances, I have not had time and until our arrival here we had no facilities by which we could forward our communications; but all arrangements have been made at this place, and as they very kindly call for our correspondence daily, it is a favor we all readily accept, and feel thankful we have an opportunity to inform our families, relatives and friends of our whereabouts. I suppose the Burlington boys write home occasionally. I thought a great deal of the Burlington boys and those from that vicinity, on account of the courage and cheerfulness with which they bore privations and hardships. Tell their folks when they write to them to inform them where I am; and no one but myself knows how often I have wished that I was with them; but as that cannot be until I an exchanged, I sincerely hope that Lieutenants Smith and Hurd will look well after the company and see that they are as well provided for as circumstances will permit.

I suppose that you are well aware of the particulars of our arrest, (Col. Devilliers, of 11th Ohio, Col. Woodruff, Lieut. Col. Neff, Capt. Austin, and Capt Hurd, of the 2d Kentucky V.I.) or at least of the different statements published. Fortunately, I saw one of the accounts of the affair, taken from the Cincinnati Commercial, by the Richmond Enquirer, reflecting in a very harsh manner on Col. Woodruff's and Lieut. Col. Neff's proceedings. I immediately wrote to my Father, and requested him to have the letter published in the Portsmouth papers, and if you see that, you will learn the truth and facts of the matter, newspaper reports to the contrary, notwithstanding.

The treatment extended towards us by Gen. Wise, the officers of his command, (particularly Capt. Jenkins) the citizens of Charleston, and on the route from Charleston to this place was the very kindest; in fact, the utmost courtesy, civility and every attention to our wants was carefully attended to; and we certainly have not anything to complain of here, only the close confinement; and you, knowing my roving disposition, can imagine how irksome it is to me.—From the fact that we five were attached to Gen. McClellan's division, and from the assurances we have received from Gen. Wise, we expected that the limits of this city would be extended to us, but as yet it has not been done. The confederate States have here including officers and privates, near a thousand prisoners, and we have received no positive information what our Government intends doing in regard to making exchanges, but from the time that has elapsed since our arrest, I am rather inclined to think they do not intend to make any exchanges; and if not, I cannot form the least idea when we will be released, but hope some arrangement will be effected that will release us on parole. As for myself, if they would accept my parole of honor, I would never attempt to escape, or join my company, until fairly exchanged.

Not wishing to tax the time of those whose duty it is to examine this, I come to a close, hoping they will find nothing to condemn.- I would be pleased to hear from you, and if you reply, direct in the care of Lieut. Col. Todd, Richmond, Virginia.

J.R. Hurd
Capt. Co. F, 2d Reg. Ky. V.M.

THE COL. JOHN W. LOWE AFFAIR

[As noted on page 137 of the original text Col. John W. Lowe of the 12th Ohio was made the scapegoat of the whole affair. This argument deserved more space so below can be found a series of newspaper articles and letters both attacking and defending Lowe, many of which were found in a scrapbook kept by the Lowe family, particularly Col. Lowe's son, Thomas Lowe. The reader may judge for themselves Lowe's guilt or innocence, but he was never formally charged with neglect.]

LETTER TO COL. LOWE'S SON FROM *CINCINNATI COMMERCIAL* EDITOR

OFFICE CINCINNATI DAILY AND WEEKLY COMMERCIAL
Fourth and Race Streets
Cincinnati, August 1st 1861

Thomas O. Lowe, Esq.

Dear Sir—Yours of yesterday is at hand. The statements made in reference to your father, have been substantiated, as I understand, by Col. Norton who was wounded in the engagement referred to, and is now or was a few days since in this city. The same charges have been made in several letters from the army in the Kanawha, published in the Cleveland papers.

We have no acquaintance with your father, and certainly no malice to gratify in the publication of such statements. On the contrary such acts as are reported were a source of mortification to us as much as to any one and only a sense of duty induced their publication in the Commercial.

If further developments should go to exonerate your father from the charges made we shall with pleasure give such exoneration publicity through our columns.

Respectfully,
M.D. Potter

PERRYSBURG JOURNAL

The Col. Lowe Affair.

We have taken some pains to investigate the matter of "cowardice" and "incompetency," which has been preferred against Col. Lowe, as evidenced in the Scary fight, but do not learn anything to warrant us in pronouncing the charge in every particular false. In the "evidence of eye-witnesses," sent us from Dayton, it would appear that Col. L. was a quarter of a mile behind, at the time Col. Norton made the charge upon the enemy; that he had "several times *sent* orders to have the charge properly supported, and that he did not know *why* his orders were not obeyed." If this be true, the duty of Col. Lowe was plain. He should have gone forward, *himself*, and seen that the order *was* obeyed.

Whether it was "cowardice" or "incompetency" that prevented him from taking the lead of his column, as Col. Norton did the five companies under his command, we of course cannot determine. However we are willing to drop the matter entirely, if interested parties are, for we think that the more it is stirred the worse it will get.

The Affair at Scary Creek and the Capture of the Colonels.

We publish, without the least hesitation, a communication which refers to our irreverent paragraph on the bagging of the three Colonels on the Kanawha. Our correspondent, in his concern for the reputation of the captured Colonels, does not fully bear in mind that we made no reflections upon their gallantry or capacity; but we could not help thinking, that Colonels who leave their General, contrary to orders, and at a time when the safety of the army may be in peril, cannot be looked to for examples or enforcement of the discipline which is indispensable to the effective service and even honor and safety of an army; and we could not help saying, partly in humorous exaggeration, of course, that it was not a bad haul of Colonels; though we are none the less concerned for their safety and future service, for their rashness has resulted in a severe case to them.

As to Col. Lowe, he was not included in the remarks on the "haul of Colonels," but it was observed that he seemed to have had very little discretion in carrying out the discretion that his orders gave him. We think this was shown by the result. He had discretion to attack or not. Had he ascertained the position and force of the battery by reconnaissance, and returned to the main body, he would have rendered effective service, but he fired away forty rounds of ammunition, and had not enough left to protect his retreat, and finishing by a charge which periled his entire command, they retreated, in disorder, at first. All this is creditable to his gallantry, but not so much so to his discretion. It was the anxiety for a fight when he saw an opportunity before him, which went in without stopping to calculate the chances, the same fault that the most of our brave officers are subject to.

The lesson of the action and the capture of the Colonels, is the absolute necessity of discipline. Our troops drill, but they do not acquire the habit of instinctive obedience of command which is called discipline, and which will give the command of their officers the supreme control of their instincts even under a surprise, or the most destructive fire.

PERRYSBURG JOURNAL
J.W. Bailey, Editor
Aug. 8, 1861

Full Particulars of the Scary Creek Fight in which Col. Norton was Wounded.

As promised in our last to give a faithful sketch of the battle of Scary Creek on the 17th July in this issue, we publish the account as we have it from an eye witness. On Sunday, July 14, Col. Norton was ordered by Gen. Cox to take a portion of his command and proceed up the Kanawha for the purpose of ascertaining the position and strength of the rebel force at or near the mouth of Cole river, 12 miles from Charleston, where it was reported the enemy were in camp and had thrown up some defenses. Col. Norton started with companies F, G, and H of his regiment by three different roads-all terminating at the bridge crossing Scary Creek. Taking the center road himself, it being the shortest route to that point, in order to be in advance of the remainder of the command and reconnoiter before they should come up. Having marched to within half a mile of Scary Creek, our approach was signaled to the enemy by the firing of five guns in rapid succession. The Colonel immediately ordered a halt of the advance guard, until the main body of his force should arrive. He gave them orders to proceed carefully when the others came up, and *he*, with five mounted men rode forward to examine the positions of the enemy more closely. On examination he found a picket guard of the enemy had been posted in an old church, and on his approach had fled, leaving behind them their dinner already cooked, their blankets, knapsacks and other accouterments. When the company came up, a careful examination was ordered of the woods adjoining the hill side. A scouting party of sixteen under Lieutenant [*Joshua L.*] Preble [*Co.* G] went forward with orders to move with great caution, and discover, if possible, the enemy's precise position. On nearing the brow of the hill at a point where the road begins to descend towards the bridge and creek Lieutenant Preble discovered the rebels drawn up in line of battle to the number of about one thousand men. At the moment the enemy perceived our scouts they opened right and left and fired at the party two six-pounders loaded with grape. The entire force of the enemy then fired by rank at the scouts, but without doing any injury. The men prostrating themselves the shots passed over them. By order of Col. Norton our men then retreated out of range of the fire of the enemy, there being but 60 of us all told-the other two companies not yet having reached us. We marched back to the junction of the central and valley roads, where we were met by Capt. [*Albert M.*] Blackman, of company H, who having heard the firing, pushed forward on the double quick to join us. We then took a cross-road and marched to the river road in order to join Capt. [*George F.*] Walker with company F, he having been ordered to take the road. On arriving at the junction of the two roads we found Capt. Walker had passed about 30 minutes before us. Col. Norton ordered a halt of the two companies, and himself set off with Sergeant Major [*D.S.*] Price and Hornman [*2nd Lt.Charles E. Hambilton?*] of Capt. George's company, to overtake Capt. Walker, and if possible, bring him off before he came upon the rebel battery. After a race of three miles with the horses on a dead run, Col. Norton came up with Capt. Walker just as he had come within an easy range of the rebel battery, but before they had thought proper to open fire. Company F then counter-marched, and joined the other companies at the junction, where they all encamped for a few hours until dark. At dark a march was ordered to three miles down the river, where we went into ambush, with the expectation that the rebels would follow and attack us. In the meantime Col. Norton wrote dispatches to Gen. Cox, who was but 9 miles distant, and sent the same post haste by Sergeant Major Price. In these messages Col. Norton stated to Gen. Cox the number and position of the enemy, the number and size of their field pieces and that he himself had been twice in full view of their entire force, and asked for re-inforcements, including Captain Cotter with his section of rifled cannon. Gen. Cox upon receipt of these dispatches, sent the balance of the 21st regiment and five companies of the 1st Kentucky, but did not send Capt. Colton [*Cotter*] and his guns as requested, and we were compelled to stay in the woods without fire or rations all night, not deeming it prudent to attack a force nearly equal to our own, and who had the advantage of position, and a battery of two six-pounders, we being without artillery. At daylight on the 15th, we marched up the river again to the junction, and there remained until afternoon, without food, until the steamers came up, when we were ordered into camp on the opposite side of the river. We remained in camp until Wednesday morning, the 11th [*17th*], at which time Col. Norton received an order from Gen. Cox to prepare to march with two companies of the 21st regiment, the 12th Ohio, and Capt. Cotter's battery with Col. Lowe in command, for Scary. We got off at 12 o'clock n.; and after a careful march of two hours, came upon the enemy's pickets, driving them in, and in a few minutes drawing the fire from the rebel battery and their entire line. We approached carelessly, with an attempt, however, to form in line, which proved entirely futile—Col. Lowe failing to give command. The rebels had planted their battery in a position commanding the road by which we were approaching, and our men being in column in the road, instead of being in line as they should have been had Col. Lowe given the proper command, were in imminent danger of being at any moment swept from the road by the enemy's guns.

At this juncture Col. Norton ordered the left wing, consisting of five companies, including the two from the 21st regiment, to fall in line in a ravine. He then ordered them forward to the brow of the hill and then gave the order to open fire, Col. Norton then designated Capt. Cotter his position upon the brow of the hill, in full view of the enemy's battery, which position he took, and immediately prepared his battery for action, and opened fire with astonishing effect. One shot from our guns struck a gun of the rebel battery directly in the muzzle, breaking out a piece of the metal, passing through and taking off a wheel from the gun carriage and the head of the 1st lieutenant in the artillery. We soon found that the great distance our position from the rebels prevented our doing much injury with our muskets, and that they being armed with Sharpe's rifles, had no difficulty in reaching us, and were wounding and killing our men with impunity. Col. Norton then ordered three companies of the 12th Ohio and the two companies of the 21st to file down the hill on our left with the intention of driving them out at the point of the bayonet from behind fences, trees, logs and a number of log buildings of which they had taken possession upon the bank of Scary Creek. These various objects formed defense for the rebel Sharp shooters, from which they were firing upon our men with deadly certainty, and with perfect security to themselves. The men filed down as directed and formed three companies on the outside of the fence next the river, and the two companies of the 21st deployed as skirmishers in the field, between the base of the hill and the fence. The companies on both sides of the fence were then ordered to move forward cautiously. When within 20 yards of the log buildings on the bank of the creek the entire command halted and were instructed to form for a charge. Col. Norton ordered them forward on the double quick with fixed bayonets, and when within fifty yards of the buildings, the front rank were ordered to fire and charge. This they did gallantly and with effect—taking several prisoners, and pricking them out of their various hiding places; while the rear rank men passing forward fired at the retreating rebels crossing on logs and over the ruins of the burnt bridge, and at all points where they showed themselves in their precipitous flight. At this juncture Lieutenant Pomeroy of company D of the 21st announced to Col. Norton with much feeling, that Capt. Allen was killed. Col. Norton ordered his body to be laid beside the fence under guard, and directed Lieutenant Pomeroy to take command of the company and bring it up for another charge; which the brave Lieutenant did almost instantaneously, and with the others made the second and lst charge, driving the rebels from their battery and putting their entire right wing and center to flight. Col. Norton finding that our center had come partly down the hill and halted in an excavation, took off his cap and turning partly around, signaled them forward to the charge, and while doing this was shot directly through the hips. The ball passed in at the right hip, just missing the end of the spine and out on the opposite hip. Col. N. being unable to give further command, was taken to one of the log buildings from which the enemy had just been driven, refusing to be taken to the rear. Before leaving the field Col. Norton sent a messenger to Col. Lowe, the principal in command, stating that the enemy had been driven from their right and center, and that he (Col. Lowe) must charge with his center and right wing, in order to sustain the left, and that this movement, if done quickly, would gain a victory, as their right and center had already retreated and they had raised a white flag upon their battery. The messenger either failed to give the message as ordered, or Col. Lowe neglected to regard it. The messenger was Lieutenant Ewing, Co. D, 21st regiment. He says he delivered the message and that Col. Lowe refused to do as requested. Hence the Federal troops were repulsed and obliged to retreat. The rebels seeing that they were not pursued and that no effort was made by our right and center to sustain us, and at this moment being re-inforced by 300 men, returned and obliged our men to retreat, leaving Col. Norton in the building to be taken prisoner. While so retreating many of our men were wounded, and some mortally, among whom was the gallant Lieut. Pomeroy who died in three days after from the effects of his wound; he being the second commanding officer in company D that was killed in this engagement—One word as to Col. Lowe. From the time the enemy opened fire upon us he gave no command. He did nothing to inspire his men with confidence. He kept well in the rear, out of the range of fire, and on but one occasion did he approach the line—where our men were firing, and then took good care to keep a log building between himself and the shots of the enemy. Had he approached them properly with his men formed in line, he could have in twenty minutes after Capt. Cotter opened fire upon the rebel battery, either by a flank movement upon their left turned their position, or by a direct charge in front and line, have completely routed them. And this with less loss of life and with much more credit to himself and satisfaction to the troops. Or had he sustained Col. Norton in his charge with the left wing by charging with his right and center after receiving the message sent him by the hand of [*1st*] Lieut. [*Matthew*] Ewing [*Co. D, 21st O.V.I.*] from Col. Norton, the day would undoubtedly have been ours. As to Gen. Cox had he sent the artillery with the re-inforcements on the Sunday previous when urged to do so by Col. Norton they could, by a march of 5 miles, have reached the enemy's position by daylight, and gained an easy victory—taking the cannon of the rebel force and undoubtedly many prisoners and routing them from their camp at the mouth of Cole river. When Gen. Cox came up with the main body, instead of stopping and going into camp as he did for six days at the mouth of the river Poca. We could have been at Charleston by Monday evening, had he so desired, and by this he would have saved the mortification of a disgraceful defeat the loss of three colonels and two captains, who, taking more interest in the battle then he, supposing the day to be ours; rode incautiously into the enemy's camp and are still detained as such. He could also have saved 6 or 8 days of valuable time, and probably the lives of several soldiers and officers and the crippling for the time being, Col. Norton himself. During the entire time Gen. Cox was lying with the main body in camp, he did not send out a scouting party, nor did he take any pains to ascertain our relative position with the enemy. He knew well that the enemy were in a place chosen by themselves as a battle ground, and they were daily becoming better and better prepared for the conflict. And even after the firing had commenced and had lasted for hours, Gen. Cox refused to send us reinforcements, or allow the balance of Col. Norton's regiment to march to the aid of their gallant Colonel; although they were under arms and chafing under confinement, impatient for the order to march and join in the battle. And after the battle, when the 21st begged him to send a party with a flag of truce to bring our dead and see to the welfare of Col. Norton, this brave General Cox indignantly replied that the enemy would have no more respect for a flag of truce than any other white rag. During the advance and battle Gen. Cox's action was rather unsoldierlike and questionable. The rebels took Col. Norton's horse, horse equipage, sword, pistols and even his boots and spurs. He then remained about three days a prisoner in a hospital, and was then released on parole until exchanged. He is now at home. His wounds though serious are not dangerous. He is now doing well and will probably be able in a few weeks to return to the army. We understand that arrangements have already been made to effect the exchange of Col. Norton for Major Patton, a rebel Major who is now on parole from our troops, and who had command at the battle of Scary Creek. Too much credit cannot be given to Capt. Cotter and Lieut. Col. White, of the 12th regiment during the entire engagement they fought bravely and like men. Poor Havens a member of Capt. Cotter's company, was mortally wounded while passing ammunition to the guns. His entire hip was shot off, and his dying words were "Boys, don't mind me; but protect the flag, and don't let it come down."

The "*Commercial*" and Colonel Lowe

An infamous paragraph appeared in the *editorial* columns of the Daily *Commercial* of Cincinnati, of the 30th ult., in reference to Col. John W. Lowe in his conduct at the battle of Scarey Creek.

All who *know* the Colonel, *know* that what is there charged is a most vile and malicious slander; and the "*Commercial*" and his *responsible* informers ought to be held answerable accordingly.

I might have sufficed the editor to speak of the slanderous rumors afloat, as an *item of news* interesting to all lovers of evil reports; but this, it appears, did not satisfy him, therefore, as far as he dare, he gives them his editorial endorsement, and connects them with a *murderous* sentence, that renders his rehearsal of them a *greater perfidy* than the original slanders.

It is time that a muzzle were put upon this ox's mouth. We do not know but that editors, who take such unwarrantable liberties with the character of our military leaders, as the "*Commercial*" has here done, should be obligated to *establish* their charges, upon the condition of suffering the traitor's doom if they fail. A law to this effect would have a healthful result, no doubt, upon the columns of very many of our daily sheets.

It is time an example were made of some of them. But may be, the public indignation, enlightened and aroused, will inflict an adequate penalty. Justice will yet be done.

The Daily Press on the *Commercial.*

The *Daily Press*, in animadverting upon the slanderous article in the *Commercial* upon the military conduct and character of Col. Lowe, remarks as follows:

"This style of trying and punishing people, of gibbeting them in the newspapers upon rumor and *exparte* testimony, is wrong and cruel. It is especially so in this case, where the party charged is absent; and we venture to say, had Colonel Lowe been known to be in this city, the *Commercial* would not have dared to give utterance to the slander."

Mr. *Daily Press*, you know your neighbor of the *Commercial*. You don't mean to say that he is a *coward*? But you *intimate* as much. You say that he would not have *dared* to have given utterance to the slander which he has uttered, if he knew that Col. Lowe was near to vindicate himself against the slanderer. Is Mr. *Commercial* such a *coward* as all that? Cowards are despicable. We would suggest that the *Commercial* be court-martialed, and if convicted of cowardice, we suppose according to his own humane code, *tenderly expressed*, he ought to be shot.

Relics from the Battle Field.

There is now in our sanctum, a musket and bayonet from Scary Hill battle ground. It is an old fashioned flint-lock musket, in a good state of preservation. On the lock are the words — "Manufacture Richmond," and the date "1810." There is also a separate bayonet — the longest we ever saw. These weapons were picked up on the battle field and brought to Xenia by Lieut. M.W. Trader [*2nd Lt. Moses W. Trader*], who is now at home on furlough.

Lieut. Trader bears evidence of the courage and presence of mind of Col. J. W. Lowe. In the hottest of the engagement—amidst the whizzing of balls the Colonel was as calm and unruffled as he had been merely reviewing his regiment at a parade.

Col. John W. Lowe

Some idle rumors, intended to disparage the official conduct of Col. Lowe, during the late battle of Scarey Creek, which we have noted, have obtained a limited circulation among a certain class of citizens, whose depravity in regard to all the movements connected with our national war is such, that they eagerly listen to, and readily believe reports which are evil, but we are slow to give them credence or to circulate reports which are good. So far as such citizens are concerned, it matters not what they believe or don't believe and we would not put ourselves to the pains of indicting a line here, upon this subject on their account.

But, it is due to this officer, as our fellow-townsman, that we should express our high gratification at the uniform testimony of correspondents for the press, and other responsible witnesses, certifying to his gallant demeanor on this trying occasion, and to the bravery and skill with which his attack upon the enemy was projected and enforced, and had not an unforeseen contingency occurred, for which he was in no way responsible, the victory would undoubtedly have been complete. As it was, it was a victory, although an incomplete one, and a victory achieved against great and unequal advantages in the enemy's favor.

May God preserve him to do deeds of greater valor still, and to win other laurels of triumph in this momentous *world-battle against the giant of oppressions and wrong*. Every page that will record, in future, the history of these conflicts of our soldiers in defense of our free Governmental institutions against our rebel subjects who have enlisted as the soldiers of a *black despotism* (the contrast of *black republicanism*) will be a page never to be obliterated. "Honor to whom honor is due."

Letter from Kanawha Valley. [*To the Xenia, Ohio* Torchlight]

Gauley Bridge, Fayette Co., Va.,
August 1st, 1861.

Editor Torch-Light — By some of the Ohio papers, I see that Col. Lowe has been most vilely slandered for his conduct during the battle of Scarry. Now I consider it my duty, as well as the duty of every honorable person who witnessed his conduct during the action, to expose these slanders.

During the whole action, Col. Lowe was in the most exposed position in the field, and, by his uniform, drew the attention of the enemy's fire right toward him, and the bullets whistled around his head like hail-stones. I stood within ten feet of him during the most of the action, and witnessed his whole conduct. As to the charge that he failed to give any orders during the fight, I would state that it was impossible to do so and be heard, as our regiment was scattered all over the ground, and it would have taken a man with a voice like thunder to have made himself heard during the heavy fire which was kept up for more than an hour.

W.H.H.[*1st Lt. William H. Hivling*],
Com'y B., 12th Reg't.

Col. McCook took command of Camp Chase on the 2d inst.

The Cincinnati *Commercial* acknowledges it lied in having charged Gen. Hill with "imbecility and cowardice" The editor also lies when he charges Col. Lowe with cowardice, and deserves to be kicked, caned and horse-whipped for his villainy. Potter's Whangdoodle Ass cannot long escape merited castigation. His buttocks are aching for a collision with bull's hide.

The *Commercial* on Colonel Lowe of the Twelfth Regiment.

The worst charge that can be made against a man upon whom a military trust has been imposed, is that of cowardice in battle. If proven, it renders the party infamous; and it even *said*, it imposes a blemish upon his reputation which scarcely any amount of retraction is able entirely to remove. The reason for this is that mankind are unwilling to believe that charges of so damaging a character will be made without testimony in every respect conclusive. They, therefore disregard retractions and counter-testimonials, upon the presumption that they are things manufactured for the charitable purpose of relieving the accused from a part of the disrepute which he has justly incurred.

Our neighbor of the *Commercial*, who saw the big gun at the Rig Raps roughed off, and foresaw on that occasion several events for whose occurrence the world is yet waiting, has, upon the strength of so extensive a military experience, assumed the airs of an oracle among us upon war and its elements, material and personal. Among other things he has exhibited a proneness to make free with the characters of gentlemen who have embarked in the service of their country, and has, on several occasions, taken the liberty to pronounce dogmatically upon their qualities and their conduct.

We admit the force of the inducement. The *Commercial* seldom attracts attention, editorially, except when it perpetrates a slander; and slanders, especially against men of standing and character, being invariably sensational, the temptation to indulge in them is very great. We do not blame the *Commercial* any more than the Lord blamed the unjust servant—acting, as it does, under the impulsion of the higher law of necessity. When a man is down, or is supposed to be down, the *Commercial* never fails to jump on him; thereby signalizing, without danger of loss, its watchfulness of the public interests and its hatred of transgressors. We, therefore, have no desire to detract from its value as an important sentinel upon the social watch tower hereabouts.

Upon the strength of certain vague, and what are equivalent to anonymous reports, the *Commercial* has been making free with the character of Colonel Lowe, of the Twelfth Ohio Regiment, a citizen of Dayton—charging that gentleman with cowardice exhibited at a skirmish upon the Kanawha. We have known Colonel Lowe, not intimately, but personally and by representation, for years. He is a respectable gentleman, and one who would not have accepted the post of Colonel had he been conscious of any want of the necessary courage to fill it properly. We do not believe the story, nor have we found any but such as accept without reflection whatever they hear or see in the newspapers, who give it any credit whatsoever.

This style of trying and punishing people, of gibbeting them in the newspapers upon rumor and *ex-parte* testimony, is wrong and cruel. It is especially so in this case, where the party charged is absent; and we venture to say, had Colonel Lowe been known to be in this city, the *Commercial* would not have dared to give utterance to the slander.

Col. Lowe.

We recently referred to the ridiculous and lying charge of cowardice, made against Col. Lowe, of the 12th Ohio Regiment, now occupying a post of honor and danger in Western Virginia. The Cincinnati Press thus speaks of the matter, which is the universal estimate of the man where he is known:

Upon the strength of certain vague, and what are equivalent to anonymous reports, the Commercial has been making free with the character of Col. Lowe, of the 12th Ohio Regiment, a citizen of Dayton—charging that gentleman with cowardice exhibited at a skirmish upon the Kanawha. We have known Col. Lowe, not intimately, but personally and by representation, for years. He is a respectable gentleman, and one who would not have accepted the post of Colonel had he been conscious of any want of the necessary courage to fill it properly. We do not believe the story, nor have we found any but such as accept without reflection whatever they hear or see in the newspapers, who give it credit whatsoever

Tomorrow we will copy from the Commercial a correspondence which should make ashamed the authors of the dastardly charges, and the editors who licked them into shape and printed them.

We deem it but necessary to say that the rumors circulated industriously by unprincipled sneaks, that Col. Lowe, of the 12th Ohio Regiment, deported himself in a cowardly manner at the recent battle of "Scary Hill," are scorned here, as elsewhere, by all who know the man. An officer who passed the ordeal of a battle field in Mexico and who was mentioned by his superiors as a "gallant officer," would not act the coward in a fight in Virginia. We ought not deign to notice the matter.

Col. John W. Lowe.

In the Commercial of last Tuesday, the 30th ult., there was a paragraph concerning the above named officer, in which he was accused, "on the authority of officers and men returned from the Kanawha," of having acted in the most cowardly manner at the battle of Scarey Creek, in Virginia. It was stated that "he had hid himself behind a house, and that, though expostulated with, he could not be induced to come from his shelter." To those who read this paragraph, and to those who have heard any rumors derogatory to Col. L., the following statements are particularly commended:

STATEMENT OF ADJUTANT ROBERTS.
Columbus, O., July 30, 1861.

Having seen several communications and editorials concerning Col. Lowe's actions in the above affair, I being his Adjutant and in the battle with him, I think it no more than just to him that I should deny these charges. Col. Whittlesey, of the Engineer corps, was detailed by Gen. Cox to accompany the expedition, and was of great service to the command. Col. W. has said that everything was done that could have been done, and it was for the want of ammunition alone that the Federal troops were compelled to retire, and not for the want of courage and bravery on the part of the officers and soldiers. (Signed)

WM. H. ROBERTS,
Adjutant 12th Regiment O.V.

STATEMENT OF PRIVATE BROWN.
Xenia, O., Aug. 1, 1861.

The subscriber was in the fight at Scarey Creek, in Western Virginia, and was stationed for a long time in a position less than fifty yards from Col. Lowe, and can bear testimony that he bore himself with the utmost bravery, standing amid a shower of balls without the least flinching or appearance of fear, and any assertion to the contrary is absolutely false. (Signed)

JOHN E. BROWN
Private Co. D, 12th Reg. O.V.

STATEMENT OF LIEUT. TRADER.
Xenia, O., Aug. 1, 1861

Having seen the statement in the Cincinnati Commercial that Col. Lowe acted in a cowardly manner at the battle of Scarey Creek, in Virginia, it is nothing more than my duty to state that it is entirely false. I was with Col. Norton and Lieut. Col. White on the left, and when we discovered the advance of the rebel reinforcements was sent by Col. White to advise Col. Lowe, who was chief in command, of their approach. I found Col. Lowe in a position as much exposed as anybody on the field, and as perfectly cool and self-possessed as if he were merely on parade. He did his whole duty, and there was no blame attached to him by any one that I heard of in the Kanawha Valley. That he dodged behind a house, or showed the least sign of fear, is entirely untrue. (Signed)

W.W. TRADER [*Moses W. Trader*]
Lieutenant Co. D, 12th Reg. O.V.

STATEMENT OF LIEUT. BROWN.
Dayton, O., August 1st, 1861.

I was in the fight at Scarey Creek in Virginia, and as there has been some commenting upon the conduct of Col. Lowe during the engagement, I wish to make a statement that justice may be done to all parities.

I was with Col. Norton on the left and was taken prisoner with him. As we were nearly a quarter of a mile from Col. Lowe's position, I am not able to say from my own observation anything about his conduct under fire, but I am convinced beyond any doubt, that the charge of cowardice is untrue because I heard nothing of it in the Kanawha country, and because the Twelfth Regiment with Col. Lowe at its head, still had the place of honor in the advance when I left a week ago.

As reports have been flying around this city and elsewhere, that Col. Norton had said as much about Col. Lowe as the "Commercial" did, I will say that I was with Col. N. during all his captivity, and came down to Cincinnati with him, and I never heard him say a word against Col. Lowe, and I don't believe he ever did. He did say, however, that "there was blame somewhere, because the left was not supported as it should have been, and that he had no doubt Gen. Cox's report would place it where it belonged. It was not for him to blame any one." I don't believe Col. Norton ever said anything about Col. Lowe's conduct under fire; because, as I have said before, we were a quarter of a mile away from him and out of sight of him all the time and could not, therefore, know any thing about it. I feel perfectly confident that when the whole truth is known, it will appear that Col. Lowe did his whole duty, and proved himself to be a gallant and efficient officer. (Signed)

ASHLEY BROWN,
1st Lieut., Co. I, 12th Reg., O.V.

It seems to the writer hereof, that Col. Norton, according to Lieut. Brown, has the proper idea in regard to awarding praise or blame to officers after a battle is over. By the official report of the Commander-in-Chief, and by that alone, should the officers and men under him be judged. And it seems not a little strange that those officers, upon whose authority the "Commercial" professes to speak, should permit themselves to charge a fellow officer, hundreds of miles away, with so heinous a crime as cowardice, when they have never dared, and never will dare to make such a charge in his presence, or complain of him to Gen. Cox.

THOMAS O. LOWE.
Dayton, O., 2d August, 1861

Letter Sent To *Cincinnati Commercial* Defending Col. Lowe

Camp Gauley, Va.
Aug. 13, 1861

Editor Cin Commercial,
Dear Sir.

We were greatly pained to see in your daily issue of 30th July an editorial statement made upon what you deemed good authority that Colonel John W. Lowe of the 12 Ohio Regiment, had played the cowards part at the Battle of Scarey fought on the 17th July

That you may know what uninterested and impartial gentlemen, present in the action, think of the Colonels conduct, I enclose their statement.

You will do but an act of justice to contradict additionally so unjust and injurious a charge.

C.B. White Lt. Col., 12th R. O.
J.D. Hines Major
H.H. Clement Lieut. Comp. A [*1st Lt. Henry H. Clement*]
W.E. Fisher Lieut. Comp. A [*2nd Lt. William E. Fisher*]
A.N. Charnell Lieut. Co. E. [*2nd Lt. Aaron N. Channel*]
D.W. Pauly Adjutant [*Daniel W. Pauley*]
A. Legg Capt. Co. E [*Andrew Legg*]
J. Whitecomb Ross Lieut. Co. F
Robert Wilson Lieut. of Co. G.
A.M. Dimoniti Lieut. Co. C [*Alonzo M. Dimmitt*]
J.L. Hilt Capt. Co. G 12th Regt. [*Joseph L. Hilt*]

CINCINNATI COMMUNICATOR
August 22, 1861

We have seen letters from Col. Charles Whittlesey of the Engineer Corps, and Capt. John B. Gibbs, member of Gen. Cox's staff, and also from Gen. Cox himself, pronouncing the rumors that Col. Lowe, of Ohio, behaved in a cowardly manner at the battle of Scarey, unfounded.

LETTER TO COL. LOWE FROM COL. WHITTLESEY

Gauley Bridge, Virginia
Aug. 4th 1860

Col. Lowe 12th Ohio Regiment

Sir -

The annexed extract from the Cincinnati Commercial of the 30th with which you have just brought to my notice does you great injustice and must certainly have originated with persons not present in the engagement at Scarey run.

I think I saw you not less than twenty times during the battle and it never occurred to me that there was any thing in your conduct to warrant a charge of cowardice.

Your respectfully,
Colonel Whittlesey

I fully confirm and endorse the statement of Col. Whittlesey—and will say that the point at which I saw Col. Lowe longest was the point that I found most uncomfortable—and so far as my observation goes—the point at which more men were wounded than at any other one point.

Ira B. Gibbs

LETTER TO COL. LOWE FROM GEN. JACOB D. COX

(Private)
Gauley Bridge, 15 Aug. 1861

My dear Colonel

I have seen with great pain the attack upon you to which you refer in your private note to me, but I have also seen the array of testimony published in your defense and really believe that the case even as now published is sufficient to enable candid persons to form a just judgment in the matter. Col. Whittlesey and Capt. Gibbs both told me they bore cheerful testimony to the courage you exhibited in the 17th ult., and I believe that all who are willing to be convinced are satisfied with their testimony.

I have great doubt whether any further publication on the subject is expedient. My own such is to let such slander kill itself, as it is almost seen to do in the long run. To continue to bring this case before the public is apt to be regarded as an extra sensitiveness which would imply consciousness of the truth of the charge, and one may do as much hurt as good by simply insisting upon the truth.

Let us rather hope that the future will give such proof of the falsity of these charges that the slander will [*illegible*] and have the effect of praise.

Very sincerely yours
J. D. Cox

Col. J. W. Lowe
Charleston

The remark that "Col. Lowe seems to have had very little discretion in carrying out the discretion that his orders gave him," does great injustice to a brace and competent officer. From the best authority obtainable at this time his orders were to reconnoiter and attack if he thought he could dislodge them. When the attack was made the number of the rebels seemed to be but 700, instead of 1,500, as the investigations of our men in the woods and underbrush afterward proved it to be. Notwithstanding the great disparity of numbers had the advantages of the enemy in position, the battle was fought gallantly and successfully by our men, up to the time of the arrival of the rebel re-enforcement and until all their ammunition was exhausted. All accounts agree that this is so; and to show that Colonel Lowe's orders were well given, and that it was no fault of his that the issue was not successful, I quote from the letter of your "Own Correspondent" in this morning's Gazette.

"As the ammunition of our boys was now getting low, an order was given to charge bayonets. The left wing, composed of the fragment of the Twenty-first and one or two companies of the Twelfth, led by Lieut. Col. White, promptly obeyed, and rushing down the hill forded the stream, which was more than knee deep, and rushed upon the enemy's entrenchments. Had the movement on the right been equally prompt, the *rebels would have been utterly routed*, but owing partly to the incompetency of their officers, and partly to the fact that they were badly disciplined, they faltered, and soon after fled."

Had the movement on the right been equally prompt, we would have heard nothing but praises of the Commander of the expedition. Unless you hold him responsible for the "incompetency" of his subordinate officers and for the arrival of the rebel re-enforcement, it seems to me your charge of "indiscretion" must fall to the ground.

E.

The Army on the Kanawha—General Cox's Brigade.

Gentlemen just from Kanawha represent the state of the army in that region as discreditable in an unusual degree. There is an utter lack of discipline. The officers give little or no attention to their duties, and the soldiers run at large, and commit with impunity depredations and wrongs upon the persons and property of the inhabitants.

We are speaking of the command of General Cox, and upon authority which we deem in every way reliable. The General is as in private life a worthy and useful citizen; but it is evident that he has no fitness for the important post of commander of an army. He has none of the qualities requisite to render him useful in the camp or in the field. Having no knowledge of his duty, he, of course, has no capacity to perform it; and his command owes its safety more to the fact that the enemy is, if possible, still more demoralized and anarchical than his own soldiers.

We regret to say these things, but it is right to say them. General Cox is only a general by title and commission. He has had some apparent successes, to which rumor, either with or without his agency, has attached considerably more importance than they deserve. Such as they were, they are not the result of any skill or vigor of this own; for of those qualities there have been, if accounts are true, none exhibited. The army upon the Kanawha evidently needs the attention of the Government; and General Cox had better retire to the walks of civil life, a sphere which, it is probable, he is admirably qualified to adorn and illustrate.

GALLIPOLIS
THURSDAY—AUG 8, 1861

The gallant 21st Regiment of O.V.M. made their appearance in our town last Thursday, on their return trip home from Kanawha. The men gave token in their sun-burned visages of having seen some service. Reports from Kanawha are highly creditable to this regiment, in regard to their strict sobriety, good order, and manly bearing. The citizens of Charleston were sorry to see them leave, fearing others sent in their place might not prove so careful in observing the rules of propriety and decorum. It was just what we expected to hear of them, judging from their conduct whilst in Camp Carrington. The boys say they are ready for a three years term, but only under other officers, and upon the express condition that they are not to be under Gen. Cox. They are unanimous in condemnation of this officer, and indeed if a tithe of their statements be true, he is certainly not the man for the position of Brigadier General. Indeed, from other sources we have long since been induced to believe that he was a "slow coach."

In times like the present, we have forborne making reflections upon the actions of our military leaders. They are sometimes unjustly blamed by men not acquainted with the facts. But in this case, hundreds of men concur in statements, which, if true, show at least that Gen. Cox has a wholesome dread of doing things in a hurry.

The affair at Scarey, according to the testimony of these men, terminated so disastrously, because of his indecision of character. The "Julia Maffit," with 300 seceshers on board, could have been taken easily by Capt. Cotter's artillery, but Gen. Cox forbade any firing until she reached the opposite shore, her rebel troops landed, and she herself set on fire by them, which Capt. Cotter under orders of Gen. Cox, by a timely shot rendered of short duration.

Many other matters they allege against him, but having no desire to tarnish the fame of Gen. Cox, "or any other man," we suffer them to pass without comment.

The Affair at Scary Creek.

Dayton, O., July 22.

Eds. Gazette: The "Gazette" has always hitherto been remarkable for its accuracy and general reliability, and in most matters it seems to be so still. In military criticism however, the friends of those who are criticized are disposed to think it too haste in pronouncing judgment. The reputation of a military man is to him dearer than his life, and those of our citizens who have gone forth to stand between our country and destruction have the right I think, to expect that their fellow citizens at home will send after them their warmest sympathy, and even though they be unfortunate, that their home newspapers will hesitate long and consider well and thoroughly all the circumstances of the case before rendering judgment as to the measure of blame they should receive. It is very easy for an editor to indite a slashing paragraph like the one headed "A good haul of colonels" in this morning's "Gazette," but it is no easy matter for those brave men and good officers to set themselves right before the community whose opinion is necessarily formed by the newspaper reports and editorial comments.

It is easy to say that Gen. Cox—a good man but not an experienced soldier—"can spare them without damage," but he has not said so and won't say so. On the contrary we have every reason to think that being deprived of the aid of such [rest of article is missing]

Camp Lowe.— Camp Lowe, Xenia, named for the lamented Colonel of the Ohio Twelfth begins to assume a military aspect. But a hundred or two are on the ground—more coming in today. Judge Wm. Mills, of Yellow Springs, the Quartermaster, is "lively as a cricket," and deservedly popular with the soldiers, who do not fear being treated in an ir *ration*-al or unhandsome manner, in any respect. They say he is no snob, but a downright good fellow, generally.

By the way, we met, last night, a soldier of the Twelfth, from Scarey Creek and Carnifex, at home on a furlough, and asked him of Col. Lowe's bearing at Scarey. He swore a blue streak over the calumny that charged him with cowardice, said he stood up firmly to the fight till seventeen rounds were fired and the ammunition gone, and then gave the order to charge bayonet. But the enemy had disappeared and a retreat was finally ordered. (penciled Oct. 22, 61)

OPERATIONS FOLLOWING THE BATTLE OF SCARY CREEK

PERRYSBURG JOURNAL
August 1, 1861

Letter from a Virginian.

Camp Pocatanlico, July 19, 1861.

Mr. J.W. Bailey—Your Wood county boys are here, and we thank God for it. They have been in the Kanawha Valley six days, and have cheered up the Union cause in Western Virginia. As a Virginian for the Union, it has been my good fortune to become acquainted with some of your boys. On the 26th day of May last, I was assailed by a guerrilla band of secessionists, with cocked rifles presented at me, the cap glistening on the tube, the finger on the trigger, and with the most horrid oaths, they said they would blow my heart out of the wrong side of me if I attempted to plow Southern soil; that no man with free-soil or northern principles should plow Jeff Davis' soil. I, as you would suppose, took the only alternative, and left for Ohio, the "land of the free and the home of the brave." Scarcely conscious of my course, I came to Gallipolis, where I found your regiment, had an introduction to Col. Norton, whose sympathy and manly treatment of me and my countrymen in the same condition, has placed us under a debt of gratitude we can never repay or find words to express. I have been more or less with your boys ever since I was with them on the 4th of July, when they made a rush upon Ripley, the county seat of Jackson county, Va. They made a gallant descent on the town in double quick time; surrounded the place, but to their utter astonishment their game was gone. Spies gave them timely notice of danger, and they went in such a hurry, that they left their breakfast on the tables in the court house. After a close examination of the place, they unfurled the stars and stripes from the lofty spire of the court house; and may they wave in the breeze of the Old Dominion as a memento of the gallant sons of Ohio as well as to the Union of a common country. On this expedition your boys signalized themselves with a nobleness of soul commonly unknown in warfare. They were often seen to almost weep when cheered by the matrons of exiled sons and husbands, which occurrence was common. They appear to be made of the best materials of nature. They have, as by instinct, every qualification that is necessary for the station they are filling, with a full appreciation of what is right, and a strong resentment against all wrongs. I have followed them on this expedition to capture Charleston, the main seat of the rebel army in Western Virginia. They are camped within 15 miles of Charleston and 13 miles of the main fortress, which is two miles below Charleston. I must now digress for a few lines to give you an explanation of the cause of my having to leave my family in the mountains of Virginia. The secessionists call me a Southern man with Northern principles. So far is truth. They also say I am an Abolitionist, which is absolutely false, so far as I understand the term. I am for leaving all the races in the world in the book of fate where they are placed, and, claiming to be of the anglo-saxon or European race, I think more of that race than of all the other races on the face of the earth. I am against the extension of slave territory or slave labor, where it comes in competition with white labor or the interests of the white race. I am a Virginian by birth, have been raised in Virginia, have never claimed citizenship in any other State; it being the place of my forefathers' graves. But living in that portion of Virginia whose proximity to Ohio and her sister Free States, the lights of their arts and science have shone upon us; they have sent the spelling book with its instructor among us; they have sent their steam mills to grind us our bread; they have shown us the equality of society, and have let us see that we have an equal right with our aristocratic brethren. And now, we of Western Virginia bound by these fraternal bonds of brotherhood to our sister State of Ohio; with the love of a common country, our interests are inseparable. Yet the "rulers," as they term themselves, have transferred us to Jeff Davis, from whom we look to your generous chivalry to interpose to keep us from being swallowed up in this great Southern vortex. While I am writing I am amidst your boys. They appear to be intent on sweeping secession from the face of the earth, whilst they, joking in all the gay vivacity of youth, innocent in their diversions, manly in their deportment, yet terrible in battle. Well may their mothers be proud of such offspring, and may their end be in peace. I must give you some of the experience of your noble boys. The enemy placed a masked battery at Scary Creek, 4 miles above this place, with the intention of destroying our boats as well as to ambuscade the advance of the army . But the vigilance of the pickets discovered it in time to keep us from being entrapped, and there was a move made to destroy the works. The assault was made with two companies of the 21st, backed by part of the 12th regiment. The action lasted upwards of two hours, in which the rebels lost between sixty and one hundred killed and their battery knocked to pieces. So they found by experience that free boys can fight on Southern soil and teach them a lesson they have long wanted instructions in. The time for which your boys volunteered has just expired, and they are coming home. In as much as it must be s source of joy to welcome them to the bosoms of friends and relatives, we who would be glad to keep them as friends and citizens as well as soldiers, have cheerfully to submit. May heaven's blessing follow them to the bosom of their friends.

Joel Cunningham

WHEELING INTELLIGENCER
July 27, 1861

FROM THE KANAWHA EXPEDITION

Pocatalico Creek, Kanawha River,
July 22, 1861

Here we are, at this date, lying around loose with a heavy storm of rain pouring down upon our devoted heads, making locomotion rather an unpleasant recreation among the Virginia hills—to your correspondent especially, in seeking for something to interest your many readers. But I fear of being unsuccessful in the present monotony of the camp. The Kentucky boys, for the want of more active service, resort to various amusements to while away the time, varying from musical concerts to sham engagements, and from chicken practice to the chase and capture of a bullock, should one unconsciously show his horns—two of whom, poor souls were made to suffer yesterday.

Quite an amusing scene occurred in the capture of one of them. Being a powerful fellow, he scattered the boys around quite unceremoniously. About one hundred men were in the chase—some armed with muskets, some with axes, some with clubs, some with stones, and others with fence rails. In his flight he upset several of the "boys," in their efforts to catch him by the horns. The cry was: Head him here—head him there—shoot—don't shoot—knock him in the head—catch him by the horns—throw a rope over him, &c, &c. After a long chase, one fellow, armed with an axe, succeeded in getting in a blow between the horns, which fetched him to the ground. The rest is soon told: Being turned over to the butcher's hands. His remains were soon disposed of.

Captain Cahill, with a squad of men, went on a scouting expedition in search of some Seceshers, living four miles from the camp. Coming upon the premises of Squire Martin, a noted Secessionist, his men charged upon a flock of ducks and chickens. The matron of the premises plead to Capt. Cahill in behalf of herself and seven children in the loss of her poultry. The gallant Captain's heart melted to her appeals; on learning her estimated value of the seizure he drew forth his purse and deposited the amount in her hand. On his return to camp, your correspondent was made the recipient of a nice duck and chicken, which was duly appreciated as a luxury in camp fare.

This morning, notwithstanding the rain, a reconnoitering party was sent up the river on one of the steamboats, and was landed for the purpose of proceeding up to the mouth of Coal River, and ascertain, if possible, where the enemy are entrenched.

The expedition was composed of the following commands: Major Leiper, with companies G and K of the First Kentucky, and Major Hines, with companies A, F and H of the 12 Ohio Regiment. They returned at 6 o'clock this evening, with the following intelligence: "After leaving the boat the column moved on up the river, without meeting with the enemy until arriving near the mouth of Coal river. Upon their appearance the enemy suddenly fled, setting fire to the bridge across Coal River as they left." Major Leiper's command succeeded in capturing one of Jenkin's dragoons and horse, and also Major Patton, the commander of the enemy's forces. Major Patton was severely wounded in the last engagement, and was there, attended by his wife.

He was left by Major Leiper, under a parole of honor, subject to exchange. Two of the wounded of the Twelfth Ohio Regiment, were found there, receiving every attention at the hands of the enemy. The camp at Coal River was found to be excellently located. Comfortable cantonments had been erected there, and every comfort and convenience had been added. The headquarters were established at the palatial residence of Beverly Tompkins, a neutral, surrounded by a beautiful grove and pleasant lawns. A council of war was held there by the Majors and Captains in command, over which presided Major Leiper, of the First Kentucky Regiment, to take into consideration the propriety of burning the camp and its surroundings.

The result of the conference was, that in consideration of the attention being paid to our wounded there, and the former attentions of Mr. Thompkins, the owner of the grounds, when Col. Norton was a prisoner and wounded with them, it was resolved to spare the premises. The burning of the bridge at Coal river, by the enemy, was wholly unnecessary, as the Federal troops in their march, will proceed up the opposite side of the Kanawha and have also the advantage of the Kanawha river as a means of transportation, which is at present in good stage and rising. The steamer Mary Cook arrived, this evening with one company of recruits for the Eleventh Regiment O.V. They also bring Information of Col. Guthrie and his command having arrived at Ravenswood. The steamer Eunice was dispatched to transport them up the Kanawha to join the main army.

Tuesday Morning, 23d July.—After a continued rain throughout the entire day yesterday, the morning of the 23d opened with a clear and cool atmosphere. The sun rose in its majesty, proclaiming a serene and pleasant day; The heavy rains have left the camp grounds in a muddy and unpleasant condition for locomotion. The "boys" throughout the camp are quite busily engaged this morning in cleaning up their arms and accouterments preparatory for active service. An accident occurred this morning from the careless use of fire arms. John E. Spicer, of Co. F. Twelfth Ohio, was shot through the arm by the accidental discharge of a pistol.—

Major Leiper was informed yesterday while at Camp Cole, of the removal of Colonels Woodruff, De Villiers and Neff, together with Captains Hurd and Austin, from the town of Charleston, to the city of Richmond.

Col. Woodruff was represented to have been effected to tears from the humiliation of his position. Colonel DeVilliers pronounced their capture as contrary to all honorable military rules. They all claim that they were treacherously ensnared into the enemy's camp, by the enemy displaying the American flag. They have been kindly treated by their captors and complain only of the mode of their capture. Col. Norton is fast recovering of his wounds, and it is supposed will soon be exchanged with Major Patton of the Confederate army. I cannot now inform you of our future movements. General Cox is at present quite busy in perfecting his movements, which will soon be completed and then onward will on the watchword. I could give you some information in regard to it, but do not think it advisable to do so at present, as it might fall into the enemy's hands, or otherwise prejudice the General's plans. When the circumstances will admit you can depend upon being fully advised by your own correspondent. The "boys" here express their gratitude for your generous and constant supply of the *Times*. C.W.B.

WHEELING INTELLIGENCER
July 30, 1861

Further News from the Kanawha Expedition

Mr. Gibner, of this city, left Charleston on the Kanawha, on Friday afternoon, and arrived here Saturday evening. He reports that Gen. Cox proceeded with great caution from Poco, and was considerably delayed by burnt bridges, which he was compelled to replace. The enemy were scattered about Charleston and vicinity in considerable numbers, but fled without firing a gun. Our troops sent several volleys after them, killing a few, and Capt. Carter, of the Cleveland artillery, fired one shot into the rebel steamer Julia Moffit, which caused her boilers to explode, and she burned to the water's edge. The rebels, under Wise, were strongly fortified below Charleston, but they evacuated their position, and left considerable plunder behind them, which was taken by Cox's troops.—They retreated to Gauley bridge, thirty-eight miles above Charleston, where it was supposed they would give battle. The position is formidable, and if they have had time to fortify it, it will require hard fighting to drive them out. Gen. Cox was pursuing them, cautiously but steadily to prevent them from establishing themselves too strongly. His rear column moved from Charleston for Gauley bridge, at 2 o'clock, Friday afternoon.

Mr. Gibner says that Wise's army was greatly demoralized, and he thinks 500 men must have deserted before they reached Gauley. Gen. Cox had four regiments—the 11th and 12th Ohio, and the two Kentucky Regiments—Col. Guthrie having joined him—besides a company of cavalry. Carter's battery of two guns, and the Ironton Artillery of two guns, making a force of 3,600 men. Capt. J.C. Lane, of this city and his company of mechanics were infinitely serviceable to Gen. Cox in rebuilding bridges. The General is extremely cautious in moving through the country, sending out scouts and skirmishers constantly in advance to prevent surprises. Mr. Gibner thought that a battle probably took place at Gauley bridge, yesterday. We are informed, however, that Wise retreated, although our information is not definite. He informed the people of Charleston that he was ordered to retire to Eastern Virginia. Meantime, an expedition consisting of three regiments, under Col. Tyler, of the Ohio 7th, had moved from Weston to cut off the rebels at Gauley. If they retreated from that position it is probable that both Cox and Tyler are pursuing them. The 21st Ohio declined to go to Gauley bridge because their time had expired.

Extracts from a Letter by Col. Lowe.

We are permitted to make the following extracts from a letter, just received by Mrs. Lowe from her husband. They will be of interest to our readers. The letter bears two dates, having, of course, been written accordingly, and sent in one envelope. The first is dated

Ten Miles Below Gauley Bridge, Kanawha Valley, July 28th—Evening

We came to Charleston in the most gallant style, our three boats filled with men, the stars and stripes flying and our band playing. It was a most glorious scene. We encamped on the bank of the river below the town, having found that Gov. Wise had cut the main cable of a most splendid river bridge. It was a perfectly unnecessary job, and did not detain us over six hours. The scenery around Charleston is beautiful, but the town is not much. We left it next day and marched through a most lovely valley, calm and quiet apparently; but the desolation of war is observed. There are many sad hearts here amongst the people. Gov. Wise has stripped them of everything they had, and left them beggared, in many instances almost starving.

Gauley Bridge, July 29th.

We left our camp early this morning and marched through a most lovely valley for ten miles to this place. I never saw such a country for defenses. High mountains, 500 feet high on either side, with nothing but a roadway for the troops to pass,—there were a dozen places stronger than the far-famed Thermopylae. Why Gov. Wise did not fight us, I cannot say, unless our fight at Scary fully satisfied him of Northern pluck and endurance. The march to day was very exciting. We began soon to meet traces of the Wise legion. We took several prisoners,—then found clothing, broken wagons, sick men,—then trees cut down to impede our way, but we did not stop long. We soon came to a steamboat they had burned, called the Kanawha Valley,—a dreadful waste of property. About 11 o'clock we came insight of the Falls, and in a half-hour we were at Gauley Bridge, but it was not there. Wise had given it to the flames. It must have been a noble structure of three spans, each as long as the Milford bridge. Everything was in the wildest confusion. Hines was in command of the advanced guard, and I was next with the Regiment. Hines got all the boats together and with Doan's and Cary's companies, crossed the river and captured 1,000 stand of arms, 400 pounds of powder, and bacon, tents, clothing, &c., in almost any quantity.

We will remain here a few days, but what our destination will be, I cannot say.

GALLIPOLIS JOURNAL
August 1, 1861

Charleston, Va., July 27.

I embrace the only opportunity offered for several days to give you some particulars relative to the movement of Gen. Cox's brigade.

From the date of this letter you will see that an advance has been made.—On Tuesday evening, an order was issued to the army at Camp Pocatallico to prepare two days' rations and be ready to march at four o'clock the following morning. The impression had somehow gone abroad in camp that no movement would be made till the latter part of the week, if then; and the soldiers had just completed various preparations for a more protracted stay; but the command was none the less cheerfully received. In a short time afterward, the camp fires were blazing brightly, and amid song and jest, the requisite amount of provender was prepared.

A dense fog which covered the valley during the night, together with the unavoidable delay incident to striking the tents of an army, prevented our departure at the hour named in the General's order; but shortly after eight o'clock we were under way. The main column of the army followed the Charleston turnpike, which runs some distance behind the hills overlooking the river, the Eleventh Ohio forming the advance, and the Second Kentucky Regiment the rear guard. The fleet of Government steamboats, containing the army stores, under the command of the genial Commodore Beltzhoover, so well known on all the Western waters, cautiously felt their way up the river, preceded on the right and left by the Twelfth Ohio, which had been detached from the main column to act as skirmishers, and prevent a surprise to the boat from masked batteries, of which our frail barks have a wholesome dread.

The afternoon was well advanced when the steamers reached the mouth of Coal Creek, only eight miles above. Here it was reported that the enemy were strongly entrenched at a point

[*page torn at this point — continues with next column*]

fight this side of Gauley Bridge, forty miles above, if there.

I had almost forgotten to say that when our fleet passed the still smoking hull of the Julia Maffitt, they found a flatboat moored by her side, a considerable quantity of army stores, which the rebels had been compelled to leave behind them in their flight. A box of shoes and another of caps, three or four barrels of flour and as many bags of corn meal, besides bacon, sugar, and a variety of articles too numerous to mention were promptly reshipped.—Some of our soldiers helped themselves to blankets, fiddles and other mementos of their sojourn in Dixie.

Charleston, which is altogether the most agreeable town in Western Virginia, is situated on a point at the juncture of the Kanawha and Elk rivers. It has, or had, a population of about twenty-five hundred or three thousand souls, and gave a large Union majority when the vote on the Secession ordinance was taken. Elk river is here spanned by a beautiful suspension bridge, which cost $30,000. To give you an idea of the vandalism of the rebel troops, I need only say that after they crossed the bridge, they cracked the wire strands that support it with axes till it was unsafe to cross, and then fired the flooring, which fortunately only burned twenty or thirty feet from the shore. This bridge is the pride of the town, and you can readily imagine that its people do not love the traitors any the better for their attempt to destroy it.

From the most reliable information we can obtain, it appears that Wise's force is not more than thirty-five hundred strong. About seven hundred of these are said to have been impressed into the rebel service. We also learn that desertions from his ranks are numerous. About one hundred are reported to have left him at this place night before last. They are also said to be indifferently armed, and poorly supplied with means of transportation. They have literally gutted several stores in Charleston, and all along our route we learn that horses, cattle, provisions, and whatever else [*page torn*] duce to their comfort or [*page torn*] flight has been seized upon without as much as saying, "by your leave."

Our forces were heartily welcomed here last evening by the Charlestonians. The star spangled banner was once more thrown to the breeze, people lined the bank of the river and cheered lustily as we passed, ladies waved their handkerchiefs, and nearly everybody seemed rejoiced to see us. The "contrabands," especially, were in their element, and caused many a shout from

[— *REMAINDER OF PAGE IS TORN* —]

GALLIPOLIS JOURNAL
August 1, 1861

Gov. Wise and son, on their retreat from Kanawha destroyed nearly all the bridges above Poca, stole every thing that was loose and burnt the steamers Julia Maffit and new Kanawha Valley. The last heard from this gang of thieves they had crossed and set fire to Gauly Bridge and were badly scared for fear Cox would overtake them. They are completely demoralized and disorderly. All the Western men deserted near the falls and are scattered through the mountains, except a few who have returned to their homes in small squads.

THE IRONTON REGISTER
August 1, 1861

Charleston, Kanawha, Occupied by the Federal Troops

We are indebted to the editor of the Clipper for the letter below from Judge Golden

Charleston, Virginia, July 27

Friend Drake; We are now encamped at Charleston. Gen. Cox moved up this river. Wise and his whole rebel army fled, tearing up and burning bridges. The wire bridge across Elk was fired, wires cut, &c. and is now impassable. Many of the rebels have deserted. The Union men here have been stripped of nearly all their property. The enemy left much of their camp equipage, provision, &c., and some arms. The rebel boat "Julia Maffit" was fired into by our troops, after having been set on fire by the rebels. She was passing up the river, loaded with wheat, provisions, troops, &c. She was soon reduced to ashes. Jenkins was killed—so his physician (our informant) says. We will start in pursuit of the rebels this morning. Before leaving, the rebels robbed the Charleston Bank. Send up some papers

FLETCHER GOLDEN
[*Capt. John S. George's Ironton Cavalry Company*]

We have other information that Jenkins (A.G.) was not killed, but badly wounded perhaps mortally—shot in the breast.

It appears that Gen. Cox, with the 1st and 2d Ky. and 11th and 12th Ohio, took the line of march from "Poco" for Charleston, July 24th; and before the arrival of the Federal troops, the valiant Wise fled somewhat precipitately, having "orders," so reported, to retire—leaving behind him a considerable quantity of camp equipage, tents, guns, knapsacks, &c., destroying bridges as he went—At our latest advices, Gen. Cox had gone some thirty or forty miles above Charleston, on the track of Wise, who was considerable distance ahead—perhaps a safe distance.

Civilian's Account From *Civil War Memories of Two Rebel Sisters* edited by William D. Wintz, (Charleston, West Virginia: Pictorial Histories Publishing Co.), 1989.

The spring of 1861 came as all other springs with its sunshine, its birds, and its flowers, yet we hailed it not with the usual joy and anticipation. Far away we could hear the rumblings of the storm that we feared would soon sweep over our beautiful valley. Fort Sumter had already fallen, there had been blood shed in Maryland, and now there had been a great stir in Western Virginia.

Mr. George Patton from Charleston had heretofore been a staunch Union man and had previously made stirring speeches in our town in favor of the Union. Recently, however, he returned speaking eloquently and calling on all sons of Virginia to rally around her flag. He was cheered lustily and how patriotic we felt as we waved our handkerchiefs. We all sang "We Will Die for Old Virginia." Altogether, this was an exciting day in our quiet little village of Coalsmouth.

Nine of our young men volunteered in Captain Patton's Company known as the Kanawha Riflemen. They were my brother Carroll Hansford, Stephen Teays, N.B. Brooks, Charlie Turner, Theodore Turner, Thornton Thompson, Tom Grant, James Rust, and Henry Gregory. The citizens of Coalsmouth gathered around the wagon to tell them good bye and to wish them "God speed." Tears were not only shed by their mothers and sisters, but many others there that day wept over the sacrifices they were about to make.

A camp had been established about two miles below Charleston by Captain George Patton of the Kanawha Riflemen, Captain John Swann of the Charleston Sharpshooters and Captain Andrew Barbee of the Border Rifles. These companies I believe were among the first that went into camp in western Virginia. They remained there until May when they were called to Buffalo about 25 miles below here. While they were there in camp, I went down to see "our boys" as did many others, thinking they might soon be sent far away. I stayed at Mrs. Wyatt's and had a pleasant visit. But then when it was determined that Buffalo might be attacked, we turned our faces homeward with many misgivings as to the future welfare of our dear ones. Sure that Buffalo would be attacked, Colonel McCausland ordered the troops to withdraw back up the valley as it would be impossible to hold the position even against a small force.

One day about sunset in early May, the steamboats "Julia Moffat" and "Kanawha Valley" came up the river with troops on board and landed below the mouth of Coal. We ladies had been molding bullets all day for the soldiers as there seemed to be a shortage.

As soon as we heard the boats had arrived, we all went down to welcome them. We all cheered and waved and their band responded by playing "Dixie" and some other pretty tunes from the boat. They then landed and marched to Camp Tompkins where they were soon joined by Captain Jenkin's company from Cabell County and other troops from Wayne and Boone counties. They were later formed into the 22nd Regiment under Colonel C.Q. Tompkins.

Then came those pleasant days like an oasis in a desert. The regiment was made up almost entirely of young men from Kanawha and adjoining counties. Our friends and relatives were all among them, and we went to and fro taking them things that would make their camp life more comfortable. We seemed to forget why they were there, and the threat of conflict seemed far away. Evening after evening we walked down to the camp to see them on dress parade and hear the music from the Kanawha Riflemen's brass band. They were well drilled, having excellent drill masters.

One morning about the last of June, I heard loud cheering down at the mouth of Coal River. I threw on my bonnet and ran in that direction as fast as I could to see what was going on. There I could see soldiers ascending the high hill across the Kanawha opposite the mouth of Coal. They were going in Indian file up the winding road and here and there through the openings in the trees could be seen different companies, each in their different uniforms. First were the Kanawha Riflemen under Captain Patton in their gray jackets, then came Captain Bailey's company in blue, and there was also Captain Barbee's company and Captain Lewis' cavalry. They all joined in singing "Virginia Boys" to the tune of Dixie. It sounded beautiful as the light breeze bore it down the mountain and across the river. Then when they sang "We Will Die for Old Virginia," it brought tears to our eyes.

They had been ordered to Ripley by the most direct route to drive back several companies of Federal troops. They had crossed over from Ohio to plunder and harass secessionists who lived in the area. There was a skirmish with three of their men killed and several wounded while none of our men were injured. They were only gone a few days but soon after, several companies were sent back to Buffalo on steamboats. Some Union men at Pt. Pleasant with the help of a few soldiers from Gallipolis, had arrested some prominent citizens. They were to be held as hostages for two Union men who had been taken by Captain Jenkins for disloyalty to the State. By the time our soldiers arrived, they found the Federal troops had returned to Ohio.

Soon after, Captain Albert G. Jenkins arrived at Camp Tompkins with his troop of Border Rangers from Green Bottom on the Ohio River. We ladies made and presented his company with a flag, it was a pretty one carefully made of the best material. Miss Sallie Lasley wrote our speech and her younger sister Allie delivered it. My father, John Hansford, held the flag unfurled to the breeze as it was presented to the company. They were all mounted and their horses were arranged in formation along the fence. They were under the shade of two locust trees that were in the yard of the old hotel near the covered bridge over Coal River. Captain Jenkins accepted it gracefully with a short and appropriate speech. We ladies stood on the lawn in front of the hotel with arms full of flowers in abundance which were showered over the officers and soldiers at the end of the ceremony.

Here I will relate an incident which occurred at the flag presentation ceremony which was very unusual for the times. When the flowers were being presented to the soldiers, one young lady having seen a small boy with the company, requested to present her bouquet to him. Captain Jenkins then called him up and he rode forward on a little mule with a rope bridle and no saddle. He wore a little cap and a very plain suit of everyday clothing. After he received his flowers, the captain introduced him as Lucian Ricketts. He said he had been adopted as a "child of the regiment" and then proceeded to tell us his story.

He said that when they were in camp at Greenbottom in Cabell County, this boy who was now only 14 years old had been drilling with them whenever he could borrow a horse. When they were ordered here to Camp Tompkins he went to his uncle's farm and appropriated this frisky little mule and began following the company. When I was told he was behind us I sent him word to return home, but he only dropped back and continued to tag along. Finding my orders disregarded, I rode to the rear and ordered him to go back home. I knew his mother, who was a widow and would surely be nearly deranged finding him gone. Another one of her sons, Albert Gallatin Ricketts, who is my namesake, is also in the company. When I began to reason with him he said "Captain, the road is free, I will ride in sight of you by day and camp nearby at night." When I told him he was too young for duty he said, "I can carry water, I can wait on you and do anything, but I am determined to go to war." We could hold out no longer and that night we voted to adopt him as "The Child of the Regiment."

He went by the name of "Cooney" Ricketts and afterwards he always rode at the head of the column beside his beloved captain who was also very fond of him. The company was camped directly across from where I lived just below Tacketts Creek. They were in great need for pistols as they could get none through the army at that time. Captain Jenkins conceived a plan to obtain some which involved the service of young Cooney Ricketts. He was furnished with a good supply of money and was set off astride his little mule in the direction of Guyandotte. Arriving in his home town he left his mule with relatives and boarded a steamer for Cincinnati. Arriving in the city, so as not to arouse suspicion, he began buying up pistols, one here and one there until he had obtained the required number. He then went out to the Union Camp Dennison where he collected important information regarding troop numbers and movements.

After his successful return with the guns, Cooney was nicely equipped with a new bridle and saddle for his mule. As he and the mule were both little, the ladies all thought him cute, sweet and brave. A great many tried to get him to return home, but all to no avail.

At Coalsmouth the pleasant summer days of July were passing and even though we were daily expecting the war to reach us we still managed to be cheerful. Our boys were yet at Camp Tompkins and the soil of Virginia up to now had not been invaded by the ruthless foe. However, a looming battle in our area was fast approaching.

My brothers would not hear to my remaining home any longer as I was already the only white female still in town. They directed that I should refugee to Paint Creek until after the battle. Ah, those were heart rending times. To go away and leave my father and two brothers behind with the enemy advancing slowly up the valley. I was to go on horseback but then Uncle Alva Hansford concluded to take me in his buggy.

Then came the question—what should I take and what should I leave. I could take very little and necessarily it was mostly clothing. All the things I prized so much had to be left and it was altogether likely I would never see the old home again or anything in it. The servants, six in number, were sent a few miles up Coal River at the farm of Frank Thompson where his Negro quarters were. It was a sad parting—all of us going in different directions, my father and brothers into battle was the worst of all.

These were the times that tried women's hearts, but I had to be brave and strong, and never a tear did I shed. Had I been allowed to stay I would have done so but everyone had refugeed. A great many had gone to the Falls of Coal to be out of the way of the battle. Indeed, people went in all directions to get out of the village as it was thought the homes would be burned if the Yankees ever got this far since our soldiers were encamped here. My brother Charley gave me his money to keep for him. I made a hole in the ground and buried all of my mother's silver and some other valuable things.

So I left home the day before the Battle of Scary, which was fought on July 17, 1861. We started in the afternoon for Paint Creek and had to drive very hard to get there that night. The road was full of refugees going up the valley and from all directions soldiers and armed civilians were going down the valley towards the advancing foe. Weeping women and sad, unhappy children were all along the road. When I got to Paint Creek I found many others in the same fix as I was.

I went to my Uncle Felix Hansford's where they received us gladly and made us as comfortable as possible although the house was full. The girls were all put up in the office building in the yard above the road. What a merry time we had, we forgot for a while that the war clouds were hovering over us. The young are so full of life and hope.

The next day we heard the Battle of Scary had been fought with the loss of three of our men and six or eight on the Federal side. It was a hot fight that lasted all afternoon. We also took several prominent officers as prisoners. Captain Patton of the Kanawha Riflemen was wounded in the shoulder and a Yankee Colonel Neff was badly wounded. *(It was Colonel Jesse Norton who was wounded, not Colonel Neff)*. Both were taken to Beverly Tompkins' house (Sunny Side) where they were both exchanged later. Colonel Gilbert Morgan captured Colonel Neff and got his navy revolver. He allowed me to shoot it, and I read where it was engraved "For Leut. Neff from his friends on Pearl Street, Cincinnati."

The Rebels (as they now call us) pulled up stakes and left Camp Tompkins three days after the battle. Of course, we thought after we had repulsed the enemy there would not be much more trouble and were quite jubilant and expected the Rebels to remain in control of the valley. But wiser ones shook their heads, the end was not yet. We soon heard our men were slowly retreating up the valley. About the 22nd of July, they began passing Paint Creek. The road was full of all kinds of wagons and buggies loaded with women and children and household goods, while cows, horses, sheep and dogs were being driven along with them.

My Uncle Felix Hansford's house was filled to overflowing all day, they must have fed hundreds of citizens. Captain Jenkins' family was among them. Toward evening, the Captain rode in with Cooney Ricketts proudly by his side. In the heat of the afternoon the yard was strewn with soldiers resting. I was well acquainted with a great number of them, nearly all were friends and relatives. My brother Carroll was among them, and we had a long talk about the situation and he told me that in all probability they would not be back in the Kanawha Valley again until spring. I gave him all the silver money I had as he said the notes I had would not be good in "Dixie."

Nobody who has not seen a retreat of an army (although in no haste at all) can conceive any idea of it. We were all standing out in front of my uncle's house looking down on the turnpike watching them go by. The cavalry and baggage wagons went by with the artillery near the last. I remember seeing five or six fine looking officers riding the finest horses I ever saw. They made a splendid appearance in their dark gray uniforms with brass buttons. They wore hats with plumes which they took off and rode with them in hand until they were completely by our group of waving and weeping women. One I noticed in particular was a very tall handsome man who rode a beautiful large black horse. Inquiring who they were, I was told they were officers of Chapman's Battery from Monroe County.

After our troops had all passed up the valley, we knew the Yankees would not be far behind. At the invitation of Cousin Martha Jane Smith, a number of us went to her house about five miles up Paint Creek. Her husband, Major J.S.F. Smith, was superintendent of the Coal Oil Works and she lived in the company house. We all went up on the railroad that ran there from the river. There was a carload of women, children and nurses. However, it was a large house with 17 rooms and we got along nicely. In a few days we heard that all the Federal Army under General Cox had passed by. So, after saying good bye to all our hospitable friends, we turned our faces homeward. When I arrived home I found my father and brother Charley and the servants safe and all things as when I left. The Federals at that time had not started disturbing the citizens and everything seemed quiet after all the excitement.

Excerpts from *The Memoirs of a Confederate Soldier, As Told to His Grandson, Samuel Hunter Austin* by Joseph Alleine Brown (Company H, 22nd Virginia Infantry), Forum Press, Abingdon, Virginia, 1940

"...The fields about Charleston were alive with drilling and other activities incident to the gatherings and enlistments of the forces destined to participate in their marvelous effort and struggle to establish their independence. Very soon one hundred and twenty young men, the flower of Virginia chivalry, were enrolled in a company known at that date as the "Kanawha Riflemen"... in their green broadcloth uniforms, equipped with the handsome Mississippi rifles and drilled to the discipline of a corps of cadets, were the popular toast of the countryside. Quartered in the Tompkins' spacious home...Each commodious room was assigned to a mess and designated by name— "The Aristocratic Seven," "The Filthy Four," "The Thieving Three," and other choice appellations described or designated the identity of the company's subdivisions.

As the summer continued, characterized by various happenings, these gallant boys were drawn nearer to the vortex of tragedy and bloodshed. One day we were suddenly surprised by the "long roll," although some days before we had been warned by ominous beating of the enemies' drums down the river after sunset and in the night. Summoned to arms and action, we proceeded down the river to Scarey Creek, which empties into the Kanawha River, where we were destined to experience the first baptism of blood in our history—if not the first battle on Virginia soil. With Captain Patton in command of the various companies from the adjoining counties, a line of nearly eight hundred men was stretched in an irregular formation from the river back into the mountains, and there waited for the belligerent forces of General Cox, who was in command of these invaders of Virginia. We had not long to wait before the two forces were joined in the deadly grip of battle. The casualties to the Confederates began almost with the first shot. Jim Welch, commanding his artillery section, was decapitated; Captain Patton in command of the Confederates was severely wounded and was carried off the field. The Confederates were surprised by the splendid personality of Colonel Jenkins who rushed into the midst of the fray with his shirt on a pole and rallied the soldiers into position. In the height of the engagement, and at its crisis, the fighting Confederates had their attention attracted up the river in the direction of Camp Tompkins by an oncoming re-enforcement. Captain Dye Hansford, mounted on a pony, and riding beside a fast approaching vehicle which proved to be a cannon of his own manufacture in his own foundry, was coming hurriedly to participate in the battle. With his four animals, it required considerable space to enable him to place the muzzle of his great weapon toward the enemy. That done, he touched off his load of missiles composed of horse shoes, spikes, and miscellaneous pieces of iron. The report of the cannon was terrific, so much so that the Federals, believing a great re-enforcement had come, decided that "discretion was the better part of valor" and fled from the field.

Never yet has the world beheld a prouder band of soldiers as we realized the first splendid victory. After the battle was over, and while the boasting was going on, a group of Kanawha Riflemen were seated around a smouldering fire at dusk. They were surprised by the approach of a considerable number of horsemen. After a short parley they discovered they were Federal soldiers, and to their astonishment found out that the group consisted of nearly all the field officers of Cox's army. These officers—Colonels, Majors, and Captains, were captured to the immense delight of the Wise Legion, and immediately transferred to the custody of the Confederate authorities at Richmond. This battle of Scarey Creek was a notable event in the beginning of hostilities and occurred on July 17, 1861, just five days prior to the battle of "Bull Run" the time when the war assumed its real importance as a great and long continued struggle for the right of Secession and the independence of the Southern States.

As hostilities in West Virginia became more important, battle after battle distinguished this section in the theatre of the great conflict. In the evacuation of the Kanawha Valley, the forces of General Wise proceeded up the river. A considerable number of us, the forces that had been engaged in the battle of Scarey Creek, battle-seized the *Julia Moffat*, a stern-wheel steamboat, to carry us to the end of the navigable waters. As we approached Charleston, nearly ten miles from that city, proceeding in fancied security, an excited commotion among the soldiers on board was explained to be caused by an eagle-eyed soldier who reported observing a Federal flag a mile or so up the river. In suppressed excitement the steamboat continued until almost opposite the dangerous locality. Then, when more thoroughly examined, and realizing that peril was imminent, Captain Wells, the commander of the steamboat, turned the bow of his vessel squarely into the bank of the right up-stream shore. When the men had all scampered up the bank and into the corn field bordering the river, a parley from each of the opposing sides disclosed the fact that the vision of the United States flag was the real sign of a Federal force. We soon learned that there were soldiers of both forces along the banks of the river, and when that was distinctly a fact, the *Julia Moffit* succumbed to flames at the hands of the Confederate soldiers. We then, proceeded through the corn field to the turn-pike, had our pace accelerated by some artillery firing of the disappointed Federals, who shot at random into the field of luxuriant corn.

This section of the Wise Legion was moving up the road, and we were congratulating ourselves on our escape from the imminent peril on the boat—made more manifest as we glanced towards the river and beheld the smoke of the burning steamer we had abandoned. Leisurely and jocularly we wended our way towards the city of Charleston. Suddenly the gathering dusk brought into view the advance guard of another Federal force—about a dozen troops unexpectedly facing us. This sudden meeting created a panic in the ranks of the retreating Confederates, and in our demoralization we precipitately clambered the mountain sides. Our officers soon succeeded in restoring order and just a few miles from Charleston, and on the turn-pike leading to the city, we resumed our march. At dark we reached the city of our homes sadly realizing we would soon be beyond home influences as the tide of war would carry us far away from our loved ones.

We decided to cross the river and bid farewell to our seemingly deserted friends. The old time ferry-boat was moored for our convenience, but just as we were expecting to be borne across the stream again, we were demoralized by the sound of fury a short distance up the river. The visible blasting of guns decided us to return and attempt to follow up the Federals who were retreating up the river. In spite of our disappointment and chagrin, we continued our march evacuating the Kanawha Valley (this was in August, 1861) to follow the great war over the Valley of Virginia. But distressed as we were to be given the sad pleasure of meeting and parting from our loved ones, we manfully pushed ahead in our enthusiasm, pledged to redeem our land from despoilers. This last spectacular incident that prevented our visits to our homes and families was the vandal act of the "Louisiana Tigers" who had seized and boarded a steamboat, with experience gained from the wharves of New Orleans, applying their river lore to managing and running the boat, they were able to avoid the thirty miles march to the head of navigation—the well known Kanawha Falls. This main part of the Wise Legion continued to retreat until they reached the Greenbrier White Sulphur Springs.

FOOTNOTES

Chapter One

1. Hull, Forrest, "Rag-Tag Southern Soldiery Swamped Charleston in '61," *The Charleston Daily Mail,* Feb. 15, 1963, n.p.
2. Summers, George, "Battle Fought at Scary Was One of the First of Civil War," *Charleston Daily Mail,* July 24, 1939, n.p.
3. Evans, Clement, ed. (Jed Hotchkiss), *Confederate Military History—Virginia* (Atlanta: Confederate Publishing Co., 1899), pp. 57-58.
4. Moore, George E., *A Banner in the Hills* (New York: Appleton-Century-Crofts, 1963), p.14.
5. Morton, Oren F., *History of Monroe County, West Virginia* (Staunton, VA: n.p., 1916) (contains the Civil War diary of Rev. S.R. Houston).
6. Moore, G.E., op. cit., p. 100.
7. "Occupation of Charleston by Union Men Described" (unknown newspaper clipping), West Virginia State Archives Collection.
8. Ward, J.E.D., *Twelfth Ohio Volunteer Infantry* (Ripley, OH: n.p., 1864), p.34.
9. Mays, James H., Lee Mays, ed., *Four Years for Old Virginia* (privately printed). The war time experiences of James H. Mays, Company F, 22nd Virginia Infantry, C.S.A., assembled by his son.)
10. Background information on George S. Patton is plentiful. The bulk of it came from the following sources: (a) Confederate Service Record of George S. Patton, National Archives, (b) Noyes Rand Manuscript Collection, Civil War, West Virginia State Archives, (c) Correspondence on the Patton Family Genealogy, Manuscript Collection, The Huntington, San Marino, California, (d) Forrest Hull, "George S. Patton, Rebel," *Holland's Magazine of the South,* May 1945, (e) Stan Cohen, "Colonel George S. Patton and the 22nd Virginia Infantry," *West Virginia History,* n.p., n.d., (f) Stan Cohen, "The Original George S. Patton," *Civil War Times,* June 1961, Vol. 3, No. 3.
11. Majority of information on the Kanawha Riflemen came from (a) Issues of the *Kanawha Valley Star,* West Virginia State Archives, (b) "A list of those persons who have joined the Kanawha Rifle Company," Manuscript Collection, West Virginia State Archives, (c) "Kanawha Riflemen," Manuscript Collection, West Virginia State Archives, (d) Val Husley, "Men of Virginia—Men of Kanawha—to Arms," *West Virginia History,* Vol. 35, 1973-74, (e) William Clark Reynolds, "Diary of William Clark Reynolds" (a private in the Kanawha Riflemen), Union, Kentucky?, West Virginia University Collection, Morgantown, West Virginia.
12. Eskew, Garrison Laidlaw, "Monument Erected to Memory of Kanawha Riflemen, Youths Who Battled in Civil War 60 Years Ago," *Charleston Gazette* (June 4, 1922).
13. Original charter of the Kanawha Riflemen, Manuscript Collection, West Virginia State Archives.
14. Eskew, op. cit.
15. Noyes Rand Manuscript Collection, Civil War, West Virginia State Archives (Noyes Rand was an original member of the Kanawha Riflemen.)
16. Description of the Kanawha Riflemen's uniform is based upon various reports by veterans after the war; the detailed, although sometimes questionable, newspaper columns of Forrest Hull, as well as "Veteran Writes Letter about Thrilling Events" (Thomas Jeffries), *Charleston Daily Mail,* Oct. 25, 1925.
17. Gallagher, D.C., "D.C. Gallagher on Civil War in the Valley," *Charleston Gazette,* July 12, 1925.
18. Eskew, op. cit.
19. Jeffries, Thomas, "Veteran Writes Letter about Thrilling Events," *Charleston Gazette,* June 4, 1922.

20. The Kanawha Spectator, Vol. I., n.p., n.d., n.p.
21. Moore, Frank, *The Civil War in Song and Story 1861-1865* (New York: Peter Fenton Collier), 1882 reprint of 1865 ed., p.523.
22. Cook, Roy Bird, "A.G. Jenkins—A Confederate Portrait," *West Virginia Review,* May, 1934.
23. Sedinger, James D., "Diary of a Border Ranger" (unpublished), West Virginia State Archives. (Sedinger was an original member of the Border Rangers, Company E, 8th Virginia Cavalry, C.S.A.)
24. *Ibid.*
25. United States War Department, *War of the Rebellion: A Compilation of the Official Records of the Union and Confederate Armies* (128 vols.) Washington D.C., Government Printing Office, 1880-1901 (hereafter referred to as *Official Records*), Series I. Vol. 2, p.788 (Robert E. Lee to John McCausland, April 29, 1861).
26. Reynolds, William Clark, "Diary of William Clark Reynolds" (a private in the Kanawha Riflemen), Union, Kentucky?, West Virginia University Collection.
27. *Official Records,* Series I, Vol. 2, p.791 (John Brooke to C. Dimmock, April 30, 1861).
28. *Ibid,* p.800 (R.S. Garnett to C.Q. Tompkins, May 3, 1861).
29. Tompkins, Ellen Wilkins (ed.), "The Colonel's Lady: Some Letters of Ellen Wilkins Tompkins: July-December 1861," *Virginia Magazine of History and Biography,* Oct., 1960 (#69), p.387-419.
30. Obituary of C.Q. Tompkins, West Point Annual Reunion, June 14, 1877; C.Q. Tompkins' vita from Cullum's *West Point Biographical Register;* Military Service Records, National Archives.
31. Kanawha Riflemen Company Orders No. 1 for May 6, 1861, read: (1) This command will assemble for parade on Saturday next, the 11th day of May, in fatigue jackets and winter uniform pants, at 2½ o'clock P.M., precisely; arms and accoutrements in order for inspection, (2) The leader of the band will report and cause the first call to be beat, at fifteen minutes past 2 o'clock P.M. the same day—By order of Capt. Patton; E.S. Arnold, O.S.
32. *Kanawha Valley Star,* May, 1861.
33. Eskew, op. cit.
34. Devil Anse Hatfield fails to show up on the service records for the Sandy Rangers or the Logan Wildcats, although he attended veterans reunions of the Wildcats after the war. Certainly they would not have permitted his attendance had he not served with them.
35. Hull, op. cit.
36. Movement of troops from Charleston to Buffalo is detailed in the "Diary of William Clark Reynolds" (a private in the Kanawha Riflemen), Union, Kentucky?, West Virginia University Library (hereafter referred to as "Diary of William Clark Reynolds").
37. Catherine B. Broun Diary (#2389), Southern Historical Collection, Chapel Hill, North Carolina (reprinted in part in *West Virginia Heritage Encyclopedia,* edited by Jim Comstock, and titled "Civil War Letters from the Kanawha Valley," Richwood, West Virginia, 1968).
38. "Diary of William Clark Reynolds."
39. Letters Received, 1861, V.M.I. Archives: John McCausland to Francis Smith, May 16, 1861.
40. Beverly Randolph Wellford Papers (1773-1907): John McCausland to Major Crenshaw, May 17, 1861: Virginia Historical Society.
41. Evans, Clement A., general editor, *Confederate Military History: Virginia,* (Atlanta: Confederate Publishing Company., 1899), p.59.
42. *Official Records,* Series I, Vol. 2, p.888 (Tompkins to Garnett, May 27, 1861).
43. *Ibid.,* p.888 (amended message).
44. Manuscript Collection, Museum of the Confederacy, Richmond (E.C. Phelps to C.Q. Tompkins, May 29, 1861).
45. *Official Records,* Series I, Vol. 2, p.50 (C.Q. Tompkins to Governor John Letcher, May 30, 1861).
46. *Ibid.,* p.895 (R.S. Garnett to W.B. Blair, May 31, 1861).

Chapter Two

1. Canfield, S.S., *History of the 21st. (Ohio) Regiment* (Toledo, Vroorman, Anderson, Bateman), 1893.
2. Shirey, Mervin, *The Battle of Scary Creek* (Riley Dawson Publishing, St. Albans, WV), 1932, p.12.

3. __________, *History of Gallia County, Ohio,* p.29.
4. *Ibid.*
5. Horton & Teverbaugh, *History of the 11th O.V.I.* (Dayton, Ohio, W.J. Shuey), 1866, p.21.
6. Scott, William Forse, *Col. Philander P. Lane of the 11th O.V.I.* (privately printed), 1920.
7. *Ibid.*, p.12.
8. Cox, Jacob D., *Military Reminiscenses,* 2 Vol. (New York, Charles Scribner's & Sons), 1900, Vol. 1.
9. Warner, Ezra J., *Generals in Blue, Lives of the Union Commanders,* 1964.
10. Ward, J.E.D., *Twelfth Ohio Volunteer Infantry* (Ripley, Ohio), 1864, p.17.
11. *Ibid.*
12. Davidson, Henry M., *History of Battery A of First Regiment Ohio Volunteer Light Artillery* (Milwaukee: Daily Wisconsin's Steam Printing House), 1865.
13. Dyer, Frederick H., *Compendium of the Rebellion* (Dayton, Ohio: Morningside Bookshop), 1978 reprint (original printing, 1908).
14. Ohio Roster Commission, *Roster of Ohio Soldiers 1861-1865* (Cinn., Ohio Valley Publishing-Mfg. Co.), 1866, Vol. I.
15. (Kentucky) Adjutant General's Report for 1861, p.557.
16. Union Soldiers and Sailors Monument Association, *The Union Regiments of Kentucky* (Louisville, KY), 1897, p.282.
17. *Ibid.*, p.
18. Johnson, R.R. and C.C. Buel, eds., *Battles and Leaders of the Civil War,* 4 vols. (New York: Century, 1887-88), Vol. I, p.137 (Jacob D. Cox, "McClellan in West Virginia").
19. George E. Moore, *A Banner in the Hills* (Appleton-Century-Crofts: New York), 1963, p.53.
20. Elijah Beeman Letters Collection, Cabell County Public Library, Huntington, WV (original in the possession of Leona Waller Bree).
21. *Ibid.* (original in the possession of Leona Waller Bree).
22. *Ibid.* (original in the possession of Maxine Beeman Snyder).

Chapter Three

1. Camp Tompkins at Coalsmouth should in no way be confused with the Federal camp, also known as Camp Tompkins, established on the Gauley Mount estate of Col. Christopher Q. Tompkins in the fall of 1861.
2. Wintz, William, "Historical Bus Tour of the Lower Kanawha Valley," *Upper Vandalia Historical Journal.*
3. Bahlmann, William, "Down in the Ranks," *Journal of the Greenbrier Historical Society,* Oct. 1970, Vol. II, No. 2, p.43.
4. *Ibid.*, p.46.
5. Shirey, Mervin R., *The Battle of Scary Creek,* Riley Dawson Publishing, St. Albans, WV, 1932, p.12.
6. Bahlmann, "Ranks," p.47.
7. Letters Received 1861, V.M.I. Archives (Patton to Smith, June 4, 1861).
8. *Official Records,* Series I, Vol. 2, pp.656-657 (McClellan to Townsend, June 1, 1861).
9. *Ibid.*
10. James Welch Manuscript Collection, Civil War, West Virginia State Archives (Hale to Welch, June 7, 1861).
11. *Official Records,* Series I, Vol. 2, pp.908-909 (Cooper to Wise, June 6, 1861, with addition of June 10.)
12. Wise, John S., *End of an Era,* (A.S. Barnes & Co., Inc., New York) 1965 reprint, p.177.
13. Stutler, Boyd, *The Civil War in West Virginia,* Education Foundation, Inc., Charleston, WV, 1963, p.52.
14. Cutchins, John A., *A Famous Command: The Richmond Light Infantry Blues,* Garrett & Massie, Richmond, 1934, p.75.
15. Tompkins Family Papers, Virginia Historical Society.
16. Wise, Barton H., *The Life of Henry Wise* (New York: McMillan & Co.), 1899, p.
17. Cutchins, p.77.
18. James Welch Manuscript Collection, Civil War, West Virginia State Archives.
19. *Ibid.*
20. *Ibid.*
21. *Ibid.*

22. Tompkins Family Papers, Virginia Historical Society.
23. *Ibid.*
24. James Welch Manuscript Collection, Civil War, West Virginia State Archives.
25. *Ibid.*
26. Tompkins Family Papers, Virginia Historical Society.
27. *Ibid.*
28. *Ibid.*
29. *Ibid.*
30. *Ibid.*
31. *Ibid.*
32. *Ibid.*
33. *Ibid.*
34. James Welch Manuscript Collection, Civil War, West Virginia State Archives.
35. *Official Records,* Series I, Vol. 2, p.994 (Chilton to Wise, June 21, 1861).
36. Wise, John S., *End of an Era,* p.171.
37. Jones, Beuhring H., "My First Thirty Days Experience as a Captain." *Southern Literary Messenger,* Vol. 37, No. 2, 1863.
38. *Official Records,* Series I, Vol. 2, p.951 (Beckley to Richardson, June 25, 1861).
39. James Welch Manuscript Collection, Civil War, West Virginia State Archives.
40. *Ibid.*
41. Cutchins, p.79.
42. Stutler, p.52.
43. "True Story of the Wise-Littlepage Affair," unknown newspaper clipping, West Virginia State Archives Collection.
44. *Official Records,* Series I, Vol. 2, p.1012.
45. Galbraith, Julia, *History of the Cross Lanes Area,* compiled for Women's Club of Cross Lanes, 1976.
46. James Welch Manuscript Collection, Civil War, West Virginia State Archives.
47. Letters Received 1861, V.M.I. Archives (McCausland to Smith, June 28, 1861).
48. Confederate Records Group 109, Records of the Army of the Kanawha; Letters Sent by General Henry A. Wise, June 1861–August 1864 (Harvie to Cooper, June 29, 1861).
49. Evans, Clement, ed., *Confederate Military History (West Virginia),* Robert White, p.25.
50. *Official Records,* Series I, Vol. 2, p.737 (Pierpont to McClellan, July 1, 1861).
51. Telegrams and other correspondence from/to Commander in Chief (Ohio governor), 1861 (Norton to Dennison, July 7, 1861), Ohio Historical Society.
52. *Official Records,* Series I, Vol. 2, p.674 (McClellan to Townsend, June 11, 1861).
53. *Ibid.,* p.706 (McClellan to Townsend, June 19, 1861).
54. *Ibid.,* p.195 (McClellan to Townsend, June 23, 1861).
55. For a much more detailed account of the Pryce Lewis adventure in the Kanawha Valley the reader should refer to the following works: Harriet Shoen, "Pryce Lewis, Spy for the Union," *Davis and Elkins Magazine,* March/May 1949; Alan Pinkerton, *Spy of the Rebellion,* New York, 1883; Harnett T. Kane, *Spies for the Blue and Gray,* Hanover House, Garden City, New York, 1954; James D. Horan, *The Pinkertons: The Detective Dynasty That Made History,* Crown, New York, 1957. All quotes used in this manuscript are from the Harriet Shoen work.

Chapter Four

1. Confederate movements about Ripley at this time are well detailed in (a) John A. Cutchins, *A Famous Command: The Richmond Light Infantry Blues,* Garrett & Massie, Richmond, 1934, pp.79-80; (b) "Diary of William Clark Reynolds" (a private in the Kanawha Riflemen), Union, Kentucky?, West Virginia University Library Collection; (c) W.C. Clark, "The Journal of a Soldier of 1861," *West Virginia Review,* 1930, Nov. (based upon the diary of Joab Smith of the Jackson County Border Rifles).
2. "Memoir of a Youthful Confederate," *Jackson County Miscellany,* Jackson County Historical Society.
3. Reid, Whitelaw, *Ohio in the War,* Vol. 2, 1868, p.148.
4. Clark, W.C., "The Journal of a Soldier of 1861," *West Virginia Review,* November 1930 (hereafter referred to as W.C. Clark, "Journal").
5. Ironically, although historians have generally agreed that July 4th is the date Wise left

Charleston, the General's Captain and Assistant Adjutant General for the Wise Legion (or Brigade), E.J. Harvie, reported to Col. J.H. Richardson at Gauley Bridge that Wise departed on the morning of July 6. The dispatch is found in Confederate Records Group 109, Records of the Army of the Kanawha, Letters Sent by Gen. Henry A. Wise, June 1861–August 1864, National Archives.

6. Clark, W.C., "Journal."
7. "Diary of William Clark Reynolds."
8. Moore, Frank, *The Rebellion Record* (New York: G.P. Putnam), 1861-71.
9. Tompkins Family Papers, Virginia Historical Society.
10. *Ibid.*
11. *Ibid.*
12. *Ibid.*
13. "Diary of William Clark Reynolds."
14. *Official Records,* Series I, Vol. 2, pp.211-212 (John Connell to George McClellan, July 8, 1861).
15. *Jackson Countians in America's Wars 1775-1918,* Jackson County Historical Society.
16. Confederate Records Group 109, Records of the Army of the Kanawha, Letters Sent by Gen. Henry A. Wise, June 1861–August 1864 (Harvie to Cooper, July 2, 1861), National Archives.
18. *Ibid.* (Wise to Cooper July 2, 1861).
19. Letters Received, V.M.I. Archives, McCausland to Smith, July 3, 1861.
20. James C. Welch Manuscript Collection, Civil War, West Virginia State Archives.
21. Confederate Records Group 109, Records of the Army of the Kanawha, Letters Sent by Gen. Henry A. Wise, June 1861–August 1864 (Harvie to Richardson, July 6, 1861).
22. James C. Welch Manuscript Collection, Civil War, West Virginia State Archives.
23. Confederate Records Group 109, Records of the Army of the Kanawha, Letters Sent by Gen. Henry A. Wise, June 1861–August 1864 (Harvie to Wise, July 8, 1861), National Archives.
25. *Ibid.* (Harvie to Bucholtz, July 9, 1861).

Chapter Five

1. *Official Records,* Series I, Vol. 2, p.197 (McClellan to Cox, July 2, 1861).
2. Cox, Jacob D., *Military Reminiscenses,* Vol. I, p.61.
3. *Official Records,* Series I, Vol. 2, p.737.
4. *Ibid.*
5. *Ibid.*, pp.239-240 (Garnett to Deas, July 1, 1861).
6. *Ibid.*, pp.240-242 (Garnett to Deas, July 6, 1861).
7. *Ibid.*, p.200 (McClellan to Townshend, July 6, 1861).
8. Confederate Records Group 109, Records of the Army of the Kanawha, Letters Sent by General Henry A. Wise, June 1860–August 1864 (Harvie to Adler, July 11, 1861), National Archives.
9. James C. Welch Manuscript Collection, Civil War, West Virginia State Archives.
10. Cox, J.D., *Military Reminiscenses,* Vol. 1, p.64.
11. *Ibid.*, pp.64-65.
12. Horton & Teverbaugh, *History of the 11th O.V.I.* (Dayton, Ohio) 1866, p.27.
13. Cox, J.D., *Military Reminiscenses,* Vol. 1, p.65.
14. *Ibid.*
15. Ward, J.E.D., *Twelfth Ohio Volunteer Infantry,* p.23.
16. *Ibid.*, p.25.
17. "The Story of W.A. Burdett, Rich in Civil War History," *Hurricane Breeze,* July 16, 1964.
18. Horton & Teverbaugh, *History of the 11th O.V.I.*, p.26.
19. Tompkins Family Papers, Virginia Historical Society.
20. Horton & Teverbaugh, *History of the 11th O.V.I.*, p.27.
21. *Official Records,* Series I, Vol. 2, p.202 (McClellan to Townsend, July 10, 1861).
22. *Ibid.*, p.203 (McClellan to Townsend, July 12, 1861).
23. *Ibid.*, p.203 (McClellan to Townsend, July 13, 1861).
24. Manuscript Collection, Museum of the Confederacy, Richmond, Virginia (Patton to Tompkins, July 13, 1861).
25. *Ibid.*
26. Confederate Records Group 109, Records of the Army of the Kanawha, Letters Sent by

General Henry A. Wise, June 1861-August 1864 (Harvie to O.J. Wise, July 13, 1861).
27. *Ibid.* (Harvie to unknown officer, July 13, 1861).
28. Tompkins Family Papers, Virginia Historical Society.
29. Many accounts state there were only four companies involved.
30. Estimates have ranged from 350 to 600.
31. Capt. A.G. Jenkins' whereabouts at this time are uncertain.
32. Ball, Frank, "Uncle Billy Miller, 90 Years Old, Recalls Battle of Mud River," unknown newspaper clipping, James 'Slim' Combs Collection.
33. *Ibid.*
34. Ball, Frank and J.W. Miller, "Now and Then—Mostly Then," *West Virginia Review,* Jan. 1935.
35. Ball, Frank, "Uncle Billy Miller."
36. Moore, Frank, *The Rebellion Record,* Document 86, "The Fight at Barboursville, Virginia," p.285.
37. Ball, Frank and J.W. Miller, "Now and Then—Mostly Then."
38. Ball, Frank, "Uncle Billy Miller."
39. Ball, Frank and J.W. Miller, "Now and Then—Mostly Then."
40. Ball, Frank, "Uncle Billy Miller."
41. *Official Records,* Series I, Vol. 2, p.299 (McClellan to Townsend, July 19, 1861); McClellan gives the date of the battle at Mud River as July 16 which fails to coincide with other verified accounts of the affair.
42. Patton, G.S., "A Brief and Imperfect Account."
43. "Diary of William Clark Reynolds."
44. Confederate Records Group 109, Records of the Army of the Kanawha, Letters Sent by Gen. Henry A. Wise, June 1861-August 1864 (Wise to Gen. ? , July 14, 1861), National Archives.
45. *Ibid.*
46. Horton, Joshua, and Solomon Teverbaugh, *History of the 11th O.V.I.,* pp.33-35.
47. *Official Records,* Series I, Vol. 51, p.1.
48. *Official Records,* Series I, Vol. 2, p.210.
49. Confederate Records Group 109, Records of the Army of the Kanawha, Letters Sent by Gen. Henry A. Wise, June 1861-August 1864 (Harvie to Cooper, July 15, 1861), National Archives.
50. *Ibid.* (Wise to Cooper, July 15, 1861).
51. *Official Records,* Series I, Vol. 2, pp.290-291 (Wise to Lee, July 17, 1861).
52. *Official Records,* Series I, Vol. 51, Pt.1, p.420 (Cox to McClellan, July 16).
53. Letter to West Virginia State Archives—from Simms family decendants relating to activities at Scary Creek prior to the battle, West Virginia State Archives.
54. Simms Family History (unpublished), Courtesy Emma Simms Maginnis.
55. Cox, Jacob D., *Military Reminiscenses,* Vol. I.
56. Godfrey Family Papers; U.S Army Military History Institute, Carlisle Barracks, Pennsylvania.
57. Confederate Records Group 109, Records of the Army of the Kanawha, Letters Sent by Gen. Henry A. Wise, June 1861-August 1864 (Wise to Walker, July 16, 1861), National Archives.

Chapter Six

1. Special credit must go to Putnam County historian William Wintz who has done extensive research on the geographic, physical, and historical aspect of the Scary Creek community, particularly in various issues of *The Upper Vandalia Historical Journal.*
2. Patton, George S., "A Brief and Imperfect Account of the Action at Scary Creek, Manuscripts Collection, The Huntington, San Marino, California.
3. Maginnis, William H., "Scary Creek Really Earned Its Name," *Charleston Newspapers,* July 16, 1950.
4. Wintz, William, "The Scary Curse of Scary Creek," *Upper Vandalia Historical Journal.*
5. Maginnis, William H., "Scary Creek Really Earned Its Name," *Charleston Newspapers,* July 16, 1950.
6. Journal of Albert Gallatin, as reviewed in William Wintz's, "The Scary Curse of Scary Creek," *Upper Vandalia Historical Journal.*
7. "Occupation of Charleston by Union Men Described," unknown newspaper clipping,

West Virginia State Archives Collection.

8. Sedinger, James D., "Diary of a Border Ranger" (unpublished), West Virginia State Archives Collection.
9. Patton, George S., "A Brief and Imperfect Account of the Action at Scary Creek," Manuscripts Collection, The Huntington, San Marino, California (hereafter referred to as "A Brief and Imperfect Account").
10. Ward, J.E.D., *Twleftb Ohio Volunteer Infantry* (Ripley, Ohio), 1864, p.27.
11. Simms Family History (unpublished), Emma Simms Maginnis Collection, Winfield, WV.
12. *Ibid.*
13. Whittlesey, Col. Charles, *War Memoranda: Cheat River to the Tennessee 1861-62* (Cleveland, Ohio), 1884, p.19 (hereafter referred to as "War Memoranda").
14. Patton, George S., "A Brief and Imperfect Account."
15. *Ibid.*
16. "Millard Phillips of Huntington Was Youngest Soldier in Southern Army," *Huntington Herald-Advertiser,* July 8, 1928.
17. "Battle of Scary," as told by Kanawha Rifleman Levi Welch, *West Virginia Historical Quarterly,* Vol. I, No. 1.
18. Ward, J.E.D., *Twelfth Ohio Volunteer Infantry,* p.28.
19. Elijah Beeman Letters Collection (Beeman to his parents, July 20, 1861), Cabell County Public Library.
20. Moore, Frank, *The Rebellion Record* (New York: G.P. Putnam), 1861-71, Document 99 as reported in the "Cincinnati Gazette."
21. *Ibid.*
22. Welch, Levi, "Battle of Scary Creek," *West Virginia Historical Quarterly,* Vol. I, No. 1.
23. Moore, Frank, *The Civil War in Song and Story, 1861-1865* (New York: Peter Fenton Collier), 1882, p.228.
24. Thompson, Cameron L., "The Battle of Scary," *Confederate Veteran,* June, 1918, no. 26 (Cameron was a member of the Kanawha Riflemen).
25. Ward, J.E.D., *Twelfth Ohio Volunteer Infantry,* pp.31-32.
26. *Ibid.,* p.32.
27. *Ibid.,* p.31.
28. Patton, George S., "A Brief and Imperfect Account."
29. Bahlman, William F., "Down in the Ranks," *Journal of the Greenbrier Historical Society,* Oct. 1970, Vol. II, No. 2, p.48.
30. Collins, J.H. (letter), "The Irrepressible," May 3, 1894 (reprinted in *The Upper Vandalia Historical Journal*).
31. Elijah Beeman Letters Collection (Beeman to his parents, July 20, 1861).
32. Moore, Frank, The Rebellion Record, Document 99 as reported in the *Cincinnati Gazette.*
33. Whittlesey, Col. Charles, *War Memoranda,* p.19.
34. Ward, J.E.D., *Twelfth Ohio Volunteer Infantry,* p.28.
35. Welch, Levi, "Battle of Scary Creek," *West Virginia Historical Quarterly,* Vol. I, No. 1.
36. Ward, J.E.D., *Twelfth Ohio Volunteer Infantry,* p.29.
37. Whittlesey, Col. Charles, *War Memoranda,* p.20.
38. Simms Family History (unpublished), Emma Simms Maginnis Collection.
39. Whittlesey, Col. Charles, *War Memoranda,* p.20.
40. *Ibid.,* p.21.
41. Ward, J.E.D., *Twelfth Ohio Volunteer Infantry,* p.30.
42. Wintz, William, "Notes, Quotes, and Antidotes on the Battle of Scary," *Upper Vandalia Historical Journal.*
43. Welch, Levi, "Battle of Scary Creek," *West Virginia Historical Quarterly,* Vol. I, No. 1.
44. Mays, James H., *Four Years for Old Virginia,* Lee Mays, ed. (privately printed), p.12.
45. Some accounts report this as having transpired as early as 4 P.M. but such time does not hold up against eyewitness accounts.
46. J.H. Collins (letter), "The Irrepressible," May 3, 1894 (reprinted in *The Upper Vandalia Historical Journal*).
47. Ward, J.E.D., *Twelfth Ohio Volunteer Infantry,* p.30.
48. Wallace, G.S., *Cabell County Annals and Families* (Garrett and Mossie), 1935, p.319.
49. Ward, J.E.D., *Twelfth Ohio Volunteer Infantry,* p.30.
50. Moore, Frank, *The Rebellion Record,* Document 99.
51. Tompkins Family Papers, Virginia Historical Society.
52. Whittlesey, *War Memoranda,* p.23.

53. Tompkins Family Papers, Virginia Historical Society.
54. Whittlesey, *War Memoranda,* p.23.
55. Bahlmann, William F., "Down in the Ranks," *Journal of the Greenbrier Historical Society,* Oct. 1970, Vol. II, No. 2, p.49.

Chapter Seven

1. Sedinger, James D., "Diary of a Border Ranger" (unpublished), West Virginia State Archives.
2. Wallace, G.S., *Cabell County Annals and Families,* (Garrett & Mossie, 1935).
3. "Diary of William Clark Reynolds."
4. Mays, James H., *Four Years for Old Virginia,* p.13.
5. Patton, George S., "A Brief and Imperfect Account."
6. *Official Records,* Series I, Vol. 2, p.291 (Wise to Lee, July 18, 1861).
7. Patton, George S., "A Brief and Imperfect Account."
8. Poem: "The 21st at Stones River," by Kate Brownlee Sherwood: printed in the "Diary of Jacob Adams, Private in Company F, 21st O.V.I.," *Ohio Archeological and Historical Quarterly,* October 1929.
9. Sedinger, James D., "Diary of a Border Ranger," West Virginia State Archives. (It must be noted that this incident probably took place in the days prior to the battle of Scary Creek. Some accounts have said as early as July 1, although that date would appear to be too early. Since Sedinger is the only Confederate participant to leave a written account, his use of July 18 as the date of the expedition is applied herein, although it is almost undoubtedly incorrect. Also, the use of the names Blagg and Holloway for the ship's captain and pilot is apparently Sedinger's attempt at using fictitous names, although there is a small probability that they are the correct names.)
10. Many of the Rebels would have a chance to return this name later in the war when driving the Yanks out of White Sulphur Springs.
11. Confederate Records Group 109, Records of the Army of the Kanawha, Letters Sent by Gen. Henry A. Wise, June 1861-August 1864 (Wise to Tompkins, July 19, 1861).
12. Bahlmann, William, "Down in the Ranks," *Journal of the Greenbrier Historical Society,* Oct. 1970, Vol. II, No. 2, p.49.
13. *Official Records.*
14. Shoen, Harriet, "Pryce Lewis, Spy for the Union," *Davis and Elkins Magazine,* May 1949, p.31.
15. *Ibid.,* p.32.
16. Letter to author from Ruth Ellen (Patton) Totten.
17. Harriet Shoen, "Pryce Lewis," p.34.
18. *Official Records.*
19. Moore, Frank, *The Rebellion Record,* Document 119½—"Occupation of Charleston, Va.," p.402.
20. Summers, George W., "Burning of Confederate Boat and Supplies Was Bold Stunt," *Charleston Newspapers* unknown clipping, West Virginia State Archives.
21. Summers, George W., *Pages from the Past* (Charleston, West Virginia), *Charleston Journal,* 1935 ("Boat Burned with Cargo to Prevent Its Capture," pp.60-62.
22. Sedinger, "Diary of a Border Ranger."
23. Whittlesey, *War Memoranda,* p.25.
24. Mays, *Four Years for Old Virginia,* p.15.
25. *Ibid.,* p.16.
26. Jones, Beuhring H., "My First Thirty Days Experience as a Captain," *Southern Literary Messenger,* Vol. 37, No. 2, 1863.
27. *Ibid.*
28. *Ibid.*
29. *Official Records,* Series I, Vol. 2, p.1011 (Wise to Lee, August 1, 1861).
30. Confederate Records Group 109, Records of the Army of the Kanawha, Letters Sent by Gen. Henry A. Wise, June 1861-August 1864 (Wise to Cooper, August 1, 1861), National Archives.
31. *Ibid,* (Wise to Loring, August 1, 1861).
32. Tompkins Family Papers, Virginia Historical Society ("Record of the Revolution," an unpublished history of the war, by Col. Christopher Q. Tompkins).

33. Moore, Frank, *The Rebellion Record,* Document 119½, "Occupation of Charleston, Va."
34. Cox, *Military Reminiscenses,* p.74.
35. West Virginia Historical Records Survey, *Calendar of the Francis Harrison Pierpont Letters and Papers in West Virginia Depositories,* Charleston, West Virginia, 1940.
36. Whittlesey, *War Memoranda,* p.25.
37. Hotchkiss, Jed., *Confederate Military History - Virginia,* (Clement Evans, ed.), (Atlanta, Confederate Publishing Co., 1899), p.57.

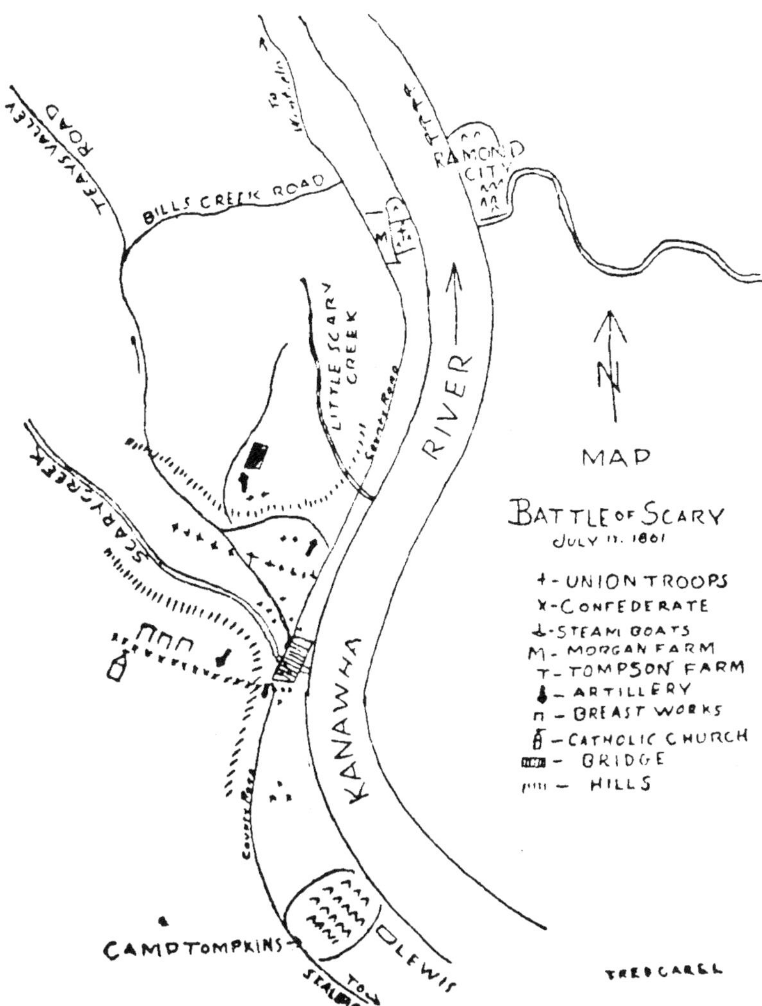

A CONTEMPORARY MAP OF SCARY

Drawn in 1932 and obviously based upon the Mays map. The Catholic Church shown did not exist at the time of the battle. It was built by the Claire Alphonsine Vintroux family in 1881 and burned in 1900. — From Mervin Shirey's **The Battle of Scary Creek**

APPENDIX A

A REPORT OF KILLED, WOUNDED AND CAPTURED AT THE BATTLE OF SCARY CREEK

—CONFEDERATE—

22ND VIRGINIA VOLUNTEER INFANTRY	
Lt. Col. George S. Patton	severe wound in the left shoulder
Co. A - Putnam County Border Rifles	Pvt. John T. Dudding—wounded by a cannonball, taken to a Charleston hospital
Co. K - Fayetteville Rifles	—Charles Blake—mortally wounded, died July 18 —William C. Fellers—mortally wounded —Warren Jones—slightly wounded —Jonathan Weaver—slightly wounded
Kanawha Artillery/Hale's Battery	—2nd Lt. James C. Welch—killed
46TH VIRGINIA VOLUNTEER INFANTRY	
Co. D - Border Guard	—John Mallory—wounded —Theophilus Smith—a 17 year old from Petersburg "killed while carrying the flag"
8TH VIRGINIA CAVALRY	
Co. E - Border Rangers	—Capt. Albert Gallatin Jenkins—slight head wound
	TOTAL: 4 killed 6 wounded

—FEDERAL—

12TH OHIO VOLUNTEER INFANTRY (3 years service)		AGE	
Co. A -	Roy Fairchild—wounded in the thigh	--	
	Roderick Schlosmiller—wounded slightly	--	
	Pvt. James Shaffer—wounded in the thigh	25	
Co. D -	Pvt. William P. Taylor—killed	21	
	Pvt. Warren C. Timberlake—mortally wounded	21	died July 17
Co. F -	Pvt. Jabez Turner—killed	40	

Co. G -	Corp. Jacob Banker—mortally wounded	20	died July 19
	Corp. Fredrick Hanford—killed	19	
	Pvt. Benjamin Hebble—killed	22	
	Capt. Joseph L. Hilt—wounded	20	
	Pvt. John McNeely—killed	24	
Co. H. -	colored cook—wounded in the shoulder	--	
Co. I -	Pvt. William Jackson—killed	--	
Co. K -	Capt. James Sloan(e)—wounded	40	

21ST OHIO VOLUNTEER INFANTRY (3 months service)

	Col. Jesse S. Norton—wounded in the thigh	35	
Co. D -	Capt. Thomas G. Allen—killed	25	
	2nd Lt. Guy Pomeroy—mortally wounded	27	died July 18
Co. K -	Corp. William Bishop—wounded	20	
	Pvt. George W.C. Blue—killed	26	
	Pvt. John Mercer—mortally wounded	23	
	Pvt. James M. Miller—wounded	24	
	Pvt. Barton Smith—mortally wounded	18	died July 21

CAPT. CHARLES S. COTTER'S INDEPENDENT BATTERY
OHIO VOLUNTEER ARTILLERY (3 months service)

Pvt. John P. Haven—mortally wounded	18	died July 22

CAPT. JOHN S. GEORGE'S INDEPENDENT CO.
OHIO VOLUNTEER CAVALRY (3 months service)

Pvt. Richard Lambert—killed

CAPTURED

Col. Charles DeVilliers—11th Ohio Volunteer Infantry
Col. William E. Woodruff—2nd Kentucky Volunteer Infantry
Lt. Col. George W. Neff—2nd Kentucky Volunteer Infantry
Capt. George Austin—Co. B - 2nd Kentucky Volunteer Infantry
Capt. John R. Hurd—Co. F - 2nd Kentucky Volunteer Infantry
Col. Jesse S. Norton—21st Ohio Vol. Inf. - wounded and captured on field
Capt. Ashley Brown—Co. D - 12th Ohio Vol. Inf. - remained to tend to Norton

TOTALS: 15 killed — 9 wounded — 7 captured

A REPORT OF THE KILLED AND WOUNDED IN THE BATTLE OF BARBOURSVILLE (MUD RIVER)

JULY 14, 1861

CONFEDERATE

Absolom Ballenger (or Ballengee)—local militia - broken leg
James Reynolds—civilian volunteer - mortally wounded
Col. J.J. Mansfield—local militia - knocked from his horse

FEDERAL - 2ND KENTUCKY VOLUNTEER INFANTRY

Co. A -	Pvt. John Donnovan—mortally wounded - died July 20
Co. B -	Pvt. John Burns—wounded
	Pvt. John Jordens—killed
	Pvt. Barney McEroy—killed
	Pvt. James Patterson—wounded
	Pvt. John Reynolds—wounded

Co. F. - Pvt. Elihu Harper—wounded
Pvt. Jackson Sigman—wounded
Co. K - Pvt. John G. Hempfling—wounded

Although historians have generally accepted that the 2nd Kentucky had five killed and eighteen wounded, available records fail to bear this out, as shown above, although slight wounds were rarely reported.

TOTALS: Confederates - 1 killed
2 wounded

Federals - 3 killed
6 wounded

KILLED IN BATTLE AT RED HOUSE JULY 12, 1861

(Although the Ohio Roster Commission, in their *Roster of Ohio Soldiers 1861-65,* credits this event as having taken place on July 12, in all probability these men were killed July 14 during the accidental firing of rifles while crossing the Kanawha River as a relief party to Col. Jesse S. Norton at Scary Creek.)

1ST KENTUCKY VOLUNTEER INFANTRY - Co. G
Pvt. John Dugan
Pvt. Alexander Mordecai
Pvt. John W. Robins

STATUS REPORT

This is the original status report of Confederate and State forces serving under Gen. Henry A. Wise filed on July 8, 1861 and used as the basis for the abstract presented in *Official Records,* Series I - Vol. 2, pg. 293.

Cavalry

The Valley Rangers comd. by Capt. Brock, has, rank and file	49
Caskies Mounted Rangers " " Caskie	54
Total now here and in service	133
Company comd. by Capt. Tate (not arrived) is supposed to have rank and file	64
Total Cavalry reported	197

Infantry

Richmond Blues, comd.	by Capt.	Wise,	has, rank and file	94
White Sulphur Rifles	" Capt.	Morris	" "	57
Biernes' Sharpshooters	" Lieut.	Rowan	" "	65
Company comd.	by Capt.	McComas	" "	94
" "	" "	Thrasher	" "	68
" "	" "	Buster	" "	72
Jackson Avengers	" "	Jones	" "	89
Company comd.	by "	Lowrie	" "	94
Total of Infantry in service				633

Company of Capt. Hammond has rank and file	64
" comd. by Capt. Crank "	59

Company from Pittsylvania has rank and file	108
1st Appomattox Co. (supposed to have)	64
2nd " " "	64
Total of Infantry as reported	992

Kirby's Co. of *Artillery* supposed to have rank and file	50 men

Total of Cavalry as reported		197
" " Infantry "		992
" " Artillery "		50
Total of Brigade yet reported		1239
Total of Cavalry arrived	133	
Total of Infantry arrived	633	

Total of forces arrived and on duty	766
Total of Brigade arrived and on duty	766
Volunteer forces of Virginia	2097
Total under your command	2863 men

STATUS REPORT — FEDERAL

Troops serving under Gen. Jacob D. Cox in the Kanawha Valley during the movement to Scary Creek included:

11th Ohio Volunteer Infantry
12th Ohio Volunteer Infantry
21st Ohio Volunteer Infantry
1st Kentucky Volunteer Infantry
2nd Kentucky Volunteer Infantry
Capt. Charles S. Cotter's Independent Battery Ohio Volunteer Artillery
Capt. William S. Williams' Independent Battery Ohio Volunteer Artillery (consolidated with Cotter's Artillery on July 2 with Williams acting as 1st Lieutenant)
Capt. Seth J. Simmonds' Battery (1st Kentucky Independent Battery)
Capt. John S. George's Independent Company Ohio Volunteer Cavalry

Most of the infantry were properly trained, uniformed, and armed. On July 11 Gen. Cox reported from Point Pleasant that Capt. George's cavalry were armed with Sharps carbines, single barrell pistols, and sabers, but had no uniforms, horse equipage, and had unreliable caps of the self-primers. Cox also reported Cotter's artillery as having two brass six-pounders, rifled, with a supply of ammunition, unfixed, but no sufficient caps for the James shell, and four horses to each caisson and gun.

ADDITIONAL INFORMATION FOR THE SCARY CREEK BATTLE CASUALTY LIST

— CONFEDERATE —

22ND VIRGINIA INFANTRY

Co. A - Putnam County Border Rifles

Pvt. Henry Burns - deserted

Pvt. Madison Crago [Craigo] - severe wound in hip and thigh by musketball

(Pvt. Harrison Crago, his twin brother, was left to nurse Madison)

Pvt. James W. Lanham - 36 - captured

Pvt. Beverly O. Marcum - 26 - wounded by musketball

Pvt. John Wallace - severe wound of mouth and jaw by musketball

Pvt. Thomas D. Webb - 36 - suffered scrotal hernia extricating himself from mud and water at Scary Creek

Co. H - Kanawha Riflemen

Pvt. James B. Noyes - left to nurse Patton

Company Unknown

John G. Boggess - 25 - wounded/minie ball passing through right lung

36TH VIRGINIA INFANTRY

Co. A - Buffalo Blues

Pvt. George H. Bailey - leg wounded/amputated

Lt. Nicholas Wills - captured and escaped same day

KANAWHA ARTILLERY

Two horses injured

— FEDERAL —

12TH OHIO VOLUNTEER INFANTRY

Co. D Corp. Abram King - 21 - wounded in temple

Co. G 1st Lt. Robert Wilson - 27 - wounded

These additional statistics would indicate the total documented Confederate and Federal casualties at Scary Creek would be:

	CONFEDERATE	FEDERAL
	4 killed	15 killed
	12 wounded	11 wounded
	4 captured	7 captured
	1 deserted	
	2 horses injured	
Total:	21 and 2 horses	33

At the Battle of Barboursville Col. Joseph Jefferson Mansfield, 120th Virginia Militia, was wounded in the back and died three days later

APPENDIX B

COMPANY ORDERS #1 FOR THE KANAWHA RIFLEMEN

KANAWHA VALLEY STAR
April 30, 1861

Kanawha Riflemen

Company Orders #1
April 26, 1861

1. In compliance with the requisition of a Proclamation of the Governor of Virginia dated at Richmond the 19th of April 1861, this command will hold itself in readiness for marching orders.

2. In case such orders shall arrive, each one must provide himself with the following articles at least in addition to dress and fatigue uniforms, to wit: two shirts, four collars, two pair of socks, two pair of drawers, one blacking brush and box (to any two files), two pair white Berlin gloves, one quart tin cup, one white cotton haversack, one case knife, fork and spoon, two towels, two hankerchiefs, comb and brush, and tooth-brush. Some stout linen thread, a few buttons, paper of pins and a thimble, in a small buckskin or cloth bag.

3. There being no knapsacks in the possession of the company one ordinary sized carpetsack will be allowed to every two men, for the purpose of holding such of the above articles as are not in constant use. The knife, fork, spoon, haversack and tin cup, must be worn about the person, the first three and the last articles to the waist belt. Immediately after the receipt and promulgation of marching orders, the carpet sacks, duly packed, must be delivered to the Quartermaster Sergeant, neatly marked with the names of the two owners. Each file will procure a comfortable blanket and upon the receipt of orders, send the same into the Quartermaster Sergeant, shaped into a neat and compact bundle conspicuously marked with his name.

4. It is earnestly recommended that all under clothes should be woolen, especially the socks, as cotton socks are utterly unfit for marching in, and all files should wear woolen undershirts. Shoes, sewed soles, and fitting easily, but not too loosely to the foot, coming up over the ankle, are infinitely preferable to boots, and should be made strong and servicable.

5. By the liberality and patriotism of the residents of Charleston (one of them a lady) flannel cloth (grey) has been furnished for fatigue Jackets, and provision made for cutting them, all members of the company are hereby required at once to have their measures taken and Jackets cut by Mr. James B. Noyes, tailor. Many ladies have kindly undertaken to make them up. All members of the company are required to have their Jackets finished by Wednesday afternoon next at the latest. By like liberality of another resident, cloth for haversacks has been procured, and they have been cut out by another lady. They will be delivered by the Quartermaster Sergeant, and they must be finished by the same evening.

6. Assistant Surgeon Joseph Watkins will immediately, upon the receipt of marching orders, prepare and put in portable form an ample supply of medicines, and be prepared to hire medical aid whenever required on the march or in transit or in camp. He will also provide himself with appropriate instruments, & c. In this connection the undersigned gratefully acknowledges on behalf of the company the liberal offer of a citizen of this town, to furnish free of charge all medicines required.

7. Quartermaster Sergeant John Dryden will immediately, on the receipt of marching orders, procure the necessary transportation for the baggage of the command and necessary camp utensils and fixtures, and in case the order shall require a march overland, will lay in at least six hundred rations, and provide for their transportation; the ration being one pound and a half of pork or beef (as much of the latter as can be purchased fresh), eighteen ounces of meat and one-fourth pound of corn meal, and to each one hundred rations the following articles, ten pounds of rice, six pounds of coffee, twelve pounds of sugar, one gallon of vinegar, one pound of star candles, four pounds of soap and two quarts of salt. Private Joseph M. Brown is hereby detailed as an assistant to the Quartermaster and will report to him accordingly.

8. The band will go as a band, and are as such until further orders, will carry their instruments with them, but in every other respect will govern themselves by the preceeding directions.

8. (9) The undersigned, in issuing these prepatory orders has but little doubt that the services of this command will be required to aid in driving the invader from the soil of Virginia, but has none that every Rifleman will respond cheerfully and with alacrity to the call of his State, and be prepared to do his duty bravely under the grand old flag of Virginia.

GEO. S. PATTON
Captain

FEDERAL NON-COMBAT CASUALTIES AND INJURIES IN THE KANAWHA CAMPAIGN

1ST KENTUCKY VOLUNTEER INFANTRY

Co. A - Pvt. Theodore W. Allen—died July 10, drowned in the Ohio River near Maysville, Kentucky;
Co. D - Pvt. John Thompson—discharged July 25 at Ravenswood, was discovered to be a woman (not a casualty, of course, but interesting);
Co. F - Pvt. Daniel Martin—died June 15 at Camp Clay;
Co. G - Pvt. Frank Taylor—died July 7 at Camp Dennison;
Co. H - Pvt. Martin Foley—drowned July 9 in the Ohio River;
Pvt. William Garrish—drowned July 31 at Kanawha Falls.

2ND KENTUCKY VOLUNTEER INFANTRY

Co. C - Pvt. Henry Helming—accidentally wounded at Guyandotte on July 11;
Co. F - Pvt. James Gray—died July 21 of accidental wounds at Poca.

21ST OHIO VOLUNTEER INFANTRY

Co. B - Pvt. Joseph Collins—drowned July 29 while bathing in the Elk River;
Pvt. William Honeywell—died July 4 at Gallipolis;
Pvt. Miles S. Montross—died July 21 at Gallipolis;
Co. E - Pvt. James Spitsnale—died June 25 at Gallipolis;
Pvt. John W. Walters—died July 25 at Gallipolis;
Co. I - Pvt. William Lacey—died June 9 at Gallipolis.

BIBLIOGRAPHY

BOOKS AND PAMPHLETS

Atkinson, George W. and Alvaro F. Gibbons, *Prominent Men of West Virginia* (Wheeling, WV, W.L. Gallin, 1890).

Bowman, Mary Keller, *Reference Book of Wyoming County History* (Parsons, WV, McClain Printing, 1965).

Canfield, S.S., *History of the 21st (Ohio) Regiment* (Toledo: Vroorman, Anderson, and Bateman, 1893).

Carrington, Henry B., *Ohio Militia and the West Virginia Campaigns* (Boston: R.H. Blodgitt Co., 1904).

Callahan, James Morton, *History of West Virginia* (Chicago and New York: American Historical Society, Inc., 1923).

Cohen, Stan, *The Civil War in West Virginia: A Pictorial History* (Charleston, WV: Pictorial Histories, 1976).

Comstock, Jim, *West Virginia Heritage Encyclopedia,* Vol. II and Supplemental Vol. 6 (Richwood, WV: Heritage Foundation, 1968).

Cox, Jacob Dolson, *Military Reminiscenses* (New York: Charles Scribner's & Sons, 1900), Two Vol.

Cromie, Alice Hamilton, *A Tour Guide to the Civil War* (New York: E.P. Dutton & Co., Inc., 1964).

Cullum, George, *Biographical Register for West Point of the Officers and Graduates* (New York).

Cutchins, John A., *A Famous Command: The Richmond Light Infantry Blues* (Richmond, Garrett and Massie, 1934).

Davidson, Henry M., *History of Battery A: First Regiment Ohio Volunteer Light Artillery* (Milwaukee: Daily Wisconsin's Steam Printing House, 1865).

Dyer, Frederick H., *Compendium of the Rebellion* (Dayton, Ohio: Morningside Bookshop, 1908) (Reprint 1978).

Donnelly, Shirley, *Historical Notes on Fayette County* (Oak Hill, WV: privately printed, 1958).

Ellis, Garland, *Saint Albans, West Virginia* St. Albans: Dawson Printing, 1977).

Evans, Clement A., general editor, *Confederate Military History* (13 volumes) (Atlanta: Confederate Publishing Co., 1899). Particular emphasis on the Virginia volume and the West Virginia volume.

Hale, John P., *History of the Great Kanawha* (Madison, Wisc.: Bryant, Fuller and Co., 1891).

Hardesty, H.H., *Hardesty's History of Putnam County* (1883).

Horan, James D., *The Pinkertons: The Detective Dynasty That Made History* (New York: Crown Publishing, Bonanza Books, 1957).

Horton, Joshua, and Solomon Teverbaugh, *History of the 11th O.V.I.* (Dayton, Ohio: W.J. Shuey, 1866).

Humphreys, Milton, *Military Operations in Fayette County 1861-1863* (privately issued by Charles A. Goddard, 1931).

Jackson County Historical Society, *Jackson Countians in America's Wars 1775-1918* (Ripley, WV, 1978).

Johnson, Robert U., and C.C. Buel, editors, *Battles and Leaders of The Civil War*, 4 volumes (New York: Century, 1887-88). Particular emphasis on Volume I article: "McClellan in West Virginia," Jacob D. Cox.

Kane, Harnett, *Spies for the Blue and Gray* (Garden City, NY: Hanover House, 1954).

Laidley, W.S., *History of Charleston and Kanawha County, West Virginia*, (Chicago: Arnold Publishing Co., 1911).

Lang, Theodore F., *Loyal West Virginia from 1861 to 1865* (Baltimore: Deutsh Publishers, 1895).

Mickle, William E., *Well Known Confederate Veterans* (New Orleans, 1915).

Miller, Francis, T., *The Photographic History of the Civil War* (10 volumes): A.S. Barnes and Co., 1957 (reprint—originally published in 1911).

Moore, Frank, *The Rebellion Record* (12 volumes) (New York: G.P. Putnam, 1861-71).

Moore, George E., *A Banner in the Hills* (New York: Appleton-Century-Crofts, Meredith Publishing, 1963).

Morton, Oren F., *History of Monroe County, West Virginia* (Staunton, Virginia: 1916).

Peters, J.T., and H.B. Cardens, *History of Fayette County, West Virginia* (Charleston, WV: Jarrett Printing Co., 1926).

Pinkerton, Alan, *Spy of the Rebellion* (New York: 1883).

Pollard, Edward A., *Southern History of the War* (New York: Charles B. Richmond, 1866).

Reid, Whitelaw, *Ohio in the War* (2 volumes) (Cinn., New York: Moore Wilstach and Baldwin, 1868).

Reynolds, W.C., *Diary of William Clark Reynolds: A Private in the Kanawha Riflemen* (Union, KY [?]: 1956 [?]). (A copy is located in the West Virginia University Library, Morgantown, WV.)

Ryan, Daniel J., *The Civil War Literature of Ohio* (Cleveland, Ohio: 1911).

Scott, William Forse, *Colonel Philander P. Lane of the 11th O.V.I.* (privately printed, 1925).

Shetler, Charles, *West Virginia Civil War Literature* (Morgantown, WV: West Virginia University Press).

Shirey, Mervin R., *The Battle of Scary Creek* (St. Albans, WV: Riley Dawson Publishing, 1932).

Shirey, Mervin R., ed., *Big Sewell Mountain Country* (published by the American History class of Nuttall High School, 1934).

Stutler, Boyd, *The Civil War in West Virginia* (Charleston, WV: Education Foundation, Inc., 1963).

Summers, George W., *Pages from the Past* (Charleston, WV: Charleston Journal, 1935).

Swain, G.T., *History of Logan County* (Logan, WV: 1927).

United States War Department, *War of the Rebellion: A Compilation of the Official Records of the Union and Confederate Armies* (128 volumes) (Washington, D.C.: Government Printing Office, 1880-1901).

Union Soldiers and Sailors Monument Association, *The Union Regiments of Kentucky* (Louisville, KY: 1897).

Wallace, G.S., *Cabell County Annals and Families* (Garrett and Mossie Publishers, 1935).

Wallace, Lee A., Jr., *A Guide to Virginia Military Organizations 1861-65* (Richmond: Virginia Civil War Commission, 1964).

Ward, J.E.D., *12th Ohio Volunteer Infantry* (Ripley, Ohio: 1864).

West Point Military Academy, *Annual Reunion June 14, 1877* (New York: West Point).

West Virginia Historical Records Survey, *Calendar of the Francis Harrison Pierpont Letters and Papers in West Virginia Depositories* (Charleston, WV: 1940).

Whittlesey, Col. Charles, *War Memoranda: Cheat River to the Tennessee 1861-62 (Cleveland, Ohio: 1884).*

Wintz, William, and Ivan Hunter, *History of Putnam County* (Upper Vandalia Historical Society, 1967).

Wise, Barton H., *The Life of Henry Wise* (New York: McMillan and Co., 1899).

Wise, John S., *End of an Era* (New York: A.S. Barnes and Co., Inc., 1965) (reprint).

MAGAZINES AND JOURNALS

William F. Bahlmann, "Down in the Ranks," *The Journal of the Greenbrier Historical Society,* Vol. 2, No. 2, Oct. 1970.

Clarice Lorenz Bailes, "Jacob Dolson Cox in West Virginia," *West Virginia History,* No. 6, Oct. 1944.

Frank Ball, "The Battle of Barboursville," *West Virginia Review,* June 1945.

Frank Ball and J.W. Miller, "Now and Then—Mostly Then," *West Virginia Review,* Jan. 1935.

Stan Cohen, "The Original George S. Patton," *Civil War Times,* Vol. 3, No. 3, June 1961.

Stan Cohen, "Col. George S. Patton and the 22nd Virginia Infantry," *West Virginia History.* 1961.

Roy Bird Cook, "Albert Gallatin Jenkins—A Confederate Portrait," *West Virginia Review,* No. 11, May 1934.

Roy Bird Cook, "The Civil War Comes to Charleston," *West Virginia History,* No. 23, Jan. 1962.

Roy Bird Cook, "Scary—First Battle in the Great Kanawha of the Civil War," *West Virginia Review,* No. 4, Dec. 1926. Reprinted as "First Battle in the Great Kanawha," in *Confederate Veteran,* No. 39, April/May 1939.

J.M. Ferguson, "The Battle of Scary, West Virginia," *Confederate Veteran,* No. 25, Nov. 1917.

Forrest Hull, "George S. Patton, Rebel," *Holland's Magazine of the South,* May 1945.

Val Husley, "Men of Virginia—Men of Kanawha—to Arms," *West Virginia History,* Vol. 35, 1973-74.

Beahring H. Jones, "My First Thirty Days Experience as a Captain," *Southern Literary Messenger,* Vol. 37, No. 2, 1863.

Claude M. Morgan, "Action at Scary Creek," *West Virginia State Magazine,* Dec. 1959.

Obituary—for Price Lewis, "The Death of a Famous Spy," *Americana,* New York, No. 7, Feb. 1912.

Peggy Robbins, "Pinkerton," *Civil War Times Illustrated,* Jan. 1977.

Harriett Shoen, "Pryce Lewis, Spy for the Union," *Davis and Elkins Magazine,* March/May 1949.

Cameron L. Thompson, "Battle of Scary," *Confederate Veteran,* No. 26, June 1918.

Levi Welch, "Battle of Scary," *West Virginia Historical Quarterly,* Vol. 1, No. 1, Jan. 1901.

William Wintz, "Notes, Quotes, and Anecdotes on the Battle of Scary Creek," *Upper Vandalia Historical Journal.*

William Wintz, "Historical Bus Tour of the Lower Kanawha Valley," *Upper Vandalia Historical Journal,* April 1974.

William Wintz, "The Scary Curse of Scary Creek," *Upper Vandalia Historical Journal.*

William Wintz, "More on the Battle of Scary" (the letter of J.H. Collins), *Upper Vandalia Historical Journal,* July 1973.

Thomas Broun, "Reminiscences of Major Thomas L. Broun," *Confederate Veteran*, No. 9, 1901.

Robert Barnwell, "First West Virginia Campaigns," *Confederate Veteran*, No. 38, April-May 1930.

"Diary of Jacob Adams, Private in Company F, 21st O.V.I.," *Ohio Archeological and Historical Quarterly*, October 1929 (contains the poem "The 21st at Stones River," by Kate Brownlee Sherwood).

NEWSPAPERS AND NEWSPAPER ARTICLES

"Bahlman Gives History of Men Serving in '61," *Charleston Gazette*, Sept. 17, 1922.

Ball, Frank, "Uncle Billy Miller, 90 Years Old, Recalls Battle of Mud River," unknown clipping, James "Slim" Combs collection.

Conley, Phil, "Capital Area Held by South in Civil War," *Charleston Newspapers*, Oct. 7, 1938.

Conley, Phil, "General Wise's Campaign in Kanawha Area," *Charleston Daily Mail*, July 24, 1938.

"Days When Valley was Scarred from Battle Recalled in Detail by Confederate Soldier," *Charleston Gazette*, July 19, 1953.

Donnely, Shirley, "Death Stalked Patton's Family," *Beckley Post-Herald*, Aug. 15, 1970.

Donnelly, Shirley, "Mat Masters Marked Bailey's Grave," *Beckley Post-Herald*, July 21, 1969.

Donnelly, Shirley, "Rebels Won Small Victory at Scary Creek," *Charleston Newspapers*.

Eskew, Garnett Laidlaw, "Monument Erected to Memory of Kanawha Riflemen, Youths Who Battled in Civil War 60 Years Ago," *Charleston Gazette*, June 4, 1922.

"Flag of Logan Wildcats is in Custody of O. McDonald," *Logan Banner*, Sept. 24, 1929.

"Future Presidents Stationed in City During Civil War," *Charleston Newspapers* (CW—WVa—Folder 5).

Gallagher, D.C., "D.C. Gallagher on Civil War in the Valley," *Charleston Gazette*, July 12, 1925.

Hull, Forrest, "Civil War in the Kanawha Valley Saw Many Engagements....," *Charleston Gazette*, Jan. 10, 1926.

Hull, Forrest, "Rag-Tag Southern Soldiery Swamped Charleston in '61," *Charleston Daily Mail*, Feb. 15, 1963.

Hull, Forrest, "Rebels' Kanawha Commander, Wise, Was Brave but Inept," *Charleston Daily Mail*.

Kanawha Valley Star, June 4, 1860—July 2, 1861, Microfilm Collection, West Virginia State Archives.

Maginnis, William, "Scary Had More Than a Battlefield to Hold Interest and Affection of Older Residents," *Charleston Gazette*, July 23, 1950.

Maginnis, William, "Scary Creek Really Earned Its Name," *Charleston Newspapers*, July 16, 1950.

"Millard Phillips of Huntington was Youngest Soldier in Southern Army," *Huntington Herald-Advertiser*, July 8, 1928.

"Occupation of Charleston by Union Men Described," *Charleston Newspapers* (CW—WVa—Folder 5).

Pfahler, Herbert, "Memorial for Riflemen of '61 is Dedicated," *Charleston Gazette*, June 4, 1922.

"Soldiers Liked Kanawha Camp," *Charleston Daily Mail* (CW—WVa—Folder 5).
Stutler, Boyd, "The Fight at Scary Creek," *Charleston Gazette-Mail,* Feb. 22, 1959.
Summers, George W., "Battle Fought at Scary Was One of First of Civil War," *Charleston Daily Mail,* July 24, 1939.
Summers, George W., "Burning of Confederate Boat and Supplies Was Bold Stunt," *Charleston Newspapers* (CW—WVa—Folder 4).
"The Story of W.A. Burdette—Rich in Civil War History," *Hurricane Breeze,* July 16, 1964.
"Ancient Confederate Flag Found at Logan," unknown clipping.
"First Trench System Built in Defense of Barboursville," unknown clipping, (CW—WVa—Folder 2).
"Kanawha Campaign in 1861 Might Have Had Different Result....," unknown clipping, Feb. 12, 1929.
"Lt. Gen. Patton's Grandfather Led Valley Riflemen," unknown clipping, West Virginia State Archives.
"True Story of the Wise-Littlepage Affair," unknown clipping (CW—WVa—Folder 2).

NOTE: Notations such as CW—WVa—Folder 1 indicate they are to be found in the newspaper clippings file in the West Virginia State Archives under the subject heading Civil War—West Virginia, followed by the particular folder number in which it is found. Also, as some clippings were borrowed from private collections there exists no information on them.

MANUSCRIPT COLLECTIONS AND UNPUBLISHED PERSONAL NARRATIVES

"A list of those persons who have joined the Kanawha Rifle Company," Manuscripts Collection, West Virginia State Archives.
"A Brief and Imperfect Account of the Action at Scary Creek," by George S. Patton, Manuscripts Collection, The Huntington Gallery and Library, San Marino, California.
"Ann Bailey"—a poem by Mr. Charles Robb, United States Cavalry—typescript copy which appeared in the Cleremont, Ohio *Courier* on November 7, 1861, Marshall University Library, Huntington, West Virginia.
Beverly Randolph Wellford Papers 1773-1907 (John McCausland Letter), Virginia Historical Society.
Catherine B. Broun Diary (No. 2389), Southern Historical Collection.
Confederate Military Records: Unit Records, 22nd Virginia Infantry, Department of Military Affairs, Adjutant General's Office, Virginia State Library.
Correspondence on the Patton Family Genealogy, Manuscripts Collection, The Huntington Gallery and Library.
"Diary of a Border Ranger," James D. Sedinger, Co. E, 8th Virginia Cavalry, unpublished personal narrative, West Virginia State Archives.
Godfrey Family Papers, United States Army Military History Institute.
"Kanawha Riflemen," Manuscripts Collection, West Virginia State Archives.
Letter to West Virginia State Archives, from Simms family descendents relating to activities at Scary Creek prior to the battle, West Virginia State Archives.
"Memoirs of Leroy Wesley Cox: Experiences of a Young Soldier in the Confederacy," unpublished personal narrative, Manuscripts Collection, Virginia Historical Society.
"Simms Family History," unpublished, courtesy Emma Simms Maginnis, Winfield Road, West Virginia.
Telegrams and other correspondence from/to Adjutant General (Ohio), 1861.
Telegrams and other correspondence from/to Commander in Chief (Ohio governor),

1861, Ohio Historical Society.

"The Battle of Scary Creek," Mrs. Nancy Beckwith, Washington, West Virginia, Paper submitted to the West Virginia State Archives.

The Elijah Beeman Letters, Cabell County Public Library, Huntington, West Virginia.

The James Clark Welch Papers, Civil War Collection, West Virginia State Archives.

The Museum of the Confederacy Library (includes correspondence of E.C. Phelps, George S. Patton, and Christopher Q. Tompkins).

The Noyes Rand Papers, Civil War Collection, West Virginia State Archives.

"The Part Taken by Putnam County in West Virginia During the War 1861-65," James Frederick ("Fed") Connor (Connor was a black servant that accompanied Confederate troops from Putnam County), West Virginia State Archives.

The Virginia Military Institute Archives (includes correspondence of Superintendent Francis Smith with John McCausland, and George S. Patton).

Tompkins Family Papers 1800-1871; Tompkins Family Papers 1792-1869. Included in these two collections: Correspondence of Christopher Q. Tompkins, George S. Patton, and Henry A. Wise, Virginia Historical Society.

Tucker Family Papers (No. 2605), Thomas Broun letter of July 16, 1861, Southern Historical Collection, University of North Carolina.

INDEX

for original edition only

TERRANCE DAVID LOWRY

Born in 1949, Lowry is a 1967 graduate of South Charleston High School where he worked on the school newspaper. Graduated in 1974 with a B.A. in History from West Virginia State College. Studied Civil War History at Marshall University Graduate School. Professional musician since 1966. Contributing music editor for *The Charleston Gazette* 1970-75. Music editor for *The Charleston Gazette* 1977-78. Two years with the Circulation Department of *The Atlanta Journal*. Published his first book, *The Battle of Scary Creek: Military Operations in the Kanawha Valley, April-July1861* in July of 1982. Has also published *September Blood: The Battle of Carnifex Ferry* (1985); and two volumes in the Virginia Regimental Series *22nd Virginia Infantry* (1988) and *26th (Edgar's) Battalion Virginia Infantry* (1991); and *Last Sleep: The Battle of Droop Mountain November 6, 1863* (1996). Has also had Civil War articles published in *North South Trader, Wonderful West Virginia,* and *Confederate Veteran* magazines, as well as the *West Virginia Hillbilly.* A contributor to the *Time-Life* series of books and an avid collector of Civil War memorabilia. Employed for 20 years with the circulation department Charleston Newspapers, Inc. *[Photo by Tom Wills, Charleston, WV.]*